FLORA FRASER was named after Flora Macdonald and grew up in London and Inverness-shire. She is the author of *Beloved Emma: The Life of Emma, Lady Hamilton*; *The Unruly Queen: The Life of Queen Caroline*; *Princesses: The Daughters of George III*; *Venus of Empire: The Life of Pauline Bonaparte* and *George & Martha Washington: A Revolutionary Marriage*, which won the 2016 George Washington Prize. She lives in London.

Beloved Emma: The Life of Emma, Lady Hamilton
The Unruly Queen: The Life of Queen Caroline
Princesses: The Daughters of George III
Venus of Empire: The Life of Pauline Bonaparte
George & Martha Washington: A Revolutionary Marriage

'PRETTY YOUNG REBEL'

The Life of Flora Macdonald

FLORA FRASER

BLOOMSBURY PUBLISHING

LONDON • OXFORD • NEW YORK • NEW DELHI • SYDNEY

BLOOMSBURY PUBLISHING
Bloomsbury Publishing Plc
50 Bedford Square, London, WC1B 3DP, UK
29 Earlsfort Terrace, Dublin 2, Ireland

BLOOMSBURY, BLOOMSBURY PUBLISHING and the Diana logo are trademarks of
Bloomsbury Publishing Plc

First published in Great Britain 2022
This edition published 2023

A catalogue record for this book is available from the British Library

ISBN: HB: 978-1-4088-7982-5; PB: 978-1-4088-7985-6; EBOOK: 978-1-4088-7984-9;
EPDF: 978-1-5266-5679-7

2 4 6 8 10 9 7 5 3 1

Typeset by Newgen KnowledgeWorks Pvt. Ltd., Chennai, India
Printed and bound in Great Britain by CPI Group (UK) Ltd, Croydon CR0 4YY

To find out more about our authors and books visit www.bloomsbury.com
and sign up for our newsletters

Contents

For Robert Gottlieb,
dear friend and *Avid Reader*

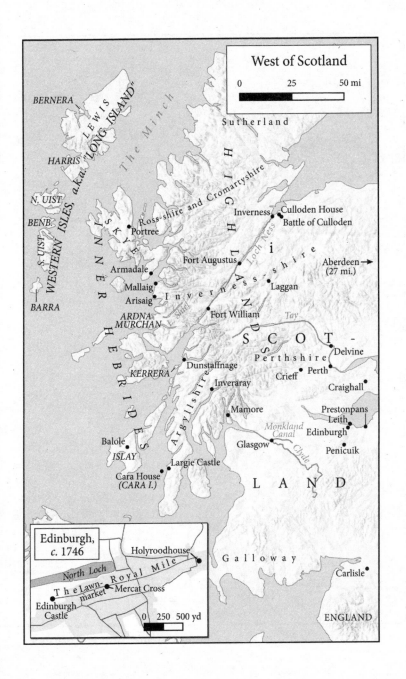

West of Scotland

0   25   50 mi

BERNERA
LEWIS
HARRIS
a.k.a. "LONG ISLAND"
N. UIST
BENB.
WESTERN ISLES,
S. UIST
BARRA

The Minch

Sutherland

H I G H
Ross-shire and Cromartyshire

S K Y E
Portree

I N N E R

Armadale
Mallaig
Arisaig
ARDNA-
MURCHAN

Inverness
Culloden House
Battle of Culloden

Loch Ness
Fort Augustus
Inverness-shire
Laggan
Aberdeen →
(27 mi.)

Sound of
Fort William

L A N D S

Tay

S C O T-

Perthshire
Delvine
Perth
Crieff
Craighall

H E B R I D E S
KERRERA

Dunstaffnage
Inveraray
Mamore

Argyllshire

Prestonpans
Leith
Monkland
Canal
Edinburgh
Penicuik

Balole
ISLAY
Largie Castle
Cara House
(CARA I.)

Glasgow
Clyde

L A N D

Galloway

Carlisle

ENGLAND

Edinburgh, c. 1746

Holyroodhouse

North Loch

The Lawn-market
Royal Mile
Mercat Cross

Edinburgh
Castle

0   250   500 yd

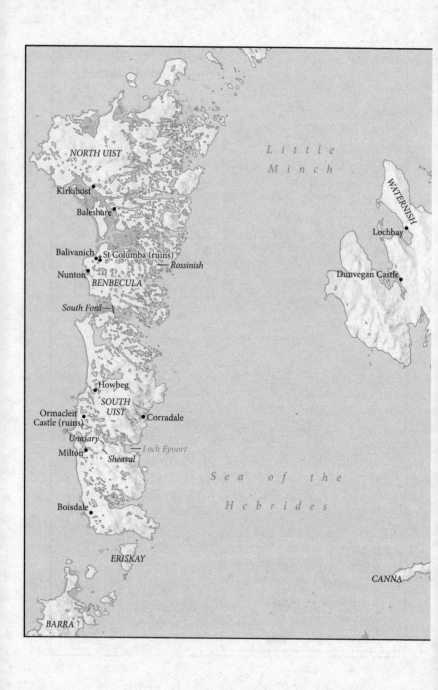

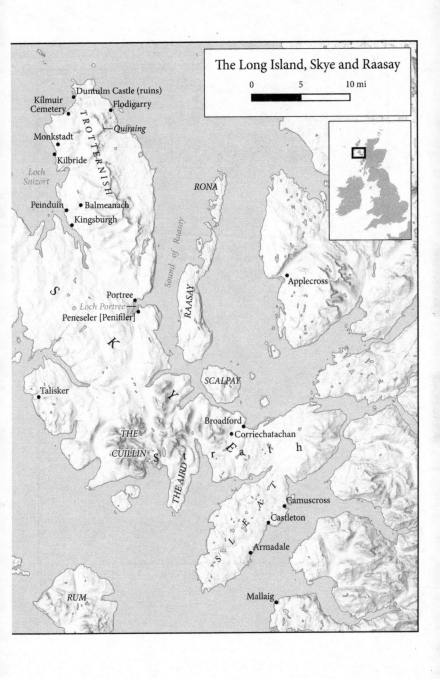

The Long Island, Skye and Raasay

0   5   10 mi

Duntulm Castle (ruins)
Kilmuir
Cemetery
Flodigarry
Quiraing

Monkstadt
TROTTERNISH

Kilbride

Loch
Snizort

Peinduin   Balmeanach
Kingsburgh

RONA

S

Sound of Raasay

Portree
Loch Portree
Peneseler [Penifiler]

RAASAY

Applecross

K

SCALPAY

Talisker

Y

THE
CUILLIN
S   THE AIRD   t   r   E a   t   h

Broadford
Corriechatachan

Camuscross

Castleton

S L E A T

Armadale

RUM

Mallaig

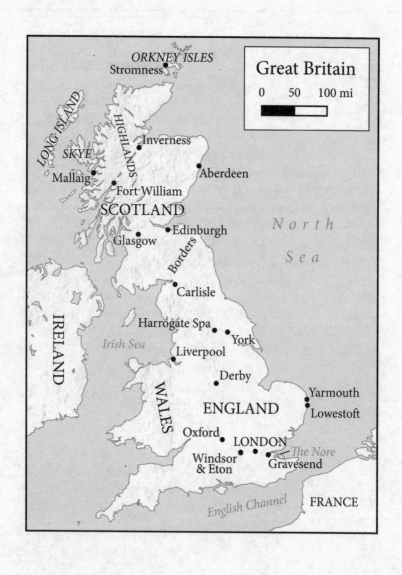

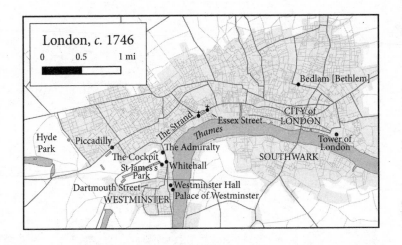

London, *c.* 1746

0   0.5   1 mi

Bedlam [Bethlem]

CITY of LONDON

The Strand
Thames
Essex Street

Hyde Park
Piccadilly

Tower of London

The Admiralty

SOUTHWARK

The Cockpit
St James's Park
Whitehall

Dartmouth Street

Westminster Hall
Palace of Westminster

WESTMINSTER

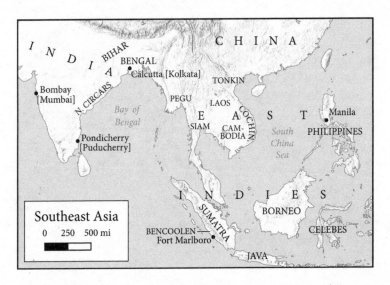

Southeast Asia

0   250   500 mi

I N D I A
BIHAR
BENGAL
Calcutta [Kolkata]

C H I N A

N. CIRCARS

TONKIN

Bombay [Mumbai]

PEGU
LAOS

Bay of Bengal

E
A
S
T

COCHIN

Manila

SIAM
CAM-BODIA

PHILIPPINES

Pondicherry [Puducherry]

South China Sea

I   N   D   I   E   S

SUMATRA

BORNEO

CELEBES

BENCOOLEN
Fort Marlboro

JAVA

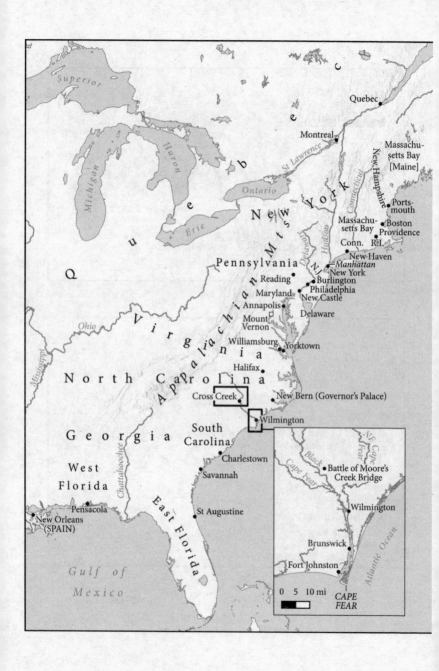

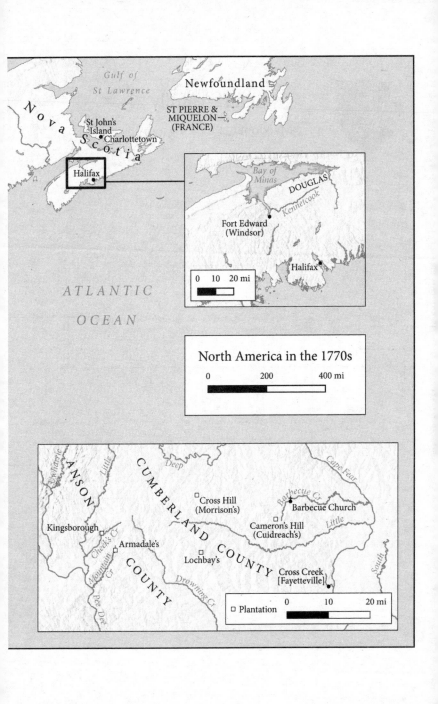

North America in the 1770s

Allan's Family

Macdonalds of Kingsburgh

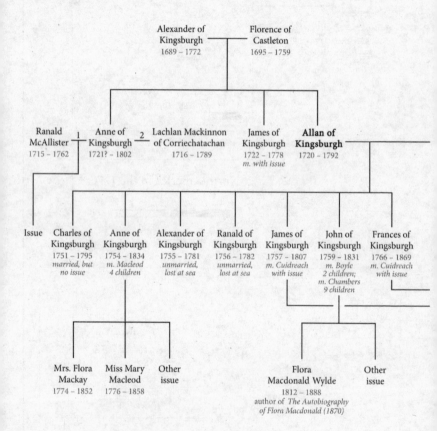

Alexander of Kingsburgh
1689 – 1772

Florence of Castleton
1695 – 1759

Ranald McAllister
1715 – 1762

1

Anne of Kingsburgh
1721? – 1802

2

Lachlan Mackinnon of Corriechatachan
1716 – 1789

James of Kingsburgh
1722 – 1778
m. with issue

Allan of Kingsburgh
1720 – 1792

Issue

Charles of Kingsburgh
1751 – 1795
married, but no issue

Anne of Kingsburgh
1754 – 1834
m. Macleod 4 children

Alexander of Kingsburgh
1755 – 1781
unmarried, lost at sea

Ranald of Kingsburgh
1756 – 1782
unmarried, lost at sea

James of Kingsburgh
1757 – 1807
m. Cuidreach with issue

John of Kingsburgh
1759 – 1831
m. Boyle 2 children; m. Chambers 9 children

Frances of Kingsburgh
1766 – 1869
m. Cuidreach with issue

Mrs. Flora Mackay
1774 – 1852

Miss Mary Macleod
1776 – 1858

Other issue

Flora Macdonald Wylde
1812 – 1888
author of *The Autobiography of Flora Macdonald* (1870)

Other issue

Flora's Family

Macdonalds of Balivanich and Milton and Armadale

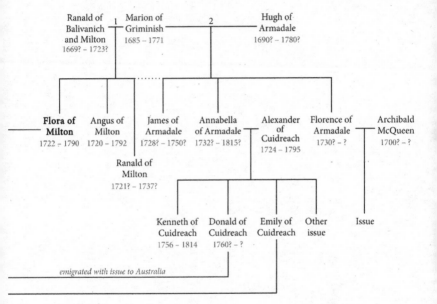

Ranald of Balivanich and Milton 1669? – 1723?

Marion of Griminish 1685 – 1771

Hugh of Armadale 1690? – 1780?

Flora of Milton 1722 – 1790

Angus of Milton 1720 – 1792

Ranald of Milton 1721? – 1737?

James of Armadale 1728? – 1750?

Annabella of Armadale 1732? – 1815?

Alexander of Cuidreach 1724 – 1795

Florence of Armadale 1730? – ?

Archibald McQueen 1700? – ?

Kenneth of Cuidreach 1756 – 1814

Donald of Cuidreach 1760? – ?

Emily of Cuidreach

Other issue

Issue

emigrated with issue to Australia

Glossary

See Family Tree for Flora's close relations, and Maps for many locations.

Ardnamurchan   Captain Alexander Macdonald of Ardnamurchan; commandant 2nd Battalion of Royal Highland Emigrants, Fort Edward, Windsor

Armadale   Hugh Macdonald of Armadale; Flora's stepfather

Baleshare   Hugh Macdonald of Baleshare; Sleat tacksman on North Uist

Boisdale   Alexander Macdonald of Boisdale, South Uist; Old Clan's half-brother

Castleton   Donald Macdonald of Castleton; Skye militia officer

Cuidreach   Alexander Macdonald of Cuidreach; husband of Annabella, Flora's half-sister

Delvine   John Mackenzie of Delvine; Edinburgh lawyer for the Sleat estates

Donald Roy   Captain Donald Roy Macdonald; Jacobite officer, Skye; brother of Baleshare

Kingsburgh   *see* **Old Kingsburgh** for pre-1773; Allan Macdonald of Kingsburgh; Flora's husband after 1773

the Knight   Sir Alexander Macdonald of Sleat, Skye; baronet and chief of Macdonalds of Sleat

Lady Clan   Lady Clanranald; Old Clan's wife

Lady Margaret   Lady Margaret Macdonald; the Knight's wife

the Laird   Norman Macleod of Macleod; chief of Clan Macleod, died 1771; *see also* **the Macleod**

Lochbay   Alexander Macleod of Lochbay; Flora's son-in-law; husband of Annie

the Lochiel   chief of Clan Cameron

Lord Macdonald   the Knight's son, Alexander; succeeded his brother as baronet; later ennobled

the Macleod   chief of Clan Macleod; until 1771, Norman Macleod of Macleod; from 1771, grandson of same name

Mrs Mackenzie   wife of John Mackenzie of Delvine, Edinburgh lawyer

Milton   Flora's father Ranald of Balivanich and Milton; died 1723/5

Milton, *also* **Young Milton**   Angus Macdonald of Balivanich and Milton; Flora's brother

Neil   Neil MacEachen, later Macdonald; Flora's cousin who recruited her to help the Prince

Old Clan   Ranald Macdonald, styled Lord Clanranald; chief of Clanranald Macdonalds

the Old Fox   Simon Fraser, Lord Lovat; chief of Clan Fraser

(Old) Kingsburgh   Alexander Macdonald of Kingsburgh; Sleat factor; Flora's father-in-law

Old Mackinnon   John Mackinnon; chief of Mackinnons on Skye

Old Raasay   Malcolm Macleod; head of Macleods of Raasay; father of Rona

O'Neill   Colonel Felix O'Neill; Jacobite officer and the Prince's companion

Rona   Old Raasay's son, John Macleod; from 1761, 'Raasay', head of Macleods of Raasay

Sir James   the Knight's heir; Sir James Macdonald of Sleat from 1746; died 1766

Talisker   John Macleod of Talisker; Skye militia officer

Young Clan   Ranald Macdonald; Old Clan's eldest son

PLACES

Scotland

Armadale   home of Flora's stepfather and mother till 1771; in 1773, occupied by Lord Macdonald

Balivanich   tack on Benbecula tenanted by Flora's father, then by her brother

Benbecula   part of Long Island; island immediately north of South Uist

Corradale   glen on South Uist tenanted by MacEachen family; Prince's refuge

Dunvegan   Skye seat of the Macleod

Flodigarry   Skye tack; Flora's first married home

Kingsburgh   Macdonald of Kingsburgh home; Flora's second married home

Long Island   local name for Western Isles or Outer Hebrides, island chain including North Uist, Benbecula and South Uist

Milton tack on South Uist tenanted by Flora's father, then by her brother

the Minch channels between the Long Island (the Uists and Benbecula) and Skye, and between the former (Lewis and Harris) and the mainland

Monkstadt the Knight's seat on Skye

Nunton Old Clan's seat on Benbecula

Peinduin Flora's final home on Skye

Rossinish peninsula on Benbecula forming a natural harbour

Skye, *also* **Isle of Skye** one of Inner Hebrides, island chain

Sleat south-west peninsula, Skye; also estates of the Knight and heirs

South Uist one of chain of islands comprising Long Island, sometimes used to denote Benbecula as well; Clanranald land

Strath Mackinnon country, south-eastern Skye

Trotternish northern peninsula, Skye; Sleat land

Waternish north-western peninsula, Skye; Macleod land

Western Isles name then current for Outer Hebrides; *see* Long Island

North America

Cameron's Hill home of Cuidreach and Annabella Macdonald, Cumberland County, NC. Near modern-day Johnsonville, Harnett County, NC

Cheek's Creek home to Allan and Flora, Anson County, NC. Now in Montgomery County, NC

Cross Creek town populated by Highland Scots, Cumberland County; modern-day Fayetteville, NC

Fort Edward   home to 2nd Battalion of Royal Highland Emigrants in Windsor, Nova Scotia

Halifax   town in North Carolina; also capital of Nova Scotia, British colony

Kenneth Black plantation   home to the Lochbay Macleods in Cumberland County; in modern-day Southern Pines, Moore County, NC

Mountain Creek   Hugh Macdonald of Armadale's plantation, Anson County, NC; Montgomery County, from 1779

Nova Scotia   British maritime province or colony; province in present-day Canada

Reading   Pennsylvanian residence of Allan and Alexander 'Sandy' Macdonald when on parole

Windsor   town in Nova Scotia, home to 2nd Battalion of Royal Highland Emigrants, later 84th Regiment

Author's Note

Such Highland names as Macdonald and Macleod were spelt in multiple ways in the eighteenth century, as is still the case today. I have, for simplicity's sake, adhered to one spelling of each clan name both in quotations and in my own narrative. I have also in general standardised eighteenth-century punctuation so that it does not present difficulties for the modern reader. In a few cases I have let the original punctuation give a flavour of how English – and Scots – were written and spoken during Flora Macdonald's life. I have for the most part similarly standardised spelling.

Lastly, dates in the book prior to 1752 are given Old Style, following the Julian calendar, and from that year New Style, reflecting the introduction of the Gregorian calendar in Britain and an adjustment to the start of the year in England and Wales.

Acknowledgements

I wish to thank Her Majesty The Queen for granting me access to the Royal Archives at Windsor, where I consulted the Stuart and Cumberland Papers when I was a Mount Vernon-Georgian Papers Fellow in 2017. I am grateful to Oliver Walton, Allison Derrett, Roberta Giubilini, Julie Crocker and Lynne Beech, among others in the Round Tower who advised and assisted me.

I owe Douglas Bradburn – President of George Washington's Mount Vernon, formerly Director of the Washington Library there – a great debt of gratitude for granting me that Fellowship, with the approval of Georgian Papers Programme directors Arthur Burns, of King's College London, and Karin Wulf, of the Omohundro Institute, College of William & Mary. Their encouragement, thoughtful advice and practical help were invaluable. The contributions of many other Fellows to the Programme have in addition greatly enriched my understanding of the Atlantic world in which Flora Macdonald lived.

I would also like to thank Kevin C. Butterfield, now Washington Library Director; Stephen A. McLeod, Mary V. Thompson and Samantha Snyder at the Library; Anthony King, then at the Library; Susan P. Schoelwer and James P. Ambuske at George Washington's Mount Vernon; and Andrew Lambert, Patricia Methven, Angel-Luke O'Donnell and Samantha Callaghan, all of King's College London, for many stimulating conversations and much assistance.

I am grateful to Jeffrey Flannery, Head of the Reference and Reader Services in the Library of Congress Manuscript Division, since retired, for suggesting fruitful lines of enquiry; and to Gordon Turnbull, General Editor of the Yale Boswell Editions, an expert guide to the papers in his care. Additionally, I thank Adrienne Sharpe and colleagues in the Beinecke Library, Yale, for much assistance. I am also grateful to Sue Geale at the Museum of the Isles, Armadale Castle, Isle of Skye, who facilitated my reading of the Macdonald of Sleat papers, and to the Museum for permission to quote from the Macdonald estate papers there, and to the National Library of Scotland, the Duke of Argyll and Sir Alexander Muir-Mackenzie for permission to quote from the Campbell of Mamore and Mackenzie of Delvine papers. In addition, I thank the staff at Adam Matthew Digital for kindly allowing me temporary access to its Colonial America website in 2020.

I would especially like to thank the following who have kindly shared their work or knowledge with me: T. Cole Jones of Purdue University, Indiana; Chris E. Fonvielle, Jr, of the University of North Carolina; Kimberly Sherman, of Cape Fear Community College, NC; Roger Knight and fellow members of the Cumberland Society; Nicholas Haslam; Laura Lindsay of Christie's, London; Michael Nash of Marine & Cannon Books, Wirral; Tom and Hannah Duguid of Turcan Connell, Edinburgh; Lowell Libson of Libson Yarker; and Nicola Solomon, of the Society of Authors.

I would also like to thank the individuals named and other kindly archivists, librarians and curators or experts at the following institutions: Shruti Patel, since retired, Kate Heard, Kathryn Hughes and Karen Lawson, Royal Collection; Phyllis Mitchell, Walker's Shortbread Ltd, Aberlour; Helen Woollison and Celine Luppo McDaid, Dr Johnson's House, Gough Square, London; Catherine Muir, Benbecula History Society; Dora Petherbridge and Ralph McLean, Archives and Manuscript Collections, National Library of Scotland; National Records of Scotland; Alison Diamond, Inveraray Castle Archives; National Archives, London; North Carolina Museum of History, NC; Heinz Archive, National Portrait Gallery, London; British Library; British Museum; Caitlin Curtis Pieper,

Red Hill, Patrick Henry National Memorial, VA; London Library; Lewis E. Lehrman, Chairman, and James G. Basker, President, Gilder Lehrman Institute of American History; Kaitlyn Pettengill, Historical Society of Pennsylvania; Michele L. Frederick, North Carolina Museum of Art, NC; National Museum of Scotland, Edinburgh; Susan Pockmire, Moore County Historical Association, NC; New-York Historical Society, New York; Lisa Adams, Berks History Center, Reading, PA; Nathan Pendlebury, National Museums Liverpool; Georgina Eliot and Viola Fazzi, Sotheby's, London; National Archives Washington, DC; Alison Mason and Catherine MacPhee, High Life Highland; Vanessa Martin, West Highland Museum, Fort William. In addition, I thank the following who shared with me valuable information: Iain Craik; Alasdair MacEachen; Zack Bacon; Susan T. Block; and Joanne Watson, independent textile historian. I would also like to express my gratitude to Irene Baldoni, Cecily Motley, Lesley Robertson Allen, Rosanne Blair and Hannah Goodall.

Michael Fishwick, my editor at Bloomsbury, offered enthusiasm and wise counsel throughout the years in which I researched and wrote '*Pretty Young Rebel': The Life of Flora Macdonald*. Georgina Capel, my literary agent, was ever encouraging when I was at the coalface and Peter James, a stern but kindly critic, interrogated the manuscript with characteristic expertise. It was a pleasure to work with Mike Athanson, who has provided maps of rare quality and the family tree, and with Cecilia Mackay, who conducted invaluable picture research. I also thank, at Bloomsbury, Kieron Connolly, Elisabeth Denison, John English, David Mann and Phil Beresford for their meticulous attention to the book when in production.

I am very grateful to my daughter, Stella Powell-Jones, who was a lively companion on walks and drives in the Hebrides. My mother, Antonia Fraser, as ever offered sage historical and professional advice, while my brother-in-law, Mark Jones, suggested numerous avenues of research to explore. I thank my cousins Simon and Petra Lovat for their generosity in sharing family lore and artefacts, and my brother Benjie, Daisy and Peter Soros, and my cousins Tessa

Keswick and Virginia Fraser also for illuminating and entertaining covnversations about Flora Macdonald. Stella and Alex, Simon and Tommy, you are all a source of wise counsel and, like Flora Grace Ingrid and Wolfgang Robert, of joy and respite too.

Flora Fraser
London, May 2022

Prologue

I cannot remember a time when I did not know the story of Flora Macdonald. I was named after her and grew up at Eilean Aigas, a house on an island in Scotland with palace doors and wooden thrones carved by the Sobieski Stuarts. Occupants during the reign of Queen Victoria, these brothers claimed to be legitimate descendants of Bonnie Prince Charlie, and they were loaned this remote retreat on the River Beauly by the Lord Lovat of the day, the better to research their claim to the British throne. During their stay the Sobieski Stuarts dressed in full Highland regalia and were rowed in a royal barge to worship in the local Catholic church which we attended in our turn.

Not only on The Island, as we termed our home, but everywhere around in my childhood and adolescence there were reminders of the 'Forty-five, the civil war that raged in Scotland in 1745–6 when the Stuart Prince roused support for his bid to wrest the British throne from the House of Hanover. Stones on Culloden Moor the other side of Inverness marked the battle positions of Frasers and other local clansmen who fought under Charles Edward in a last and fatal reckoning in April 1746 with troops commanded by William, Duke of Cumberland. Disdain for the latter's butchering ways in that engagement was later expressed by the naming of a weed seen in every hedgerow as Stinking Willy. Bonnie Prince Charlie, by contrast, appeared in a portrait often reproduced in books, a pale and lovely Prince Charming. Flora Macdonald, who came to his aid at a time of great need, was a local heroine, her statue standing outside Inverness Castle, and her grave face and neat figure provided an image familiar to me from childhood on tartan boxes, on postcards and in engravings.

At Beaufort Castle nearby loomed a Hogarth painting of the Old Fox, a Lovat forebear whose son was 'out' in the 'Forty-five with the Prince. Westward in Glen Strathfarrar this clan chief lurked in the wake of Culloden, hoping, like the Stuart Prince, to escape government detection. Lovat, apprehended, became the last peer to be executed on Tower Hill; Charles Edward, with the aid of Flora Macdonald and others, escaped to the Continent where he was to die in 1788 without ever returning to Scotland.

I imbibed Robert Louis Stevenson's *Kidnapped* and other books focusing on the Prince or on his supporters skulking in the heather. Flora Macdonald's bravery in voyaging with Charles Edward disguised as her Irish maid between the Western Isles and Skye attracted my attention. When I came to read, however, the works of John Prebble and others which dispelled romantic myths about the Prince, I turned away from Jacobite history and to other realms of the past. Had I not chanced upon her image when looking for illustrations for my book, *George & Martha Washington: A Revolutionary Marriage*, I might never have been drawn back to consider the life of Flora Macdonald. There, among a sheaf of American revolutionaries' portraits, was an image of Flora Macdonald familiar to me as hanging in the Scottish National Portrait Gallery in Edinburgh. What had she, a Jacobite heroine of 1746, to do with these patriots across the Atlantic in the 1770s and later?

Dimly I remembered Dr Johnson and Boswell visiting Flora on a journey they made to the Western Isles, and her telling them that they were lucky to catch her, as she was off to America. My curiosity aroused, I looked up the date and found that she acted as hostess to the pair in September 1773, eighteen months before the outbreak of the Revolutionary War. A quick search revealed that Flora emigrated to North Carolina the following year, and was subsequently also in New York and Halifax, Nova Scotia during that conflict. Furthermore, while Flora had been imprisoned as a Jacobite rebel in the 'Forty-five, her husband and four of her sons fought as loyalist officers for George III.

I returned to my task of securing illustrations for *George & Martha Washington*, but my mind was made up. I would next write about my namesake. What I discovered and what I present here is almost stranger than the Jacobite fiction I read as a child. It has caused me to think deeply about Scottish and American nationalism and the nature of loyalism as a function of emigration. Most of all, while as a child I hero-worshipped Bonnie Prince Charlie, now I admire Flora Macdonald unreservedly.

PART ONE

Rebel

A Fugitive Prince
1745–1746

The Western Isles, or Outer Hebrides, are remote and wind-lashed maritime lands. A strand of rough diamonds, they lie off the west coast of mainland Scotland in the Atlantic Ocean, on the outer edge of Europe. The ground, at the mercy of the ebb and flow of the ocean and washed by driving rain much of the year, can appear more water than land. Lewis and Harris, North Uist, Benbecula and South Uist, Eriskay and Barra are some of these islands' names. In the mid-eighteenth century, during the reign of George II, they were known locally and collectively as the Long Island, and were the private fiefdoms of Macdonald, Macleod and other clan chiefs.

White beaches and fertile shores dominate the low-lying western coastline of sprawling South Uist and of diminutive Benbecula to the immediate north. On the other side of a spine of hill, glen and moor, the precipitous eastern coastline is rich in rocky inlets and coves, providing safe anchorage for vessels. In the mid-1740s a Macdonald chieftain generally known as Old Clan but properly Ranald Macdonald of Clanranald, XVIIth Captain of Clanranald, styled Lord Clanranald, held feudal sway here, and lived in peace with two powerful neighbours on the Isle of Skye – Sir Alexander Macdonald of Sleat and Norman Macleod, head of Clan Macleod.

These last two chiefs were more often called, respectively, 'the Knight' – though Sir Alexander was really a baronet – and 'the Laird'. Wars with their ancestors and with other clan heads on the mainland had once occupied Old Clan's forebears. Moreover, an earlier Clanranald chief had died in battle in 1715 on the Scottish mainland, while endeavouring to restore an exiled Stuart prince to the British throne and displace the ruling House of Hanover. For thirty years thereafter, however, the Long Island was tranquil. Inhabitants of the Clanranald lands confined their attention to raising black cattle, a hardy native breed, for sale in Highland markets and growing such crops on their tacks, or farms, as would withstand the harsh climate.

Centuries before, Scottish kings had conferred lands in this Atlantic archipelago upon forebears of Old Clan, the Knight and the Laird. In the clan system that had since then evolved in the Highlands, tacksmen, or gentlemen farmers from collateral branches of the main Clanranald line held their land on long leases from their kinsman chief. In turn they provided smallholders known as the common sort with exiguous acres in exchange for an amalgam of labour, rent and produce. Bovine disease and drought, rather than the might of other clans or government troops, were now feared by these islanders, richer or poorer. In summer the tacksmen grazed their livestock inland, in the glens that abounded there and above a maze of freshwater lochs. In winter they pastured their cattle on low ground, close to their farms. The wealthier among them had stone houses and dined on roast meat and drank French wine and brandy, as did Old Clan at Nunton, his seat on Benbecula. Herdsmen occupying dwellings that were sometimes little more than huts made a diet of bread, oats, cheese and barley more palatable by the addition of whisky.

In the summer of 1746, notwithstanding these decades of peace, the atmosphere on South Uist and Benbecula was febrile. Militia raised on behalf of the Crown by the Knight and the Laird from their lands on Skye and on the Long Island guarded the fords in the shallows between South Uist and Benbecula. The Minch, a channel some thirty nautical miles wide between the Long Island and Skye, was 'pestered with the English navy', as a South Uist native later remembered with feeling. The vessels in question, he observed, had been 'sent there a purpose to hinder the prince or any of his party to make their escape'.[1]

The royal personage in question is known to history as Bonnie Prince Charlie. Then a fugitive with a price on his head, to his pursuers he was the Young Pretender. The limelight had shifted from his father, James Edward Stuart, a prince, dubbed the Pretender at the time of his bid to seize the British throne thirty years earlier and now often referred to as the Old Pretender. In the wake of a failed attempt on the British throne in 1745, Prince Charles had since late April 1746 been 'skulking' – moving about stealthily – in a variety of refuges on the Long Island, among them Corradale, a secluded glen in South Uist on Clanranald land. The chief of those territories and his brother, Alexander Macdonald of Boisdale, supplied bread and brandy, shirts and local information; and the latter took charge of plans to secure the Prince's escape to the Continent. Although the Knight was steadfast in his support for the government, his wife, Lady Margaret Macdonald, sent secretly to Charles Edward in his Corradale retreat copies of the *London Gazette*, containing valuable domestic and foreign intelligence.[2] Many others, including several militia officers on South Uist and Benbecula, came to know and keep secret his identity over the course of these weeks. When fifteen Royal Navy ships hovered off the coast in mid-June, however, and a party of regular (commissioned) officers, landing on South Uist with orders to hunt down the Young Pretender, took Boisdale prisoner, real danger threatened.

At this point, when all seemed lost, a private message from Hugh Macdonald of Armadale came to the loch where the royal party was 'lurking [concealed]'. This Skye tacksman was an officer in one of the militias raised the previous autumn by the Knight. Armadale, as he was known, declared himself, 'though an enemy in appearance, yet … a sure friend in his heart', and made a novel and daring suggestion for the Prince's deliverance: 'As it seemed now impossible for him to conceal himself any longer in the country', the officer volunteered 'to send his stepdaughter, Miss Florence

[Flora] Macdonald', then on South Uist, 'to Sleat' in Skye where he and her mother lived. If His Royal Highness would 'dress in women's clothes, that he might pass for her [Flora's] servant maid' on the voyage, Armadale advised, the disguised Prince was sure 'to be protected by Lady Margaret Macdonald' on that island across the Minch. The Knight's second wife had been bred to favour the exiled Stuarts by her mother, a Scottish countess. Finally, the Skye militia officer proposed that Neil MacEachen of Howbeg, a cousin of Flora's then with Charles Edward, be appointed to take care of both mistress and 'maid' on the journey. This scheme of Armadale's 'pleased the prince mightily', and he was 'very impatient to see it put into execution'.[3] It was envisaged that, in place of Boisdale, secret adherents to the Stuart cause on Skye would further plans to land and conceal him on the mainland, until a passage to the Continent might be effected.

Charles Edward Louis Philip Casimir Stuart had come from the Continent the previous summer to threaten the Hanoverian dynasty, now established on the British throne some thirty years. James VII of Scotland and II of England and Ireland, Charles Edward's grandfather, had been deposed in 1688, after he had turned Catholic and fathered a male heir, James Edward, with his second wife, who was also of that faith. Amid fears that the country would turn Catholic upon the later accession of the infant Prince of Wales, the Stuart monarch was exiled to France with his Queen and male heir. The Protestant Mary Stuart, the elder of James II's daughters by his first wife, supplanted her father on the throne with her husband, William of Orange, and legislation followed which excluded Catholics from the British throne. The Stuart female line only came to an end in 1714, with the death of James's younger daughter, Queen Anne, then childless, and Elector Georg of Hanover, her nearest Protestant relation, succeeded to the British throne as George I. His son, George II, now ruled in the United Kingdom.

These Hanoverian kings from Germany did not please all in Scotland, whether Protestant or secretly Catholic. Other than during the Commonwealth and Protectorate years of 1649–60,

Stuart monarchs had reigned there since 1371 and in England and Ireland since 1603. Although the exiled James II had died in 1701, periodic attempts were made after 1714, with the aid of France, to restore the 'rightful' Stuart line to the British throne in the shape of his son, James Edward Stuart. All had failed. Most recently, an invasion force sent across the English Channel by the French King in 1744 had been driven back by storms, and Louis XV thereafter declined to offer further aid to his fellow Catholic prince. He continued, however, to recognise the Stuart exile as James VIII of Scotland and III of England. Pope Benedict XIV and the papal court in Rome, where James Edward had now long resided and brought up his sons, Charles Edward and Henry Benedict, followed suit.

Styled the Chevalier by his supporters and the Pretender by the Hanoverian government, the Stuart princes' father was, in the 1740s, pious, sickly and old before his time. Nevertheless, he and his adherents, termed Jacobites, 'Jacobus' being the Latin for James, still dreamed of his restoration to the British throne and centred their hopes in James's elder son as agent for that change. Charles Edward was an ambitious young man in vigorous health. Covert encouragement from the Scottish Highlands led him to leave his paternal home in Rome for Paris and there in the summer of 1745 plan a daring attempt on the Hanoverian throne. The outcome of this venture, which has come to be known as the 'Forty-five or the Rising of 1745, was to visit upon Georgian Scotland and England civil war and government retribution that lasted into the following year. When the Stuart heir slipped out of France, however, and landed in July 1745 in Clanranald country on the west coast of Scotland, he had with him only seven companions – four of whom had no previous military experience.

The Prince's unheralded arrival in Scotland took both Highland chiefs and the Hanoverian government by surprise. The country people in Arisaig, where the Prince came ashore, were thunderstruck by the royal apparition in their midst. A member of a nearby parish was questioned by her minister: 'What number of people is with him?' 'Six men and himself,' the woman answered, 'but word is sent to all the Highland chiefs about.'[4]

The Prince wrote to one of these powerful beings, who had at their command varying numbers of fighting men, on 8 August: 'I am come with a firm resolution to restore the King my father or perish in the attempt.'[5] For all his lack of French support, when he raised his father's standard at the head of Loch Shiel on 19 August he persuaded Macdonald, Cameron and Stewart chiefs and lairds to lead out hundreds of their clansmen in the Stuart cause. More Scots of different clan septs, or branches, committed to this 'rebel army' as it passed through the Highlands on its way south to Edinburgh, where the Prince intended to rally all his adherents in the north. Foolhardy in many respects, Charles Edward's latter-day scheme for a Stuart restoration had this advantage: only a skeleton government army defended the United Kingdom in the summer of 1745. The greater part of George II's forces had been concentrated, for two years now, in Flanders fighting the French. In consequence, although the Hanoverian government ordered 'a reward of thirty thousand pounds' to be bestowed on 'any person who shall seize and secure the eldest son of the Pretender',[6] the Jacobite brigades passed on their way unchecked.

The Prince entered the ancient Scottish capital in triumph on 17 September and took possession of Holyroodhouse, the palace once occupied by, among others of his ancestors, Mary Queen of Scots and her son, James VI of Scotland and I of England. Margaret Pringle, a young gentlewoman, observed: 'Ye windows were full of ladies who threw up their handkerchiefs and clap'd their hands and show'd great loyalty to the Bonny Prince.' Some of these enthusiasts wore white roses, emblems of the Jacobite Stuart cause. Reviewing his men on horseback, Charles Edward himself sported a white cockade, or rosette, in his hat and carried a sword with a finely wrought silver hilt. He acknowledged spectators 'with an air of grandeur and affability ... In all my life', wrote Miss Pringle, 'I never saw so noble nor so graceful an appearance as His Highness made ...' While many of the Highlanders who had come south wore the plaid and kilt which were their customary attire, Charles Edward appeared in costly 'Lowland ... dress' – a grosgrain coat 'trimmed with gold lace and a laced red waistcoat and breeches'.[7]

Acting as Regent, Charles Edward proclaimed his father James VIII of Scotland. Days later he was again with his troops in the field. Although he had grown up a petted prince at the papal court, he showed himself uncaring of privation, writing to his father on 20 September:

> 'Tis owing to … my conforming myself to the customs of those people [the Highlanders] that I have got their hearts to a degree not to be easily conceived by those who do not see it. One who observes the discipline I have established would take my little army to be a body of picked veterans … I keep my health better in these wild mountains than I used to do, in the Campania Felice [fertile region, south of the Papal States], and sleep sounder lying on the ground than I used to do in the palaces at Rome.[8]

When intelligence reached London of the Prince's singular victory the following day at Prestonpans outside Edinburgh and of 'the late unhappy defeat' there of the Hanoverian General Sir John Cope, the government was confounded. The news 'gives a very great alarm here', the Secretary of State for Scotland informed Duncan Forbes of Culloden, Lord President of the Court of Sessions in Scotland. However, a 'very considerable body of troops, with artillery', Lord Tweeddale continued, had begun their march north from London to the Scottish Borders and Edinburgh, and further troops had been ordered home from Flanders.[9]

Enlisting more supporters after he crossed the English border on 31 October, the Prince aimed to end his journey at Westminster. Although he attracted other followers as he passed through the northern towns of England, his campaign foundered at Derby, a hundred miles short of London. In December lack of funds and dwindling numbers in the rebel army forced his retreat back north.

Pursuing him was the King's younger son, William Augustus, Duke of Cumberland. Having returned to England from Flanders in November, he was appointed by his father Commander-in-Chief in Scotland, succeeding Cope. In his early twenties, like his remote cousin the Prince, Cumberland was little tried in battle and had scant experience of army administration. But, unlike Charles Edward, he had at his disposal trained government troops and a fleet of ships in northern waters commanded by Thomas Smith, a proficient commodore. In the early months of 1746, redcoats – Hanoverian troops – and rebel parties disputed control of the Scottish Highlands, the Jacobite army occupying the town of Inverness in February. A short time later, Cumberland's men reached Aberdeen, only eighty miles further down the east coast. A reckoning was sure to come once these government forces had progressed northward in early April.

On a bleak moor near Culloden House, home of Lord President Forbes, the Duke and his redcoats defeated the Prince's army on 16 April. The action lasted barely an hour. Hundreds of Highlanders were killed, others wounded, and at least 400 were taken prisoner. The government claimed that any savagery displayed by their troops on the battlefield was justified. They had, they affirmed, intercepted a letter, written before the engagement, in which the Prince had directed that 'No quarter [mercy]' be shown to the enemy side.[10] Nonetheless, not all who thereafter called the Duke 'Butcher' Cumberland were Jacobites.[11]

Rebel officers and clansmen without the wherewithal to travel further returned to the vicinity of their Highland homes, and there they lurked in the hills, supplied by their families. Many of them had been badly wounded and were tended in secret by local surgeons. Other, wealthier chiefs and lairds who had come 'out' for the Stuart cause made for the west coast of Scotland. There they skulked while waiting to ship out to France and a more comfortable asylum.

The Prince himself had yielded to the pleas of his generals, and left the Culloden moor after the tide of battle turned irreversibly against his rebel army. That night, drinking deep at a refuge on Loch Ness with Lord Lovat, head of Clan Fraser, he yielded to the heady notion that the day's defeat was a mere setback, a 'ruffle'. In the course of a long political career, the Prince's septuagenarian host had sometimes supported the Hanoverian Crown, at other times the exiled Stuart line. Swayed by the Old Fox, as Lovat was known, Charles Edward sent out instructions that night to rebel chiefs, as yet at liberty, to rendezvous the following day. A letter to one clan head read, 'We have suffered a good deal; but hope we shall soon pay Cumberland in his own coin.'[12] A very few hours saw the Prince regret the venture and instead make for the west coast in order to seek transport back to France. Although Lovat was subsequently to confer with his brother chiefs about the possibility of a further stand, the conclave ended in confusion. Each of them retreated to an inaccessible recess of his own country, where he might best hope to escape detection.[13]

They were wise to seek concealment. Parties of Hanoverian officers and militiamen fanned out across moor and glen from Fort Augustus on Loch Ness and from Fort William on the west coast. While the Prince was their main quarry, they were also intent on taking prisoner and dispatching for trial those others still at large who had 'levied ... war against his Majesty'.[14] An Act of Proscription, hastily passed, provided that both chiefs and clansmen, whether participants in the rebellion or not, were to surrender all their 'warlike weapons' on penalty of transportation to 'his Majesty's plantations beyond the seas'.[15] The Hanoverian forces were aggressive in their searches for both rebels and contraband and were, in the words of one observer, 'sent out ... to ravage, burn and plunder all before them ... The most heart-rending scenes of misery began to present themselves.' The womenfolk, children and older relations of those who had been out with the Prince were expelled from their homes, which, be they chieftains' mansions or herdsmen's huts, the soldiers subsequently burned. They confiscated, too, for the benefit of the government garrisons, cattle belonging to rebel families. As the officers and men went about their work, increasing numbers of Highlanders, homeless and 'almost starved to death with hunger and cold', wandered the hills.[16] Lesser rebels were enjoined to give themselves up and surrender any cache of arms they might still have.

It was becoming increasingly dangerous for the Prince to stay on the mainland. Two of his former staff officers, both veterans of war on the Continent, urged that he 'quit that country [Scotland] for good and all … there was no appearance [likelihood] of succeeding further'.[17] A Skye sea captain promised to find transport to France on the Long Island in the Hebrides. Having arrived on the west coast of Scotland the previous year in an imposing French ship, Charles Edward left it on the evening of 26 April in an open boat rowed by eight oarsmen. With him travelled his valet, his two confessors, or priests, and the two officers, John O'Sullivan and Felix O'Neill, an Irishman.

Donald Macleod, the Skye captain who was at the helm of the vessel, successfully slipped through the cordon of ships guarding the west coast and bore his royal passenger to various harbours on the Long Island in search of transport to France. When none was offered immediately, in mid-May the royal party sought temporary sanctuary in the Clanranald lands on South Uist. In common with the Knight and the Laird, the Clanranald chief had declined to come out with his clansmen in the Rising. His fellow lairds on Skye, indeed, had likened the Prince's quest, without French support, to 'Don Quixote's expedition'.[18] However, Old Clan's forebears had been prominent in past Risings and the chief's heir, Young Clan, now in hiding, had campaigned with the Prince since his landing on the west coast the previous summer. Moreover, Old Clan's wife was the sister and daughter as well as the mother of Jacobite rebels. Island lore holds that it was she who dared her husband not to afford asylum to the Stuart scion. At any rate, the Macdonald chief directed that Neil MacEachen, his young kinsman and tutor to junior Clanranald children, harbour the royal party at a bothy, or cottage, in Corradale. Old Clan's brother Boisdale was charged with the task of securing the Prince's safe passage to the Continent.

Upon arrival at Corradale, Charles Edward appeared 'extraordinarily well pleased' with the MacEachen refuge, his host was later to write. 'He sat upon a seat of green turf that was made up for him that evening and after taking a refreshment of gradan [rough] bread and cheese, and goat's milk, upon which he fed very heartily, he desired his feet to be washed, being extreme dirty, and very much galled by his night walk.' This done, the Prince 'smoked a pipe of tobacco and went to bed, which being heather and green rushes, he slept soundly till twelve the next day'.[19]

MacEachen was also to recall the Prince taking 'a vast delight, when it was a good day, to sit up[on] a stone that was before the door of the house with his face turned towards the sun'. His companions feared that he would 'get a headache'. The Prince, however, a veteran of Roman heat, said that 'he knew himself what was good for him, better than they could describe, that the sun did him all the good in the world'.[20]

Old Clan dispatched a cook from Nunton to serve the royal party in the glen, and Lady Clan sent fresh linen and provisions. The Prince 'took care to warm his stomach every morning with a hearty bumper of brandy, of which he always drank a good deal', Neil noted.[21] Indeed, one of 'the gentlemen of the country',[22] who paid clandestine visits to the princely retreat, remarked that, where drinking was concerned, the Prince 'had the better ... even of Boisdale himself, notwithstanding his [the latter's] being as able a bowl man [carouser] ... as any in Scotland'.[23]

Neil MacEachen, meanwhile, as he later recorded, went 'straggling every day about the neighbouring towns [townships] for intelligence, and ... never missed to come in seasonable time with what news' – about the government pursuit – 'he gathered among the people'.[24] Colonel O'Neill, too, paid several visits to Nunton, where he encountered Neil's cousin, Flora Macdonald. Staying on the Long Island that summer with her brother, Angus Macdonald of Balivanich and Milton (known as Milton), she frequented the company of Lady Clan. On one occasion, 'introducing a conversation ... about him [the Prince]', O'Neill asked Flora 'what she would give for a sight of the Prince'. She was circumspect in her reply, saying only that 'as she had not that happiness before, she did not look for it now, but ... a sight of him would make her happy, though he was on one hill and she was on another'.[25]

In early June the Prince's life of comparative ease came to an end. The Duke of Cumberland having made Fort Augustus, on the mainland, his headquarters, received credible information there that the Prince was skulking somewhere in the Western

Isles. Commodore Thomas Smith, who commanded the naval
ships stationed on the north-west coast of Scotland, dispatched
those vessels to 'pester' the Minch. Other Royal Navy ships ferried
detachments of redcoats from the mainland to the Long Island.
Additionally, 200 Macdonald and Macleod militia from Skye began
a diligent search of islands including South Uist and Benbecula
and prepared to guard 'the coasts and fords in the country'. It
'seemed next to a miracle [for the Prince] to have been able to
escape', Neil was later to observe,[26] and the royal fugitive removed
with his companions for some days to an uninhabited island close
to Benbecula.

Old Clan had now been called by the Duke to Fort Augustus,
but in his place Lady Clan brought 'plenty of bread and other
meats' when she visited, so as 'to have the honour of seeing him
[the Prince], before he left the country'.[27] Plans for that departure,
in the hands of Boisdale, foundered, however, after that laird was
arrested at his house in mid-June, for illegal possession of arms.
Furthermore, his wife sent word a few days later to Charles Edward,
then in hiding barely a mile away, that Captain Caroline (sic) Scott,
a feared 'regular' officer, with a party of redcoats, was expected at
her home 'by ten o'clock next day'. Further news came that this
officer and his men, upon their arrival, had tied Lady Boisdale, her
daughters and the household 'neck and heel' in order to extract a
confession 'of the Prince's being in the country'. This intelligence
'struck such terror into the minds of the timorous crew', who had
previously minded the boat the Prince kept with him, that they
sank the vessel and abandoned the royal party. Charles Edward
and his companions, hemmed in by militia and regular troops,
with no means of transport to escape from the island, were now
in what Neil justly called a 'desperate situation'.[28] At this juncture,
however, there arrived the 'country gentleman' to whom Armadale,
now guarding the fords of Benbecula, had entrusted that private
message for the Prince. Dangerous as was the 'scheme' the militia
Captain proposed for all participants, it at least offered a solution
to Charles Edward's predicament. This last fugitive encampment
was struck, and O'Sullivan and those local men who had previously

staffed it departed, the Irishman ultimately to make his way to the safety of the Continent. In company with O'Neill and guided by MacEachen, the Prince headed for the 'north end of the country', where Flora was to be found, on the evening of Friday 20 June.[29]

Partly educated in Paris, Neil was no seasoned rebel. As Nunton domine or dominie, a Scots term for a teacher or tutor, from the Latin for master, he had previously been held by other kinsmen to be 'very timorous'. However, he had now successfully guarded the Prince for weeks while he lay in hiding. The audacity of his further actions in concert with Flora would evoke further admiration.[30] The Clanranald tutor directed their steps to where 'Miss Flora lived [was staying] with her brother in a glen near Locheynort [Loch Eynort]', a sea loch on the eastern side of the island. As Neil informed the Prince, they 'had all their cattle a-grazing' there at this time. The Prince straightaway declared that he 'would needs go to see her and tell her of the message he had from her stepfather' Armadale.

The light of a full moon that night illumined the few hours of darkness granted by the summer solstice in this northern clime. Fearful of discovery, keeping off the skyline and encumbered with sword belts and pistol holsters, shirts, linen and provisions, the royal party trudged onward. When pasturing his livestock in the summer, Flora's brother occupied a sheiling, or summer shelter, at Unasary on Sheaval, a hill that rose above Loch Eynort. Towards this 'little house' Charles Edward and his companions bent their steps. Flora Macdonald, meanwhile, was asleep inside this hillside refuge, all unaware that a Stuart prince would, within hours, invoke her aid in a desperate venture.[31]

Ill Met by Moonlight
June 1746

Although Flora Macdonald was soon to spring to prominence, the life of this young Highland gentlewoman had been free of remarkable incident until the summer of 1746. While there is no record of her birth, later information makes clear that she was born some time in 1722 or 1723, so was then aged about twenty-four.[1] Her children were to glory in her descent from Somerled, Lord of the Isles, and from Robert II, first of Scotland's Stuart kings.[2] More prosaically, her father, Ranald Macdonald, was a close kinsman of Old Clan and his forebears, and occupied tacks at Balivanich on Benbecula and at Milton on South Uist. A notable man in his time, who had earlier married a Sleat chieftain's widow, Milton died when his children by his second wife, his sole issue, were in their infancy. Flora, however, continued to be known as Milton's daughter and her brother, Angus, in due course, as Young Milton or Milton.[3] A second brother, Ranald, did not reach his majority.

Following her first husband's death, Flora's mother, Marion Macdonald, married one Hugh Macdonald, who had earlier soldiered successfully on the Continent and who was an expert swordsman and shot, although he had only one eye. A Skye man, and close kin to the Knight, Flora's new stepfather appears to have attracted considerable hostility on the Long Island. It was long held that he was the 'abductor' of Marion Macdonald in 1728, and that he had forced her into marriage in his native land.[4] If so, the union was fruitful and stood the test of time.

A brother having inherited the lease of his own family tack on Skye, Hugh Macdonald applied his considerable acumen to cultivating the Milton and Balivanich tacks on the Long Island until his stepson Angus should reach his majority and take over those leases. The Milton farm comprised low ground and hill country, whereas the Balivanich tack was located on a Benbecula headland above a curving bay where Atlantic waves broke on white sands. The Milton children were raised in the latter place during the long winter months, and half-siblings for Flora, Angus and Ranald soon swelled the family.

In the grounds of the Balivanich tack were the remains of St Columba, an ancient Catholic church. Less than a mile away was Nunton, the Clanranald house, whose master and most of those in his territories discreetly practised that still forbidden faith. Flora's cousin Neil MacEachen chaperoned Old Clan's heir when the latter received a Catholic education in Paris,[5] but Flora was raised in the faith of her mother, whose father had been a Presbyterian cleric known as the Strong Minister.[6]

Others of Flora's maternal relations kept fine state at their home in Largie, Argyllshire and on the island of Cara. They played a significant part in her life. Her brother Ranald died in the latter place when young while struggling with a cousin for possession of a gun.[7] Flora herself paid a visit 'of ten or eleven months' when she was about twenty-two to the relatives in Largie. This was, by her own admission, the only time she was absent from the Hebrides before the summer of 1746.[8] Whether at Largie or at home, she had acquired by the latter year that stock of accomplishments which distinguished a gentlewoman of the period, among them singing, dancing and embroidery.

An Edinburgh cleric was soon to describe Flora's 'behaviour in company' as 'easy, modest, and well-adjusted [composed]'.[9] In the attitudes she strikes and the steady gaze she maintains in portraits taken from life in 1747 and 1749, this well-bred manner is on view. Consistent too on the canvases of different artists are the thick, dark hair that frames her fair skin, her regular features and her blue-grey eyes.[10] She had the Celtic good looks often to be found in the Highlands. At home Flora had a stepfather who had known the great world on the Continent. She lived on neighbourly terms with Lady Clan and her daughters at Nunton, an elegant and modern house boasting an upper drawing room, a dining room and a library. 'One could not discern by her conversation that she had spent all her former days in the Highlands', that same minister remarked; 'for she talks English (or rather Scots) easily, and not at all through the Earse [Gaelic] tone [accent].'[11]

Gaelic, which had originated in Ireland long before, was all the language that the 'common sort' – herdsmen and shepherds, servants, maids and smallholders – in the Highlands and islands then knew. A strong oral tradition reflected both recent history and a faery past, when the Macdonalds ruled as Lords of the Isles. Laments for legendary chieftains and celebrations of clan victories and feats of strength were handed down through the centuries in poetry and song. Flora, in common with other inhabitants of the Long Island, grew up on a diet of selkies, kelpies and other shapeshifters – supernatural creatures which assumed the form of seals, water horses and more. Ghost stories were a staple of ordinary conversation, and there was general respect for those seers who had the gift of second sight.

As a Highland woman of gentle birth, Flora also spoke Scots, a language which had evolved in the Scottish Lowlands centuries before and which boasted a large body of literature. While Scots had once been a language distinct from the King's English, by the mid-eighteenth century it was more a variant of the latter. Speakers of both were easily intelligible to each other. The tacksmen and their families, following the lead of Old Clan, who read as deeply as he drank, and of other lairds on the Long Island and Skye, were a literate community. They stocked the libraries in their homes with books printed in both Scots and English. The women of these families, if less literate, were also generally bilingual.

Rumours long persisted that Flora's stepfather, Hugh Macdonald, fled Benbecula and South Uist after making a married woman pregnant. Most of the family, at any rate, including Flora, decamped for Skye when Hugh leased the tack of Armadale in the Sleat peninsula there in 1745 from his kinsman the Knight.[12] Sir Alexander lived at Monkstadt on Trotternish, the most northerly of the island's several peninsulas. The Macdonald chiefdom of Sleat, however, and the Sleat estates the Knight owned on Skye derived from the fertile southern peninsula of that name. The Armadale farmhouse, where Flora, her mother and stepfather and her younger half-siblings now settled, was sheltered by hills and conveniently placed – above a bay looking across to the mountainous mainland – for access to other islands. Young Milton, meanwhile, remained on the Long Island and assumed control of his patrimony.

While many others in the Highlands and islands faced capital charges after being out in the 'Forty-five, Flora's immediate family had been only marginally involved in treasonable activities. Her stepfather, now known as Armadale, had happened to be walking on the shore at Arisaig when the Prince's ship came in there in July 1745. Beyond kissing the royal hand, he had made no gesture of Jacobite support, and later that year he became a captain in a government militia on Skye.[13] Young Clan, enthusiastic for the Stuart cause, had 'carried' Flora's brother, the latter was to assert, to the Prince's first headquarters and 'pressed him strongly to join him in bearing arms for the Young Pretender'. Angus Macdonald had refused to do Young Clan's bidding, he afterwards insisted, 'nor ever did bear arms against the Government'.[14] In consequence, when Flora crossed from Skye to South Uist in early June 1746 'in order to visit her brother-german [full brother], who had about that time taken up [set up] house', she had no reason to fear the government troops and militiamen who then swarmed about the island.[15]

When later asked by government authorities 'if she had any Invitation from those who persuaded her to do what she afterwards engaged in for the young Pretender or any Body else, before she left Skye', Flora answered 'in the negative'.[16] At the time of her leaving that island, she stated, she had 'only heard he [the Prince] was somewhere on the Long Island'. Flora, like all those on the Long Island and on Skye when later questioned about their dealings with the Young Pretender, had no qualms about speaking with a forked tongue. She said nothing of what knowledge of the Prince's whereabouts she had acquired during the weeks she stayed with her brother on South Uist, nor of her acquaintance at Nunton with O'Neill, an officer known to be the Prince's constant companion. If she knew in advance of her stepfather's scheme, she never said so.

While the Prince and his companions were turning their steps towards the Macdonald sheiling at Unasary above Loch Eynort on the night of 20 June, Flora was alone or had a servant for company while she slept there, for her brother was 'not at home' at that time.[17] It was 'about midnight', she was to record in a later 'Memorial', a form of narrative employing the third person and stating a case for aid, when she awoke to find Neil MacEachen, her cousin, with her in the 'little house' on the hill. He had left the Prince and O'Neill 'at a little distance off' and was come in to urge her to rise. His companions, Neil said, wanted 'instantly to speak with her'. When Flora, years later, gave this account of her royal summons, the details were still fresh in her mind: 'She was surprised, and wanted to know what they had to say to her, but went out as fast as she could throw on some of her clothes.'[18]

At the door she met Colonel O'Neill, who boldly announced to her the scheme which her stepfather had devised, and which wanted only her agreement for its execution. She 'answered with the greatest respect and loyalty, but declined' to take part. Armadale had proposed that Flora convey her 'maid' into the hands of Lady Margaret Macdonald, the Knight's wife on Skye. Flora said that that lady's husband 'was too much her friend [for her] to be the instrument of his ruin'. Her stepfather after all leased Armadale from Sir Alexander. The former might have no scruples in proposing that his stepdaughter and the Knight's wife aid the royal fugitive, and Lady Margaret herself might be willing, but Flora held fast to her point. The Knight, then with the Duke of Cumberland at Fort Augustus, was very publicly an agent of the

Hanoverian government in their measures to discover Jacobite rebels. A scheme involving his wife in the Prince's escape would bring swift retribution from those he sought to propitiate.

The Irish Colonel continued to press her. Flora was obdurate. Moreover, O'Neill afterwards related, she 'insisted upon the risk she would run of losing her character in a malicious and ill-natured world'. Flora aired real concerns: a girl's 'character', or virginal reputation, was as much key to her future marriage as any dowry. Were Flora to consent to the proposed scheme, though her cousin Neil were to act as chaperone, ribaldry and lewd remarks about her relations with the Prince were all too likely to arise should the adventure become known. O'Neill, prone to bombast, eager to obtain Flora's consent to the scheme, exclaimed, 'If you will still entertain fears about your character, I shall (by an oath) marry you directly, if you please.'[19] At this time in Scotland, a couple had only to hold each other's hand and plight their troth for the union to be legal. Flora did not dignify this offer with an answer.

Flora may with good reason have questioned why her stepfather offered her up for sacrifice in this way. He perhaps knew he could depend on her, should she accept the challenge, to display good sense in a crisis. Moreover, though he, like Boisdale and Old Clan and Flora's own brother, had declined to come out for the Prince, none of them wished to see the Stuart scion taken on Macdonald land. Armadale's plan provided for the Prince to pass into the hands of the Knight's wife and out of those of his stepdaughter as soon as they landed in Skye.

Over thirty years later Flora recalled the dialogue that then ensued: 'She told him that as there were so many dangers to encounter, it would grieve her more that he [the Prince] should be taken along with her than in any other way, and begged he would not insist on her undertaking that service.' O'Neill responded that 'There was no other method to extricate him [the Prince] out of his present danger … Though she denied him, he was sure she would not deny himself [the Prince] as soon as she saw him.' Flora was well able to hold her ground in argument with O'Neill. 'Don't think, sir, that I am quite so faint-hearted as that comes to,' she retorted.[20]

Flora was described by one who knew her well as 'smart and lively'.[21] Another, soon to see much of her, agreed that she was 'easy and cheerful', but noted 'a certain mixture of gravity in all her behaviour which ... set her off to great advantage'.[22] Nevertheless, an audience with royalty, albeit under a dim moonlit sky and in the wilds rather than in any palace, was a challenge for this young Highlander. O'Neill whistled, and the Prince, who had been standing nearby, 'with his baggage upon his back', joined them at the door. Neil MacEachen later wrote that His Royal Highness 'saluted her [Flora] very kindly'.[23]

The royal fugitive, whom Flora saw by the light of a waxen moon, may have bent over her hand to kiss it in courtly fashion. If so, he bent low. The Prince was nearly six foot tall, and she a 'little woman ... well enough shaped'.[24] He was no longer, however, the pale, graceful youth whom Edinburgh ladies had dubbed Bonnie Prince Charlie when he rode into the Scottish capital on a gleaming black steed the previous autumn.[25] Living much in the open, and the victim of sun, rain and wind, he was now well described as 'black weather-beaten'.[26] Since coming into the Long Island, he had adopted the dress of the country – plaid, belted kilt, 'tartan hose [woollen knee stockings]' and brogues. These items, as well as his 'tartan short coat [jacket]' and undershirt, were variously stained, ragged or spattered with mud.[27] If her cousin had not vouched for this being Prince Charles Edward Stuart, Flora might well have doubted this alarming stranger's identity.

According to Neil, the Prince assured Flora of 'the sense he would always retain of so conspicuous a service'.[28] He asserted, she later recalled, that she would be 'quite safe in undertaking what he wanted', as her stepfather would provide a passport for the voyage to Skye. The different accounts of her eventual capitulation which Flora was to give over the years make clear her present qualms.[29] She 'still insisted on the danger, but her former resolution failed her', she was later to record. She at length 'with some difficulty [hesitation] agreed to undertake the dangerous enterprise', despite the risk to both her person and her character.[30] The Prince's gratitude for the 'conspicuous service' she now undertook was not to last for ever.

Nevertheless, during the ensuing days he extended to her every courtesy and was solicitous for her comfort, such as was to be had. He accorded her the appellations 'My lady' and 'Our lady', and in whatever lodging or setting outside they found themselves made sure to rise upon her coming in and going out.[31]

Flora now laid before her unexpected royal guest 'a part of the best cheer she had'. At home tacksmen owned silver and glass, and dined on beef and mutton. In their summer shelters, however, they picnicked on bread and cheese, and milked the livestock over which they watched. The fare that Flora offered the Prince included a large bowl 'full of cream'.[32] Charles Edward, who had feasted from youth at banquets in Rome and Paris and still dined, even while on campaign during the Rising, off silver and crystal, took exception to neither vessel nor contents. Old Clan had furnished 'a [dairy] cow', meat and drink, when the Prince was at Corradale.[33] Since leaving that place, however, the royal party had enjoyed rough commons. Famished after a night's journey, the Prince 'took two or three hearty go-downs [gulps]', Neil recorded, 'and his fellow-travellers swallowed the rest'.[34]

The aplomb with which Flora acted as hostess to royalty on the hill at midnight was considerable. Following the circulation, over the next century, of the accounts which Neil and the Irish Colonel committed to paper, and of those which Flora herself furnished, artists in Europe and in the United Kingdom were emboldened to depict the scene. Imagination was not lacking, on each of their parts, to supply the lack of detail and to engage the attention of the public.

Among the most successful of these depictions is that by the French artist Paul Delaroche. In *Édouard en Écosse*, the painting he exhibited at the Paris Salon in 1827, he transposed the scene from the Macdonald sheiling to a picturesque cave.[35] In the foreground among the rocks a fearsome individual on one knee and in full Highland dress is possibly intended to represent Flora's cousin Neil. Further back Flora is portrayed, standing over a seated Prince and ministering to him with a basket at her feet. This Prince, for all his recent travails, is bandbox fresh in an officer's uniform and with coiffed hair. Flora is the very image of a fine lady with a gleaming chignon, lace at her sleeve. The light catches the sheen of her silken skirt and wrap.

Delaroche made genteel what was in reality a desperate and raw encounter. So, too, did 'The Story of Flora Macdonald' in *Our Island Story*, a colourful history of the British Isles published in 1905 and lapped up thereafter by generations of children throughout the Empire: 'Many people ... helped Prince Charles, but it was a beautiful lady, called Flora Macdonald, who perhaps helped him most.' However, Henrietta Marshall, author of *Our Island Story*, continued with perfect accuracy, 'She served him when he was most miserable and in greatest danger.'[36] If none of those gathered in the Macdonald house on the hill were as splendidly dressed as those represented in *Édouard en Écosse*, Delaroche and other artists were correct when they portrayed Flora as a Highland gentlewoman.

Day had not yet broken on Midsummer's Eve when Flora, having first promised that she would send word to the Prince 'how all was going on',[37] struck out north from the sheiling for Benbecula. She meant to procure from her stepfather, whom she believed to be on duty at the fords, the passport he had promised, and then continue on to Nunton, the Clanranald seat. Her intention there was to invoke Lady Clan's assistance. Provisions were wanted for the intended expedition to Skye, and 'women's clothes', suitable for a maid, had to be fashioned. Flora's own were 'too little', she was to relate, nor, given his height, would the Prince fit those of any female in the Nunton household.[38]

Flora was baulked that day in her bid to reach Nunton, which lay fifteen miles north of the sheiling at Unasary. Transport was not an issue. Like all on the Long Island and Skye, she was accustomed to walking great distances and to riding the compact Highland ponies which negotiated rough terrain with comparative ease. Tacksmen like her brother kept and lent out these beasts which served both as mounts and as packhorses. However, upon her arrival at the northern coast of South Uist, she discovered that, while Skye militiamen, wearing a distinctive black coat over Highland dress,

were posted 'within a gun shot of each other from east to west',
her stepfather was not among them.[39] Flora 'was taken prisoner' by
some of their number, 'she not having a passport' or authority to
cross to Benbecula.[40] Only militia captains such as Armadale had
authority to provide this document.

In this first of many tests of her mettle and powers to deceive,
Flora was confident. Addressing her armed captors, she was later
to recall, she '*demanded* [to know] to whom they belonged'. When
they answered that her stepfather was their commander, 'she refused
to give any answers, till she should see their captain'. Armadale was
due on the Benbecula coast, it transpired, the following morning.
Later that day, in consequence, Flora was taken 'across the fords' at
low tide and remained in the Benbecula guardhouse overnight to
await her stepfather.[41]

Armadale was, as one in the plot was later to acknowledge, the
'grand contriver for laying and executing the scheme for the Prince's
escape in woman's clothes from the Long Island to the Isle of Skye'.[42]
Earlier in June, he had 'announced his [militia's] movements', in
advance of various searches undertaken on South Uist, 'so that the
Prince might always have the warning of them'.[43] Now, arriving
next morning, the 22nd, at the guard post, he was swift to act
upon hearing from his stepdaughter of her midnight visitors. He
furnished, as Flora was afterwards to state, 'a passport for herself,
a man-servant [Neil MacEachen] … and another woman, Bettie
Burk [Betty Burke], a good spinster, and whom he recommended
as such in a letter to his wife in Skye, as she [Marion Macdonald]
had much lint to spin'.[44] 'Betty Burke' was the fictitious name that
would serve the Prince when he was 'in woman's clothes' as Flora's
servant, 'an Irish girl'.

The letter which Armadale wrote to his wife runs as follows:

> I have sent your daughter from this country, lest she should
> be any way frightened with the troops lying here. She has got
> one Betty Burke, an Irish girl, who, as she tells me, is a good
> spinster. If her spinning please you, you can keep her till she
> spin all your lint: or, if you have any wool to spin, you may

employ her. I have sent Niel MacEachainn [Neil MacEachen]
along with your daughter and Betty Burke, to take care
of them.

   I am your dutiful husband, Hugh Macdonald
   June, 22d, 1746[45]

Flora was afterwards to state, 'If her stepfather (Hugh Macdonald
of Armadale) had not granted Miss [herself] a passport, she could
not have undertook her journey and voyage.'[46] She was, however,
now in possession of papers which would incriminate her and her
stepfather and even Neil should the plot to disguise the Prince as
Betty Burke be uncovered.

   Once the passport and letter were stowed about her person,
Flora calmly sat down to breakfast with her stepfather and a party
of others who included the Benbecula baillie, or constable.[47]
Before she could proceed on her way, however, they were to
her surprise joined in the guardhouse by her cousin Neil. The
previous day, he and his companions had skulked near Corradale,
but the Prince had become 'prodigious impatient' as the day wore
on, and still no word came from 'the lady'. He dispatched Neil in
search of Flora at Nunton, where they imagined she was by now
established. Like Flora before him, for want of a passport Neil
was halted by militiamen at the South Uist ford and detained
there till morning. He had now been sent across at low water to
be 'examined'.

   Confused to find his cousin at the guardhouse, imagining she
had already been and gone from Nunton, Neil 'called Miss aside,
and asked if everything was ready'. Flora replied that it had been
'put out of her power to go on ... that nothing was as yet done,
but that she was going off within half an hour after to consult
with the lady [Lady Clan]'. Neil, she directed, should return with
'all the haste possible' to the Prince and immediately set out for
Rossinish, a peninsula forming a natural harbour on the east coast
of Benbecula, from where it was envisaged they would embark
for Skye. Flora told her cousin that she and Lady Clan would,
meanwhile, set out from Nunton that same afternoon. They would

'carry along with them whatever clothes or provisions was requisite for the voyage'. The royal party would 'be sure to find them without fail' at the agreed rendezvous.[48] While Neil departed back across the fords in search of the Prince, Flora pressed on the few miles remaining to Nunton, where she intended to draw Lady Clan into the conspiracy.

3

'Great Fears'
June 1746

In the event, although Flora reached Nunton that Sunday afternoon, 22 June 1746, it was not till the following Saturday that she and Lady Clan set out to meet the Prince and his companions at Rossinish. Flora, who had grown up at a tack adjacent to the Clanranald seat, was close kin to its master and on easy terms with its mistress. She had already passed time at Nunton on this summer visit to the Long Island. If not from her own observation, she knew from the royal party of Lady Clan's former assistance to the Prince in hiding. She had every reason to anticipate that her hostess would aid her now. Nor was she disappointed. However, in the absence of more impetuous male conspirators, she and Lady Clan were the authors of an alternative scheme to deliver Charles Edward out of danger. They hoped to spirit the Prince to land belonging to the Knight on North Uist, which had already been searched by militiamen, where he might lurk until an opportunity arose to make for the mainland.

It was to fascinate many who knew her that Lady Clan played such a bold part in the subterfuge to effect the Prince's escape from the Long Island. She was of a nervous disposition, and the Nunton servants had, upon occasion, to nurse her through periods of lunacy.[1] However, her own sept of the Macleod clan on Bernera, another of the Western Isles, had come out for the Prince, and its chief had been among the Prince's stoutest adherents. Like Flora's cousin Neil, she proved herself sagacious and steady in her endeavour to free the Stuart scion of his pursuers.

Flora proposed 'that the Prince should go under the care of a gentleman' – Hugh Macdonald of Baleshare – 'to the northward'.[2] A tacksman on Sleat lands in North Uist, Baleshare had already acted, earlier in the summer, as secret emissary for the Knight's wife. He had brought copies of the *London Gazette*, a valuable source of domestic and foreign intelligence, to the Prince in hiding at Corradale.[3] Now Baleshare, close kin to both Old Clan and Armadale, cautiously agreed to Flora's request that he rendezvous with the Prince to discuss his providing a refuge on North Uist.

Meanwhile the Prince, Neil and O'Neill had arrived at Rossinish, having left their Corradale refuge under cover of night and having had numerous adventures aboard a small yawl belonging to some 'country people' whom Flora's cousin paid for passage to Benbecula. A nearby bothy had been appointed as the place of rendezvous with the ladies from Nunton. To reach it, they must tramp that night across boggy moorland, victims of 'vehement' rain and of a wind which blew 'directly in their teeth'. While the Prince trembled with cold, they burrowed periodically into the heather – the only shelter from the elements available – to rest.[4]

After all these travails, when Neil entered the bothy to see if the ladies had come, he found there only 'the man who took care of the house [for Old Clan], in bed with his wife'. Neil returned to tell his companions 'dismal news', learned from this individual. Twenty Skye militiamen had landed at Rossinish two days before and were under canvas about a quarter of a mile off. The Prince, previously sanguine in the face of danger, became so enraged that he was 'like to tear his clothes in pieces, not knowing where to run for safety, the enemy being everywhere'. Neil took the decision to repair to a tacksman's house some way off.[5]

Departing immediately, 'all bespattered with dirt and mud' after their night's journey, the royal party was at the farm before first light. The Prince was keen for MacEachen to head to Nunton, inform his cousin of their arrival and 'hasten her to come without any longer delay'. Neil, however, foresaw the danger to which the prince would be exposed if left only with O'Neill, 'a man who knew not one step of the country, or where to retire to in case of necessity'. In consequence, O'Neill went in his place, taking the Clanranald tacksman, whose house they occupied, as his guide. Neil noted drily that the Irish Colonel was 'mighty well pleased' with his embassy, 'not so much to further the prince's affairs, as to be in company with Miss Flora'. The officer 'professed a great deal of kindness' for that young woman, MacEachen noted, notwithstanding her earlier dismissal of his offer of marriage.[6]

When O'Neill reached Nunton, Flora revealed to him the reason why she and Lady Clan had not yet left for Rossinish. She was sure, she affirmed, that Charles Edward would be safer in North Uist than on the Isle of Skye. O'Neill thereupon dispatched his tacksman guide with a letter to the Prince, indicating Baleshare's willingness to consult. With the missive went also two bottles of wine and a roast hen from the Clanranald cellars and kitchen.[7]

Both the sustenance and the suggestion that Baleshare might prove a protector were welcome to the duo on the coast. That morning they had been forced out into the open after learning that the militiamen stationed nearby 'were accustomed to come every morning to buy milk'. Neil and the Prince spent the day wrapped in their plaids, sheltering under a rock near the shore. 'It is almost inexpressible what torment the prince suffered under that unhappy rock', Neil recalled later. It 'had neither height nor breadth to cover him from the rain, which poured down upon him so thick as if all the windows of heaven had broke open'. To complete the royal fugitive's tortures, 'there lay such a swarm of mitches [midges] upon his face and hands as would have made any other but himself fall into despair'. The attentions of these biting gnats made their victim 'utter such hideous cries and complaints as would have rent the rocks with compassion'.[8]

That evening, however, upon their return to the house, they found a good fire blazing, and the Prince's spirits revived. Stripped of his sodden plaid and other clothes, he sat down in only a shirt by the hearth, 'as merry and hearty', according to Neil, 'as if he was in

the best room at Whitehall'.⁹ The arrival of O'Neill's letter further
heartened him, as did the provisions sent from Nunton. Devouring
the roast fowl, the Prince 'took his bonnet, and drunk with it [as a
scoop] out of the loch'. He was once more 'very canty [lively] and
jocose [good-humoured]'.¹⁰

Baleshare, however, who joined the royal party later that day,
'absolutely refused', O'Neill was to write, 'receiving us [in North
Uist]'. As 'vassal to Sir Alexander Macdonald', he said, he must
decline.¹¹ Flora later stated, rather, that he 'refused the important
trust, from fear of the great dangers attending it'.¹² The North Uist
man advised instead that the Prince should revert to the former
plan of taking refuge in Skye. He should wait until the Minch
was 'clear of ships … go off in the afternoon to give him a long
night … [and] keep close by the land [coast] of Skye'. Rather than
come ashore below Monkstadt, the Sleat seat, Baleshare advised
landing close to the Cuillin, a formidable range of mountains.
Old Mackinnon, a laird who owned territory known as Strath in
the south-east of Skye, would, he counselled, see the Prince safely
landed on the mainland.

The Prince 'had his writing instruments about him', and wrote
down the names of some of those whom Baleshare indicated would
offer further assistance on Skye.¹³ The Sleat tacksman then left
for home, while the Prince sent O'Neill to acquaint Flora with
this disappointment. Reminding her of her earlier promise to be
his protector, he declared that there was now no option but to
pursue the original plan, while he and Neil made preparations for
the voyage. According to Flora, the boat to be employed was that,
earlier sunk, which the Prince had 'constantly kept with him' when
on the Long Island, in which case the 'Five men' enlisted 'for the
Boat's crew' recovered the vessel.¹⁴

Flora's efforts to evade having that 'important trust' – the
Prince's safe escape – placed in her hands were at an end. She had
amply foretold, in the midnight colloquy at Unasary, the danger in
which her stepfather's scheme would place her. There was no time
now for repining. Now was the time to act.

The Prince, Neil later wrote, 'seemed very uneasy that night' when neither O'Neill nor the ladies came 'according to promise'. He continued, 'The truth is, they could not really come sooner, as they were busy night and day to get his dress made for the prince, and whatever other things he might have occasion for.'[15]

The gown over which the ladies laboured at Nunton while Neil and the Prince waited was suitable for a maidservant, being of calico with an inconspicuous flower pattern. The sewing and enlarging of this and other items could not be entrusted to Clanranald servants, as the dimensions of the garments being produced for the outsize 'Irish maid' would undoubtedly elicit comment. In consequence, Flora and Lady Clan sewed in secret, assembling also an apron, a quilted petticoat and a 'mantle [cape] of dun camlet [wool], made after the Irish fashion'.[16] They took especial pains to stitch an elaborate cap besides. The Prince's oval visage was distinctive, and had been reproduced over the past year in countless engravings and broadsides. Although now pitted and sunburned, Betty Burke's singular face might well prove the Prince's undoing if those with whom 'she' came into contact were familiar with those royal images. The hood of the cape that Flora and Lady Clan sewed could not always be pulled up about the Irish maid's long head, but this close-fitting headdress would obscure much of his face.

On Friday morning, 27 June, Neil was informed by two of the selected crew, brothers John and Roderick Macdonald, that the vessel and the rest of their number were at the Rossinish anchorage and ready to depart. Leaving the tacksman's house, Neil conveyed the Prince to these rebels who would guide him to the bothy on the Rossinish shore. He himself posted off to Nunton, where he found that the ladies were ready to depart for their rendezvous.[17] Moreover, they had entrusted a Sleat tacksman's wife, who was travelling to Skye, with a message for Lady Margaret Macdonald, that the Prince hoped to gain that island in disguise. Though their envoy's husband was a Skye militia captain, she had no hesitation in lending her support to the coming masquerade.[18]

The group that left Nunton for Rossinish was large, and there was something of a holiday air to the outing, engaged though they were in a dangerous mission. Flora bore a bundle containing the 'apparel sufficient for his [the Prince's] disguise, viz. a flower'd linen gown, a white apron, etc.'[19] Her brother Milton and Neil, as well as O'Neill, acted as gentleman escorts and carried other baggage. The mistress of Nunton was accompanied by her eldest daughter, and John Maclean, the cook who had dressed meat for the Prince at Corradale, was of the party. He was to cook dinner on the shore. Flora later recalled that Lady Clan additionally 'provided Provisions for the voyage' – bottles of milk, bread and butter, and a bottle of wine.[20] The mistress of Nunton could offer no more. The militia these last few weeks had made so many demands on the Clanranald hospitality that the pantry and cellar were both denuded.

When in July Flora was held captive on board a naval vessel, she omitted, in her catalogue of those on this journey, her cousin Neil, who was by then in hiding, and her brother Milton. She had no wish to direct the anger of the Hanoverian general, to whom she made this confession, towards either. Similarly she did not state that, as Neil later recorded, the party, after walking some way, 'had the conveniency of a boat' – apparently supplied by Lady Clan – 'to Roshinish [Rossinish]', declining to implicate its skipper.

When the Nunton party neared the anchorage where the boat for Skye was already drawn up, the Prince was the first down to the shore to welcome the ladies upon their disembarkation. He had previously been industriously 'assisting in the roasting of his dinner' – the 'heart, liver, kidneys, etc., of a bullock or sheep' – on a wooden spit.[21] Now, entrusting the further preparation of the meal to the Nunton cook, the Prince was at his most courtly. He 'handed [escorted] the Lady Clan to the house'. Flora, her brother and Neil followed, and there they 'passed some hours very hearty and merry till supper was served'.[22] All was in readiness for the journey to Skye to begin thereafter under cover of darkness.

Hardly had the meal begun, however, when it was interrupted. One of Old Clan's herdsmen came with momentous news. General Campbell had arrived on the island. Furthermore, he was landing his men 'within three miles of them'.[23] Major General John Campbell of Mamore was a foe of calibre. Heir to the 3rd Duke of Argyll and a longstanding Member of Parliament in the government interest, he had been called back from service in Flanders in the autumn of 1745 to oppose the Jacobite army. Deputed to head the search for the Prince in the wake of Culloden, he had now entered the waters of the Long Island aboard the *Furnace*, a naval sloop which, with a cutter and other ancillary vessels, carried regular troops and Argyll militiamen.

On hearing this news, Neil recorded, 'all run to their boat in the greatest confusion, every one carrying with him, whatever part of the baggage came first to his hand, without either regard to sex or quality'. It was agreed that the Clanranald boat and the one bound for Skye should head for the far side of a sea loch where they would be secluded from view. About five in the morning, the vessels landed there and the party continued their interrupted supper, their elation at the prospect of the Prince's projected escape from the Western Isles much dimmed.[24]

Within a few hours, a further message from Nunton caused still greater alarm. A servant came to tell Lady Clan that 'General Campbell, with a party of his men, were at her house, and wanted that she should be there before twelve of the clock, otherwise … her house should suffer for all.'[25] In addition the royal party learned that John Fergusson, Captain of the *Furnace*, had arrived at Nunton the night before and had slept in Lady Clan's own bed.[26] The roles of naval and military officers had become blurred in the authorities' efforts in the Highlands to bring rebels to justice. Fergusson had recently landed on the small island of Raasay lying off the mainland east of Skye and ordered the home of its laird, who had been out in the rebellion, burned 'to ashes' and another 300 houses fired.[27] In consequence of this and other atrocities, he was widely regarded in the Hebrides as the 'most bent [intent] of any … to take the Prince'.[28]

The party on the lochside did not know that the General and Fergusson suspected nothing and were only pausing at Nunton on their way to seek the Prince in the hills on South Uist, where, in common with the Duke of Cumberland and his staff at Fort Augustus, they believed the Prince was still to be found. So Campbell's message caused alarm among those gathered at Rossinish. There was general agreement, however, that there was nothing for it but for Lady Clan to return home. There she must seek to parry any questions regarding her previous whereabouts with evasive answers. She was to do so with courage and wit.[29]

Once Lady Clan and her daughter had departed, Flora assumed control of the expedition. Although O'Neill 'insisted strongly to leave the country with the Prince', she was proof against his pleas. Unlike Neil and Flora herself, he 'being a stranger … did not speak the language of the country [Gaelic]', she observed, and 'would readily be taken [captured]'.[30] The Colonel may have spoken Irish, from which Gaelic derived, but the latter tongue was now markedly different from the former. Flora remained adamant, even when the Prince himself begged for the officer's company on the voyage. The passport she possessed was made out, she reminded Charles Edward, only for her, Betty Burke and her cousin Neil.

Flora furthermore denied the Prince's request that he secrete the pair of pistols, which he had always carried in his wanderings since Culloden, under his petticoats when he came to don female attire. She feared, if the party were searched and the 'Irish girl' was discovered to have fine firearms under her skirts, that 'she' would be uncovered as the Prince. 'Indeed, Miss,' the Prince replied, 'if we shall happen to meet with any that will go so narrowly to work in searching as what you mean, they will certainly discover me [his male sex] at any rate.'[31]

Flora was apparently amused by this remark, but did not waver in her determination that Betty Burke should carry no arms. Charles Edward gave his pistols to Flora's brother Milton for safekeeping. Angus departed, bearing away the plaintive O'Neill with him at last.[32] One of the crew later confirmed that the passengers were unarmed. On being asked, 'Had they any arms,' he replied, 'Not so much as a dirk [short dagger].'[33] The Prince was obliged to content himself with 'a short heavy cudgel' for a weapon. He volunteered that, with it, he would 'knock down any single person that should attack him'.[34]

The time had come for Charles to adopt the identity of Betty Burke. Stripping off his Highland dress, he made no difficulty about putting on the petticoat, the calico gown, the apron or the cape. He assumed the brogues offered him without complaint. He could not, however, keep his hands from adjusting his voluminous headdress, 'which he cursed a thousand times'.[35] Eventually Flora was satisfied with his appearance, and, though Betty Burke managed her skirts awkwardly, she, her 'maid' and Neil set off for the boat, which was some way off on the shore. They arrived, she was to remember, 'in a very wet condition, and made a fire upon a piece [slab] of rock', to dry as well as to keep themselves warm till night.[36] Their intention was to embark that evening.

One last alarum disturbed the final preparations. Four or five wherries came into view, approaching the shore where the royal party was established. Quickly dousing the fire which had attracted the attention of the Argyll militiamen on board the vessels, Flora, Neil and Betty Burke lay in the heather above the shore, praying that they would escape detection.[37] They were all, Flora afterwards declared, 'put ... into great Fears ... lest anybody should land there'.[38] The wherries, however, 'sailed by to the southward, within gunshot of where they lay, without ever stopping'.[39] Once the danger of discovery had passed, Flora, Neil and the Prince emerged from the heather.

There was no further incident to discompose the party waiting to embark. After the sun had set, at about eight o'clock in the evening, on Saturday, 28 June, Flora, Neil and Betty Burke took their seats in the shallop, or open boat.[40] Some twenty-four feet long, with room on board for twelve, the vessel had a shallow draught and two sails. John Macdonald was at the helm. His brother Roderick and three others – Rory Macdonald, John MacVuirich and Duncan Campbell – were at the oars. Neil MacEachen recorded, 'The weather proving calm in the beginning of the night', for want of a wind 'they rowed away at a good rate.'[41]

Flora, one of the sailors later observed, wore on the voyage a 'long jacket of English blue cloth' and a 'silk black hood'. Her 'maid' had on, he noted, 'a woman's calico gown ... a camblet yellowish long cloak, a big cape [hood] to it of the same [material].' Rory Macdonald, this oarsman, added that 'he was sworn (as he was pressed to row a boat between North Uist and Skye) not to tell anything he saw or what persons were then in the boat.' But there was no attempt on the part of the travellers to conceal the fact that Flora's servant was a man in a disguise. The crew were given to understand that the Prince was a rebel of the name of Sinclair. Recalled Macdonald, 'Flora told me she was to go to Raasay, and Sinclair was to pass for Flora's maid ... It was his [Sinclair's] and his mistress's wish to land there' at Kilbride, a harbour below the Knight's house on Skye, 'as being the nighest [nearest] place to go to Raasay'. Asked if 'Sinclair' had 'the appearance of a woman or any beard', he replied, 'Not at all for anyone would easily find him out', and 'Had little beard, and close shaved'.[42]

A century and more later would elapse before an Englishman published words to the tune of a Gaelic air, to the beat of which oarsmen rowed across a loch in Skye in the 1870s:

Speed, bonnie boat, like a bird on the wing,
Onward! the sailors cry;
Carry the lad that's born to be king
Over the sea to Skye.[43]

No record exists to indicate whether the crew of the shallop heading out to sea sang or saved their breath for the work ahead. Night, at this season thus far north, would not fall till near eleven or midnight. The period when they must then steer by the stars, if visible, would not be long, for day broke as early as night fell late. Thirty nautical miles would bring the shallop heading east across the Minch to Skye, should no storm or other peril on the sea intervene.

4

'A Man in a Woman's Dress'
June 1746

Flora Macdonald's voyage with Betty Burke to Skye was long to be remembered in the Highlands and Islands. Over seventy years later 'the mighty Minstrel',[1] James Hogg, was to take down the words of a Gaelic song recording their adventures and publish an English translation as 'Twa [two] Bonnie Maidens':

There were twa bonnie maidens, and three bonnie maidens,
Cam' owre [over] the Minch, and cam' owre the main,
Wi' the wind for their way and the corry [hollow] for their
    hame [home],
And they're dearly welcome to Skye again.

Come alang, come alang, wi' your boatie [boatman] and
    your song,
My ain [own] bonnie maidens, my twa bonnie maids!
For the nicht [night], it is dark, and the redcoat is gane [gone],
And ye are dearly welcome to Skye again.

There is Flora, my honey, sae [so] dear and sae bonnie,
And ane [one] that's sae tall, and handsome withal.
Put the ane for my king and the other for my queen
And they're dearly welcome to Skye again.

Come alang, come alang, etc.[2]

The wind picked up as the boat headed out to sea and the sails filled. Shortly after nightfall, about midnight, however, a strong westerly wind commenced blowing. At the same time a thick mist descended, which robbed helmsman John Macdonald of all sight of land or stars to steer by. In the darkness, the crew were unsure whether or not they had 'lost their course'.[3] Although the gale diminished after a time, the fog all around endured. The boatmen ended by agreeing to rest on their oars and let the boat drift till daybreak when the mist should clear. Meanwhile, a heavy rain fell and soaked passengers and crew alike.[4] Neil was to note that the petticoated Charles Edward 'all this time, was not in the least discouraged'.[5] Though no lover of the sea, he was as ever excited by the presence of danger. Flora, however, was already fatigued by the violence of the recent storm. This downpour 'distressed her much. To divert her the Prince sung several pretty songs.'[6] When Flora was later asked 'what particular songs he chanted', she named 'The King Shall Enjoy his own Again', and 'The Twenty-Ninth of May'.[7] These ballads celebrated Charles Edward's Stuart ancestors Charles I and Charles II.

Despite the adverse weather conditions, lulled by these and some other pastoral 'chaunts', Flora contrived to fall asleep on the open sea. 'Happening to awake with some little bustle in the boat' some time later, she found her tall 'maid' leaning over her, 'with his hands spread about her head'. When Flora, bewildered, asked the Prince 'what he was about', she learned from him that 'one of the rowers, being obliged to do somewhat about the sail, behoved to step over her body (the boat was so small).' Fearing that the oarsman might do 'the lady' an injury, 'either by stumbling or trampling upon her in the dark', the disguised Prince told her, he had been doing his best to 'preserve his guardian from harm'.[8]

This was not the extent of Betty Burke's solicitude for Miss Macdonald. The 'Irish maid', in common with the others in the vessel, drank from the bottles of milk which Lady Clan had supplied for the voyage. There was only the one 'half-bottle of wine' on board, however. The Prince neither had recourse himself to 'this small allowance of wine', nor would he permit any other in the boat to share in it. He 'kept it altogether for Miss Macdonald's use, lest she should faint with the cold and other inconveniences of a night passage'.[9]

Neil was the probable author later this year of *Alexis, or The Young Adventurer*, an allegorical pamphlet. The Prince was represented there by its pastoral protagonist and Flora by Heroica, a noble maiden. If that publication may be trusted, while night and mist still hung over the boat, the Prince (Alexis) dwelled in conversation with Flora (Heroica) on the barbarous treatment by 'Butcher' Cumberland (Sanguinarius) of wounded and slain Highlanders at Culloden.[10]

At daybreak on Sunday, 29 June, the crew espied the west coast of Skye and, under clear skies, took up their oars again. Coming nearer, they made for the harbour to the north, below the Knight's house, where they intended to land. However, the boatmen's travails were not yet at an end. The wind shifted about to the north and for an hour and a half 'blew … so strong in their teeth, that … it was impossible to discern whether they made any [head]way or not'. The Prince encouraged the crew on, 'saying that he would relieve him that was most fatigued'.[11]

At length the boat neared a headland, where passengers and crew could moor and rest after the night's work. The boat having been secured in a creek, Flora, the Prince and Neil ate the bread and butter they had brought with them, the sailors ate the provisions they had brought, and all drank from an icy waterfall. Embarking once more, they rounded the point to continue their journey. But now their relief at gaining Skye gave way to confusion and fear. To their dismay, the boat was now in plain sight of a party of soldiers on the sands.[12] Flora later recalled that she and her fellow passengers 'were so near the shore' that the armed men were clearly visible.[13]

Rory Macdonald was to confess, 'There were some militia or some sentry, who called to us to come ashore, which we did not … Sinclair said to row as fast as we were able.' The disguised Prince 'threatened hard' if the crew complied with the soldiers' order.[14] However, as the crew strained at their oars to get away, they saw 'a body of about fifteen [militia]men, full armed' march down from the village to join the sentry on the shore.[15] Flora feared that they would now be taken. Charles Edward calmed her fears. 'Don't be afraid, Miss, we will not be taken yet. You see it is low water … Before they can launch their boats over that rough shore, we will get in below those high rocks, and they will lose sight of us.'[16] The Prince was proved right, and the militiamen gazed impotently after the shallop as it travelled further north.

Twelve nautical miles up the coast of Skye, the vessel at last gained the Kilbride anchorage they sought at about ten in the morning. Above lay Monkstadt, Sir Alexander's seat, where Flora and Neil were to beg Lady Margaret's help with the Prince's onward journey. The Prince, in his women's garb, had escaped redcoats and militia alike on the Long Island. The perils, both maritime and military, of their voyage of over twelve hours were at an end. But new danger threatened.

The plan for the Prince's further escape, on which Flora and Neil had fixed, obliged them to leave Betty Burke in the boat with the crew. The cousins had chosen to arrive on Skye on Sunday, a day when the population of the island, including militia officers, were accustomed to spending a good part of the day in church. Nevertheless, a patrol might yet spy the newcomers. Before parting, Flora and Neil accordingly gave the oarsmen specific instructions. Should any draw near and question the identity of the female with their fellow Highlanders, the boatmen were to say that she was Miss Macdonald's maid, and 'curse her for a lazy jade [slut], what was she good for, since she did not attend her Mrs [mistress]'.[17] Thereupon the cousins set off in search of Lady Margaret. Monkstadt, her husband's commodious seat in the Trotternish peninsula with views over the Minch, was their destination.

When still some distance from the house, the pair chanced upon one of the Sleat servants. Flora asked that Lady Margaret be given a message that she was come to pay her respects and hoped that she would be received. She was, she said, on her way to her mother at Armadale, in the south of the island. The news that Flora was approaching Monkstadt and begged an interview came as no surprise to Lady Margaret. The mistress of the house 'knew her errand well enough', Neil later recorded, 'by one Mrs Macdonald, who had gone a little before to apprize her of it'.[18] Mrs Macdonald of Kirkibost, who had been earlier at Nunton with Flora and Lady Clan and was in their confidence, 'had crossed from the Long Isle only the day before (when her boat was most strictly searched for rebels)'.[19] She had, however, found no gratified recipient of her message at Monkstadt.

Lady Margaret had been the Prince's secret friend while he was on Clanranald ground on the Long Island, sending him London newspapers and other items he requested. The Knight's wife, however, had no wish at all to give the Prince sanctuary on Sleat land. Her husband was keen to present himself as loyal to the Duke at Fort Augustus, where he was now. Lady Margaret's urgent wish, on learning that the Prince was coming to beg her assistance, was to consign him into the hands of some other clan chief as soon as possible.

The Knight's wife had therefore sent for Alexander Macdonald of Kingsburgh, a Sleat tacksman who shared her husband's name and was his chief factor. The Knight had relied on Old Kingsburgh for years in a multitude of tasks. They included correspondence with lawyers in Edinburgh, the collection of rents on Skye and droving cattle to market on the mainland.[20] Sir Alexander had been hard pressed, the previous autumn, to find clansmen who would enlist for the two companies of militia which the government required him to raise. Like the Laird, whose lands and clan seat, Dunvegan Castle, lay west of Trotternish on the Waternish peninsula, the Knight found his tacksmen reluctant to join a force which might see them battling against rebel kinsmen. Old Kingsburgh's elder son was among those who came forward and served as a lieutenant.[21] When Lady Margaret looked to engineer the Prince's removal from her husband's lands, she had no hesitation in turning to the young man's father for counsel. Old Kingsburgh was now at Monkstadt, ready to do all in his power to avert catastrophe. Lady Margaret had also had the foresight to send for Donald Roy Macdonald, a former captain in the Prince's army and brother to Baleshare. Though he had incurred a severe wound in his foot at Culloden and was in hiding on Skye, the Jacobite officer set out on horseback immediately on receiving the lady's summons. The Knight's wife hoped that the resourceful Captain might play an active part in seeking sanctuary for the Prince elsewhere.[22]

Now, while Neil hovered outside the house in the guise of Flora's servant, Flora herself was admitted and taken to Lady Margaret's parlour. Here the two ladies had a hurried conversation. The letter that Flora carried from her stepfather to her mother had served merely to account for her embarkation from the Long Island with the counterfeit maidservant and Neil and their landing at Kilbride. Although this harbour on Skye was in the northern Trotternish peninsula and Flora's family home in the southern Sleat peninsula, the crossing from Rossinish east to Kilbride was relatively direct. It was entirely plausible, should they be questioned by militiamen, that the trio intended to ride south to Armadale. It had never, however, been envisaged that Betty Burke would accompany Flora south to Armadale and spin her mother's lint and wool. The mistress of Monkstadt, the travellers had hoped, would take the Prince, once more in male dress and under an alias, under her protection and facilitate his further escape to the Continent.

Flora confirmed to Lady Margaret that the Prince was now on the island and declared her hope that the chief's wife would help him to gain Portree. From this Skye harbour, it was posited, he might slip across to Raasay and, with the aid of the Macleod chief there, find passage back to the mainland and onward to France. The Knight's wife responded with calamitous intelligence. A militia officer was at breakfast elsewhere in the house with Mrs Macdonald of Kirkibost and Old Kingsburgh. Furthermore, the Lieutenant 'had three or four of his men about the house with him', while the rest of his command was 'at a small distance from the house, as he was employed to guard that part of the coast of Skye'. He was 'particularly to enquire', Lady Margaret reported, 'at every boat that should come from the Long Isle if there were any rebels on board'.[23]

Militiamen were milling about the house and on the coast. Should they only stroll along the shore, they would discover the boat which had come overnight from Rossinish and its occupants. Upon close examination, as the boatman Rory Macdonald was to declare, the Prince's womanly disguise would deceive no one: 'anyone would easily find him out'.[24] If the 'Irish maid' could be kept at a distance from onlookers, the masquerade might succeed. It was, however, essential that the Prince remove as swiftly and as far away from Monkstadt as possible.

Flora had had little sleep on the night's long and turbulent voyage from the Long Island. She was conscious that discovery of the plot in which she had become a lead conspirator might be imminent. She was nevertheless a model of composure at breakfast in the Monkstadt dining room, where she now proceeded. The Macleod Lieutenant there had been in church when the shallop had defied the order of the militiamen at the headland to come to. No intelligence of that disobedience had reached him. In consequence, the officer believed Flora to be an innocent gentlewoman, going about family business.

The Lieutenant found his new breakfast companion charming and conversational. In this he followed his fellow militiamen who had arrested Flora at the South Uist fords a week earlier and the gentlemen who had been of the company at the Benbecula guardhouse the following morning. Flora herself observed that she 'endeavoured all she could to keep up a close chit chat with Lieutenant Macleod, who put many questions to her, which she answered as she thought fit'.[25] Macleod 'asked Miss whence she came, whither she was going, what news? etc.' 'Miss' parried these questions, and the militia officer was perfectly satisfied with her nimble prevarications.[26] Furthermore, when Flora drew Old Kingsburgh to a window to confide to him the news that the Prince was on Skye and on the shore below the house, the Lieutenant was wholly unaware that anything of import had passed between the pair.[27] The factor, on hearing the news, retired from the room. Meanwhile, as Flora later told a cleric in Edinburgh, she 'could not help observing Lady Margaret going often out and in as one in great anxiety'.[28]

Flora continued to entertain the Lieutenant with the aid of Mrs Macdonald of Kirkibost. Meanwhile Donald Roy, at last nearing Monkstadt, 'spied Lady Margaret and Kingsburgh walking together, and talking in a serious way, above the garden'. Upon his coming up to them and dismounting, the lady, 'spreading out her hands', announced, 'O Donald Roy, we are ruined for ever.' She informed him that the Prince was landed 'about half a quarter of a mile from the house … If he should have the misfortune to be seized there, they [herself and Sir Alexander] would be affronted [face destruction] for ever.'

A new scheme was devised. It was settled that Donald Roy should seek out Old Raasay – Malcolm Macleod of Raasay – who ruled the island of that name and beg shelter there for the royal fugitive. Betty Burke should meanwhile spend the night at Kingsburgh's home with his mistress and her cousin and, in the morning, make for the inn at Portree. There the royal party would, were the Captain to be successful in his mission, meet with some of Old Raasay's kinsmen, who would convey the Prince, once more in male attire and under an alias, to their island. It was intended that Charles Edward should remain on Raasay until safe passage to the mainland and onward to the Continent could be secured. Flora, for her part, would proceed home.[29]

When the elements of this sketchy plan were decided, Neil returned to the shore so as to guide the Prince to a place of greater safety on the hill, and dispatch the boat and crew back to the Long Island. 'Devil a farthing but one guinea', said Rory Macdonald of the fee he received for the night journey to Skye and the voyage home. He and his fellow boatmen, however, agreed to say nothing of what they had seen or come to know during their night's work. Although only Flora, of those now conspiring at Monkstadt, had seen Betty Burke, fears were growing that she might be conspicuous by her height and awkwardness if on the high road with her mistress. It was accordingly judged best that she proceed with Neil and Kingsburgh on 'an unfrequented path across the wild country' to the latter's home, which lay ten miles down the coast of the Trotternish peninsula, while Flora took the high road there.[30] In consequence, it was to be given out at Monkstadt that 'her waiting woman [Betty Burke]' was 'so sea sick, that she chose to step slowly before [Flora] up the country'.[31]

While Kingsburgh hastened off in search of Neil and Betty, so that they could begin their journey, a pretty charade was played out in the Monkstadt dining room. Lady Margaret 'pressed Miss very much in presence of the officer' – Lieutenant Macleod – 'to stay [that night]'. The Knight's wife had not known Flora well previously. She declared, nonetheless, that the young woman 'had promised to make some stay, the first time she should happen to come there'. Flora stayed to dine, so as 'to prevent any suspicion'. She refused to remain longer, however, insisting that 'she wanted to see her mother, and to be at home in these troublesome times'.[32] She was not, of course, bound as yet for Armadale, which lay in the far south-west of the island, but for Kingsburgh and Portree. Lady Margaret, with a last show of reluctance, let her guest go, and lent horses from Monkstadt for her convenience and for that of Kirkibost's wife, who was travelling part of the way.

When Flora and those on horseback with her emerged on the high road, she saw walking ahead of them, to her dismay, Betty Burke and 'her' companions, who had yet to turn off and take the cross-country route. Soon the riders were upon the pedestrians. As Flora later remembered, Mrs Macdonald of Kirkibost, knowing the real identity of the 'Irish woman', was 'very desirous to see the Prince's countenance'. Though Betty Burke turned away so that the hood of 'her' cape obscured 'her' head, yet the tacksman's wife 'got several opportunities of seeing his face'.

Flora, anxious that the Kirkibost servants should neither inspect the 'Irish woman' closely nor 'see the route which Kingsburgh and the Prince were about to take', called upon her party to ride faster. They passed the pedestrians at a trot. Thereafter her companion's maid made free with her observation that she 'had never seen such an impudent-looked [looking] woman [as Betty Burke], and durst [dared] say she was either an Irish woman or else a man in a woman's dress'. Flora replied firmly that 'she' was indeed an Irish woman, for she had seen 'her' before.[33]

The bold comments of the Kirkibost maid, dangerous though they were for the success of the enterprise, were to become part of the lore of the Prince's adventures with Flora. Robert Chambers, historian of the rebellion, was to report the servant's further remarks thus: she 'had never seen such a tall impudent-like jaud [jade or hussy] in her life. "See," she continued, addressing Flora, "what lang [long] strides she tak[e]s, and how her coats [skirts] wamble [wobble] about her." '³⁴ To Flora's relief, the factor and his companions had now struck out across country behind her and were lost to view as the rain came on. 'So on they went,' recorded Flora, 'and the Prince and Kingsburgh went over the hills and travelled south-south-east till they arrived at Kingsburgh's house, which was about twelve o'clock at night, and they were very wet.'³⁵

It was fortunate for Flora's peace of mind that she did not know of the Prince's antics while on the moorland route that he, Neil and Kingsburgh took to the latter's house. For all their hopes to escape notice, they attracted the attention of a number of country folk straggling back home after church. The Prince himself was afterwards to admit that 'being unused to petticoats, he held them in walking up so high that some common people', whom they passed, 'remarked an awkwardness in wearing them'.³⁶ When crossing one burn, or stream, the Prince tucked up his petticoats indecently high, to prevent them from becoming wet.³⁷ After Kingsburgh had reproached him, when they came to the next burn Charles let the offending skirts hang down and float in the water. Careless in his role, he bowed when he should have curtseyed to passing strangers, although any they met, were they to realise who he was, might announce his identity to the authorities from a wish to oblige the Knight as much as to gain the vast price on the royal wanderer's head. Chambers, in the 1820s, was slick in his presentation of the problem: 'Your enemies', remarked Kingsburgh, exasperated at last, 'call you a Pretender; but, if you be, I can tell you, you are the worst at your trade I ever saw.'³⁸

When the walkers arrived at Kingsburgh, they found Flora, equally soaked and chilled. She had parted with her riding companions earlier and had arrived shortly before. All stood in need of dry clothes and sustenance. The household had long since retired for bed. Nevertheless, Old Kingsburgh sent up to his wife to beg her to descend, 'he having company to entertain'.[39]

'What company with Kingsburgh?' Mrs Macdonald asked the servant who came. 'Milton's daughter, I believe, and some company with her.' The lady of the house replied, 'Milton's daughter is very welcome to come here with any company she pleases to bring. But you'll give my service to her, and tell her to make free with anything in the house ... I am very sleepy and cannot see her this night.'

Mrs Macdonald was not to be left to slumber. In came her husband, with instructions that she must 'fasten on her bucklings [get dressed] again' and order supper for the company below. The matron woke her daughter Anne, who was in the house that night with her husband. The two ladies each later described their fear of the strange tall woman pacing the hall as they descended to retrieve the keys to various kitchen stores and cupboards. When Kingsburgh revealed the identity of the stranger, Mrs Macdonald, however, was not relieved. Her reaction had much in common with that of Lady Margaret. 'Then we are hanged,' she said. This did not prevent her providing a nourishing supper – 'roasted eggs, some collops [slices of bacon], plenty of bread and butter' – and tumblers of beer for the travellers.[40]

Betty Burke could not be seen by the servants seated with her betters. Anne McAllister, the Kingsburghs' married daughter, therefore served the company, as the Prince insisted upon her mother taking her place at table. For 'Miss', however, he reserved his greatest gallantry. Mrs Macdonald later recalled that, 'when Miss Flora at any time happened to come into the room where the Prince was, he always rose from his seat, paid her the same respects as if she had been a queen, and made her sit on his right hand.'[41] After the ladies had retired to bed, the Prince was less decorous. He sat up late with his host and luxuriated in the pleasures of brandy, punch and tobacco, till the factor protested the need for sleep. The Prince at last consented to proceed to the bedchamber which he and Neil were to occupy.

Flora was terse in her description of the Prince's night at Kingsburgh. 'He ... having got a good clean bed (which he was a stranger to for some time) slept soundly till ten o clock next morning.'[42] Flora elsewhere admitted that she was 'in pain about the Prince's lying so long in bed lest he should be overtaken by his enemies'. She could not, however, prevail upon Old Kingsburgh to awaken the royal fugitive any earlier. Charles Edward had not slept between sheets and in a bedchamber for weeks. Such accommodation as he had had, in bothies or huts, had been crude. More often than not he had slept outdoors, without shelter from the elements, and with only his plaid as covering. The Prince's host and the Kingsburgh women were awed by the presence of royalty in their farmhouse and charmed to see how long he slept in Mrs Macdonald's holland sheets. Flora, however, aware that 'the day began to be far advanced … was very uneasy, everything being prepared for the journey agreed upon'.[43]

The family was long to remember, dwell upon and treasure souvenirs associated with the brief sojourn of the Prince under their roof. Kingsburgh treated as sacred relics the battered brogues in which Betty Burke had tramped to the house. He preserved a broken pipe which the Prince had carried in his skirts, and also trophies of his late-night drinking bout.[44] The sheets on which the Prince slept were in due course folded away, unwashed, and laid up with instructions from Mrs Macdonald that she should be buried in them.[45] More immediately, once the Prince was awake, the lady of the house sought a lock of his hair, and required her daughter to cut it from his head.[46]

These delays notwithstanding, at about two o'clock in the afternoon Flora left the house with Neil and with the Prince. Portree, where they were bound, lay ten miles south-east over rough country. The Prince had not shown himself adept the day before in managing women's clothes and had attracted much unwanted curiosity. Better, it was agreed by all, for him to revert to male identity and Highland dress for the coming trek, and for any adventures thereafter. Abandoning his guise of Betty Burke, he should travel by back paths with a guide, supplied by Kingsburgh, who would know him only as a traveller in those parts, and with Neil. Flora, travelling on horseback and taking the high road, would rendezvous with them at the inn which commanded the harbour at Portree.

The time for the Prince's transformation, however, was necessarily delayed. As the 'Irish woman' had come, so 'she' must leave Kingsburgh. The servants had been kept at a distance, while Milton's daughter and the other guests were in the house, but had inevitably had sight of them. In the event that the night's adventure was found out and the household questioned about the 'company' at Kingsburgh, none of those employed there must be able to describe the clothes in which Betty Burke resumed masculine life.

Old Kingsburgh waited in a wood nearby with a 'suit of Highland clothes [plaid and hose]', a broadsword and other accoutrements. While dressing in the house for his final appearance as Betty Burke, the Prince was in high spirits. 'Oh Miss, you have forgotten my apron,' he declared. 'Where is my apron? Pray get me my apron here, for that is a principal part of my dress.'[47]

Nothing occurred to subvert the concerted plan in its first stages. 'Mistress' and 'maid' left Kingsburgh together. In the safety of the wood the Prince stripped off his female attire and assumed Highland dress. Whether now or at Portree, he gave to Flora, as mementoes of his short time in her 'service', the 'French' garters, 'of blue velvet covered upon one side with white silk, and fastened with buckles', which had held up Betty Burke's stockings.[48] Such parts of the Prince's feminine garb as were distinctive, the large dun cape included, were thrust into the heart of a bush where they would be difficult to find.[49] The gown, an ordinary 'print dress', Kingsburgh bore home to his wife, to hide in plain sight among similar items, and Flora took possession of the apron.[50]

The Prince, with Neil and a local guide, a Macdonald boy, departed for the byways which would lead them slowly to Portree. There, it was to be hoped, Donald Roy would be waiting at the inn, with news of a boat and Macleod crew to convey the Prince to Raasay. Flora, meanwhile, set out on horseback for the same place. Her journey was disagreeable. The rain streamed down continually.[51] For nine long days and eight nights now she had put her life in danger for the Pretender. Should he be put safely into the hands of the Macleods of Raasay and dispatched to that island, her part would be done. Only then could she journey on in good heart to the Sleat peninsula, where her mother, all unaware of her daughter's adventures, tended house. Meanwhile, the rendezvous at the inn was not without peril. Anyone in the public rooms there might yet recognise the Prince and denounce him and his associates.

5

'Farewell to the Lad'
July 1746

Flora, sodden from the rain and tired from the long ride, entered the inn at Portree towards evening on Monday, 30 June. The hostelry, while accommodating travellers, also served as a whisky house, or public house, and was the resort of many in the district. Captain Donald Roy Macdonald, whom she found waiting there 'by appointment', had secured a private room for the royal rendezvous, so that Charles Edward might be concealed from the scrutiny of the 'country people'.[1] While Flora was at Kingsburgh, the former rebel officer had also contracted with Old Raasay's son, John 'Rona' Macleod, that the latter would convey the Prince across the sound to the island his father ruled.[2]

Upon her arrival, Flora informed Donald Roy that the Prince was on his way, and of the direction from which he would come. The Captain gallantly stepped out into driving rain to meet him, he later recorded, but returned alone after 'about twenty minutes'. The party from Kingsburgh, he reported, was nowhere to be seen, and the wound in his foot was troubling him. However, not long afterwards, while Flora was at supper in the private room with Donald Roy, he was called to the door of the inn by the landlord. The boy who had guided the Prince and Neil from Kingsburgh was waiting there, with a message for him. A gentleman, 'a little above the house', wished for his company, the Captain was informed.

When Donald Roy reached that place, he found Charles Edward, 'wet to the skin', with Neil. He expressed his concern that the Prince 'had got such a stormy night' for his journey. The Stuart scion replied gallantly, 'I am more sorry that our lady [Flora] ... should be all abused with the rain.'[3] When the trio thereafter entered the inn, they took care to slip past the company in the public room so as not to be discovered. The inn was 'frequented by all sorts of folks, and therefore it was not safe for him [the Prince] to stay any time there', the Captain was later to state. If these country people saw a stranger, he added, 'it would make them curious to inquire who he was, and this might prove of dangerous consequence'.[4]

The Prince, 'still with the rain pouring down from his clothes', tossed off a dram of whisky on gaining the private room. Implored by his companions to 'shift [change his clothes]', he at first refused to undress, as his 'lady' – Flora – was in the room. Donald Roy and Neil, however, 'told him it was not a time to stand upon ceremonies, and ... prevailed upon him to put on a dry shirt'. Meanwhile, Charles MacNab, the innkeeper, came in and out of the room, filling orders for a supper of 'butter, cheese, bread, and roasted fish' for the new arrivals, and bringing more whisky, water and tobacco.[5]

When supper was brought in, Flora later recorded, the Prince 'fell briskly to his victuals [meal]'.[6] He regarded with disfavour, however, the 'ugly cog[gie, or bowl] containing water [that was] offered to him'. The receptacle had previously served MacNab to bail out his boat. The landlord was in the room, and Donald Roy urged the Prince, in a whisper, to 'drink out of it without any ceremony ... Though the cog looked ill, yet it was clean.' If Charles Edward showed himself fastidious, 'it might raise a suspicion about him in the landlord's mind'. The Prince complied, and 'took a hearty draught of water out of the rough cog'.[7]

Meanwhile the Macleods had gained the shore of Skye and anchored their vessel 'at a little distance from the [Portree] houses'. One of their number who shared his forename of Malcolm with the head of Clan Raasay reported that as he was walking up from the shore to announce their arrival he had 'spied three persons making towards the [whisky] house'. The trio were, he thought correctly, the royal party heading for the inn. However, in 'the darkness of the night (for it was raining excessively)', he was later to recall, he could not be certain of their identity. Accordingly he 'lurked at some distance', and sent a boy into the house with a message, asking Donald Roy 'to come out and speak with a friend'.

For a third time, the lame Captain came out into the rain. Confirming that the Prince was within the inn, he learned in turn from Malcolm that Rona and another were waiting on the shore with a boat. Promising 'all possible dispatch', Donald Roy Macdonald returned to the inn.[8] Flora and Neil there were quite as eager as Malcolm Macleod that the Prince quit the inn with celerity and be rowed over to Raasay. His Royal Highness, however, as Flora later recorded, 'was desirous to stay all night in Portree as the rain was still heavy'.[9]

From this course of action the Prince's companions forcibly dissuaded him. The innkeeper was later to tell the Captain that he had 'entertained a strong notion that the gentleman [with Donald Roy] might happen to be the Prince in disguise, for that he had something about him that looked very noble'.[10] Flora, Neil and Donald Roy had observed MacNab seizing every opportunity to loiter in the room. The Prince, giving substance to these suspicions, was careless in his monetary dealings with the landlord.

Calling for a roll of tobacco so that he could smoke a pipe before departing, Charles Edward gave MacNab a sixpence in payment. When Donald Roy asked the landlord for the change, the Prince 'smiled at the Captain's exactness, and would not be at the pain to take the three halfpence'. Fearing that this munificence would further arouse MacNab's suspicions, Donald Roy motioned to the Prince to take the 'bawbees [pennies]'. After the landlord had gone, moreover, the Captain stuffed the pennies into the 'purse [sporran]' the Prince wore with his kilt. The royal fugitive would have more use for such coins in his further skulking, the rebel officer said, than any silver.[11]

Notwithstanding this rebuke, the Prince continued imprudent while equipping himself for his onward journey. 'The unknown person supposed to be the Pretender', after offering 'a guinea to pay for a bottle of usqu'e [whisky]', according to MacNab, and receiving his change, asked for change for a further guinea. 'The landlord having no more than eleven shillings,' Donald Roy recounted, 'the Prince was for giving him the guinea for them' on the ground that 'eleven shillings would be much more useful than a guinea [twenty-one shillings] in gold could be'. His Scottish companions were horrified. 'This piece of generosity', Donald Roy represented to the Prince, must inevitably lead the landlord to suspect 'the real character of one who had been so liberal in paying a small reckoning'.[12] They scrambled between themselves instead to find the shillings the Prince wanted, rather than have him present MacNab with ten shillings gratis.

Still the Prince tried his protectors' patience. Flora later said that he evinced 'a great desire ... to have Donald Roy Macdonald along with him'. Charles Edward, about to pass into the hands of the Macleods of Raasay, was nervous. He had known safety these past months with both Clanranald and Sleat Macdonalds, and wished for the further company of a Macdonald in his future skulking. He 'began to importune the Captain to go along with him, speaking softly, lest the landlord should be near the door and overhear them'.

In vain did Donald Roy point out to the Prince that 'he would only prove a burden and distress upon him, seeing he could not skulk from place to place' in his crippled state. The Captain must needs be on horseback for any journey, however short, and so easily spotted by 'ranging parties' of regulars and militia.[13] The Prince was to press Donald Roy to accompany him further, till they parted at the boat. No totemic Macdonald, however, was with him when he entrusted his future safety to the unknown Macleods.

A genteel 1890s painting by Irishman George William Joy, titled *Flora Macdonald's Farewell*, purports to show the scene in the Portree inn where the Prince, burdened by provisions, liquid and otherwise, saluted his protectress before departing.[14] The Stuart scion, in Highland dress suitable for a ball and with ringleted locks, bows over Flora's hand. She, meanwhile, is sumptuous in a silk gown and a green velvet riding coat, embellished with gold lace. They are depicted, in best late-Victorian style, as star-crossed lovers, parting with regret.

The reality was rather different. When the Prince, weather-beaten and unkempt, at last consented to leave the inn in 'shabby men's apparel', he made a queer sight. Under his plaid, he had tied the bottle of whisky bought from MacNab to one side of his sporran belt. A 'cold hen [roast chicken]' wrapped 'in a napkin', a bottle of brandy and shirts brought from Kingsburgh hung on the other side. Charles Edward's farewell to Flora, his 'preserver' this past week, was, however, magnificent, and inspiration for any graceful depiction. He might have accorded, in the Palazzo Muti in Rome, such an obeisance to any great lady of the city. He 'saluted her, and declared, "For all that has happened, I hope, Madam, we shall meet in St. James's [the London palace where British sovereigns held court] yet."'[15] With this noble if empty gesture – Flora and the Prince were never to meet again – Charles Edward at last consented to be hurried by Donald Roy to the boat for Raasay.

Dawn was breaking on Tuesday, 1 July, when the Macleods steered across the Sound of Raasay, bearing Charles Edward to a new place of safety six nautical miles eastward. Before parting with Donald Roy on the shore, the Prince had taken from his pocket a large lump of sugar which he had carried from Kingsburgh. 'Pray, Macdonald,' he said, 'take this piece of sugar to our lady, for I am afraid she will get no sugar where she is going.' By this, Charles Edward referred with some unease – and possibly a guilty conscience – to the interrogation and incarceration that would follow if Flora's part in his preservation this past week was discovered.

The Captain refused to take it, 'begging the Prince to keep it for his own use, for that he would stand in need of it yet.' Charles Edward would not take it back. 'Upon which the Captain slip't it privately into Malcolm Macleod's hands, desiring him to preserve it for the Prince.'[16] In her fellow Highlander's estimation, Flora's needs, wherever she might be going, counted for nothing besides those of Stuart royalty.

Upon his return to the inn in the early hours of the following morning, Donald Roy was quizzed by MacNab before he was allowed to go to his rest. 'The landlord was mighty inquisitive about the gentleman that had been in his house,' Donald Roy later recorded, 'who he was, and where the Captain had parted with him.' The conspirator declared, 'in a very unconcerned way', that the stranger was 'a brother rebel, Sir John Macdonald, an Irish gentleman', who had been 'skulking among his friends, the Macdonalds of Skye'. This 'baronet' had now departed for the Scottish mainland, Donald Roy said, 'to skulk among the Macdonalds there'. He, the Captain, 'had only shewed the gentleman a little of the way he had a mind to go'. Donald Roy earnestly begged MacNab to keep this farrago of lies 'to himself as a great secret'.[17]

Flora and Neil had 'stayed behind' and 'went to bed' when the Prince and Donald Roy left for the shore, as the innkeeper was to testify.[18] James Hogg, the Scottish minstrel better known as the Ettrick Shepherd, did not let such crude facts stand in his way when he published, in 1831, the ode 'Flora Macdonald's Lament'. Later rechristened 'Flora Macdonald's Farewell' and set to a tune written by Neil Gow the Younger, the 'Lament' imagined Flora gazing after the Macleods' boat:

Far over yon hills of the heather sae green
An' doun by the corrie [hollow] that sings to the sea.
She look'd at a boat wi' the breezes that swung ...
Away on the wave like a bird on the main,
An' aye as it lessen'd she sigh'd an' she sung,
'Farewell to the lad I shall ne'er see again'.[19]

When Joy's painting, *Farewell*, was reproduced as a popular Valentine card in the early 1900s, the image was commonly inscribed with the last two lines of the opening stanza of the 'Lament':

'Farewell to my hero, the gallant and young,
Farewell to the lad I shall ne'er see again'.[20]

Written at a time when there was a revival of interest in Jacobite history, Hogg's 'Lament' did much to spread Flora's fame beyond Scotland. The myth of a romantic relationship between the Prince and Flora where there was none was reinforced.

Upon rising later that morning, Flora, her adventuring over, was eager to set off for Armadale with her cousin as escort. A good road to the Sleat peninsula led south-west from Broadford, further down the coast from Portree and in Mackinnon territory, but no boat was to be obtained to carry them to that township. MacNab supplied his own to ferry Flora and Neil across Loch Portree, and, as he later recorded, 'the people at Penefeler [Penifiler, a hamlet on the south side of that water] ... furnished horses for the lady and MacEachen'.[21] Flora was to describe the ensuing ride of over forty miles to Armadale as 'a fatiguing journey cross the country'. Her residence there offered respite after the ardours of the night voyage and the subsequent journeys on horseback and on foot that she had undertaken in poor weather this past week and more. However, though the company of her mother, Marion Macdonald, and numerous half-siblings was no doubt welcome, Flora bore alone her troubling and treasonable secret. She later declared that she 'never told her mother, or indeed anybody else, what she had done'.[22]

All Marion knew was that her eldest daughter had returned from a stay of some seven weeks on the Long Island. There she had been aiding her brother, Young Milton, in setting up house. If Flora was home earlier than expected, her presence at Armadale in early July was easily explained by such an excuse as Marion's husband had proffered in that duplicitous letter intended for the eyes of militia and addressed to his wife: 'I have sent your daughter from this country lest she should be any way frightened with the troops lying here.'[23]

For over a week Flora remained at Armadale, not knowing if government vengeance would fall upon her. She had no one in whom she might confide her anxiety about her future. Her

stepfather, that consummate intriguer, was still on duty on the
Long Island. Neil, having escorted Flora home, had vanished into
the hills. Her sex might yet prove a protection to her if her part in
the Prince's escape from South Uist and Skye became known. In
Neil's case, no clemency was to be expected.

Charles Edward, for his part, had reached the west coast of
mainland Scotland, where he was in hiding under the protection of
new Highland friends. Returning to Skye under cover of night with
Malcolm Macleod, two days after they had crossed to Raasay, the
Prince had succeeded in gaining the home of John Mackinnon of
Elgol, earlier a rebel officer, on the Aird of Strath, a south-western
promontory, on 4 July. That night Charles Edward embarked with
his host and the latter's uncle, Old Mackinnon, laird of Strath. They
landed early next morning close to Mallaig across the sound from
Armadale. O'Neill had earlier sent word to France, after parting
from the Prince, that Charles Edward urgently required rescuing.
In consequence, the Prince lurked in a succession of shelters on the
mainland, in hopes that Louis XV and his ministers would send a
ship to bring him off.[24]

The Duke of Cumberland at Fort Augustus, Commodore
Thomas Smith, commanding officer of a fleet of nineteen ships
of war on this north-west station, and General Campbell in the
Western Isles, charged with the task of locating the royal fugitive
and sometimes afloat on a navy vessel, sometimes on shore with
regulars and militia, were all as yet ignorant of the Prince's three-
week sojourn with Neil MacEachen at Corradale, South Uist.
They knew nothing of the bachelor parties there attended by
Old Clan and Boisdale and 'gentlemen of the country'. General
Campbell had alarmed the royal party gathered at Rossinish
when he ordered Lady Clan to return home to Nunton. He
had accepted, however, the mistress of Nunton's avowal that she
had been visiting one of her children then living at the home of
a wet nurse. The officer had gone on his way to South Uist to
continue the search for the Young Pretender, little knowing that
the Prince would be embarking that night for Skye. The voyage
and the Betty Burke masquerade were as yet secrets still safe with

the conspirators and the crew who had ferried the party across the Minch.

The government forces, moreover, had not the least suspicion that Charles Edward had been on the shore at Kilbride below Monkstadt when Flora dined there with Lady Margaret and the Lieutenant. Nor did they know of his night's stay, still in women's clothing, with 'Miss' and Neil at Kingsburgh. They were also unaware that the Young Pretender, under the identity of an Irish rebel baronet, had openly taken refreshment in the inn at Portree before embarking for Raasay and the mainland.

Zealous officers searching South Uist made offers of reward and threats of punishment to its inhabitants. They neither found the Young Pretender nor gained any useful intelligence about his movements from those they questioned. The Long Island and Skye, however, were alive with rumour, much of it accurate. The Laird, then on the mainland, received a letter from his factor at Dunvegan on Skye, where the latter opined on 30 June that the troops on South Uist would 'miss of their errand'. He heard that 'the young gentleman [the Prince] went from South Uist' two days earlier.[25]

The Laird did not share this information with government officers, and General Campbell, then on the *Furnace* and anchored off South Uist, remained confident of success. Writing on 3 July, his military secretary asserted, 'There is great reason to think the Young Pretender is yet there [on the Long Island] and ... there does not appear to have been any opportunities for his getting off.'[26] Two days later, still on shipboard, the General was still issuing orders for redcoats and Marines to search 'the most likely places for concealing such persons [the Prince] as are supposed to be skulking on this island [South Uist]'.[27]

Cumberland, at Fort Augustus, expressed his confidence to the Duke of Newcastle, one of the King's two Secretaries of State, that Charles Edward would soon be his captive. The Old Fox, that elderly reprobate, had recently been found, by a stroke of 'good fortune', hiding within a lochside 'hollow tree' and was now in custody at Fort Augustus. Cock-a-hoop, Cumberland gloated in a letter of 26 June to Newcastle: 'The taking [of] Lord Lovat is a greater humiliation and vexation to the Highlanders than anything that could have happened ... They had such confidence in his cunning and the strength [impenetrability] of the country [territory]', he wrote, that they thought it impossible for him 'to be taken'. Now the Fraser chief was to go south a prisoner to the Tower of London, where he would await trial for high treason.[28] How could the Prince, a stranger abroad in Scotland, not soon be likewise discovered on the Long Island?

In short, the Duke, Commodore Smith, General Campbell and those they commanded had been thoroughly bamboozled by the ingenuity and invention of those among whom the Prince had lived for six weeks. It was a long catalogue of criminals that included, besides Flora, Neil and her stepfather, the Clanranalds and Boisdale on the Long Island, Lady Margaret Macdonald, Old Mackinnon, his nephew and Old Kingsburgh on Skye, and Old Raasay and numerous Macleods on the island of that name.

The British military and naval officers, however, did not remain in ignorance of the Prince's recent movements for ever. Captain Fergusson, landing on South Uist, now employed the Barisdale, a hellish instrument of torture originally designed by a Highland laird to deter thievery, for which the naval officer had much affection.[29] Before his windpipe could be pierced by this device's vicious iron spike, a local man confessed on 6 July what most on the island now knew – that O'Neill was in hiding on Benbecula and that the Prince had left the Long Island on the 28th of the previous month. The captive 'also informed of another who was part of the crew that conducted the Young Pretender to Skye'. He named John Macdonald, helmsman, who had till now, with his fellow boatmen, kept the oath given to Neil to stay silent on returning to the Long Island from Skye. Whether put into the Barisdale irons or threatened with such treatment, the skipper now related the whole adventure to Fergusson: 'The Young Pretender left South Uist' – a term then commonly used to embrace Benbecula – 'in woman's clothes accompanied by one Miss Macdonald, daughter to Milton, and one Neil MacEachen of Howbeg in South Uist.'[30]

The naval Captain proceeded to interrogate John Maclean, the cook who had accompanied Lady Clan from Nunton and prepared dinner at Rossinish. Maclean confessed to much else, including that he 'saw some women's apparel which the Lady Clanranald brought with her ... and which the Declarant [Maclean] heard were designed for the Young Pretender to go off in'.[31]

For this joint military and naval expedition in the Hebrides, Commodore Smith had deputed to General Campbell wide-ranging powers. Upon receiving this momentous intelligence, the military officer ordered Fergusson to proceed in the cutter to Skye and wait at Monkstadt for him. Campbell then sent word to one of his officers on the Long Island 'to seize Lady Clanranald ... as also Miss Macdonald if she is returned thither'.[32] The General then departed on the Captain's ship for Skye.

By the evening of 7 July, Fergusson was ensconced at Monkstadt where Lady Margaret gave a convincing impression of shock and anger that she had been so deceived by Flora, her guest at dinner. Next morning, Donald Macleod of Talisker, a local militia officer, joined the gathering and heard of the confessions Fergusson had wrung out of the helmsman and the Clanranalds' cook. Talisker wrote to Lord Loudoun, commanding officer of all the Highland militia: 'I had some surmise that the Young Pretender had landed in this country, which made me come here early this morning, to make all the search about this surmise that was possible ... It is now certain,' he added, 'that ... he landed not far from this house in disguise along with Miss Macdonald, daughter to Mr Macdonald of Milton ... better, sister to the present Milton, a gentleman of South Uist, for whose waiting woman he passed.'[33]

While he awaited General Campbell, who was expected that night, the officer informed Lord Loudoun that he had 'sent orders to [Donald Macdonald of] Castleton', a Sleat tacksman and militia officer who lived four miles from Armadale, 'and the officer at Broadford to apprehend the young lady [Flora] and bring her here'. While pursuing Betty Burke, they were to 'look out very sharp' that no boats left the island.[34]

Flora was later to narrate that upon receiving the summons to report to Castleton at his house, 'She, a little suspicious of what might happen, thought proper to consult some of her friends what she should do in the matter.'[35] Donald Roy 'happened to be at Armadale when the message came'. He 'was of opinion that Miss should not venture upon complying' with the order, 'for that he was afraid there might be a snare laid for her'. If go she must, he counselled her, at least let her wait until the following day. Flora, however, was determined to answer the summons that day. Possibly she anticipated employing the 'smart' wit for which she was noted to deflect enquiries. After establishing 'what to say upon an examination', she set out for Castleton, which lay four miles off.

While still on the road, she met her stepfather, who was returning home after doing duty on South Uist, with his own souvenirs of the adventures with the Prince. Young Milton had confided to his stepfather's care those distinctive pistols which his sister had forbidden the Prince to carry when in the character of Betty Burke. If Flora reproached Armadale for placing her in this present danger before they parted once more, she never recorded it.[36] Soon thereafter she was seized on the road by 'an officer and a party of soldiers'. Castleton had grown impatient and dispatched them 'in pursuit of her'.[37] If she faltered at seeing this militia force, she had recovered herself by the time she and her escort reached their destination, where the Sleat tacksman examined her 'concerning what passengers came in the same boat as her'.

'She told me', Castleton was to write to the Knight, 'there were none in the boat, besides the crew, but herself, Neil MacEachen, son to MacEachen of Howbeg, and a young woman who called herself Betty Burke.' Flora had an imaginative tale ready to explain the presence of this latter passenger in the vessel. Betty had told her in Benbecula, she said, 'that she was one of those Irish persons ordered to be transported to America'. When the ship carrying her had put into the Long Island, Betty had 'made her escape'. A married woman, she had been told that her husband was on the Isle of Skye, and 'begged that she [Miss Macdonald] would be so good as to give her passage'. Flora reported that 'upon their landing [on Skye] Betty Burke went off, but that she did not know whither, neither had she seen her since that time, which was Sunday 29th June ...'

Flora, mendacious to the last, also told Castleton 'that she never saw the Young Pretender, though she often heard of that person, and had been told of his being at different places ... Since she came to Skye, she heard that he had been in Strath [the Mackinnon estates].' Her interrogator 'advised her to be ingenuous [candid] and to tell the whole truth ... It would fare the better with her.' Although Flora now knew that she was to go – as much a prisoner as any rebel who had served in the Prince's army – before John Campbell of Mamore, she was firm. She 'answered that she knew no more'. The militia Captain reported, 'This was all I could get from her ... When she meets General Campbell, I hope more can be made of her.'[38]

With an 'ensign and a party' of militia, Flora was dispatched in search of that officer, whose further interrogation she would have to parry. She was not permitted, she afterwards recorded, to bid farewell to her mother, nor did she know when she would return home.[39] At that house 'the letter which Armadale had sent along with her' on the voyage to Skye 'in the way of a passport, and in favour of Betty Burke' had been prudently burned by Flora's stepfather. He and Donald Roy briefly admired together the Prince's pistols before, as Flora was to relate, Armadale 'began a skulking [hiding in the hills]'. Donald Roy 'was obliged likewise to go a skulking, the cripple foot notwithstanding'.[40]

6

Prisoner on the *Furnace*
July–August 1746

General Campbell of Mamore had left the Long Island, on the *Furnace*, in the afternoon of 8 July. He had, however, been baulked in his hopes of reaching Sir Alexander's home on Skye the following morning. Strong winds prevented the *Furnace* from coming into the shore below that house. Instead, as George Anderson, Campbell's secretary, recorded, they anchored about midday, ten miles further down the Trotternish peninsula in the deep sea loch above which Kingsburgh stood. The General, still on board, issued a proclamation declaring that he had 'undoubted intelligence' that 'on the 28th of last month the Pretender's son passed over from the island of South Weest [Uist] to the Isle of Skye, disguised in women's clothes, and accompanying a daughter of Macdonald of Milton'. Campbell required those he addressed 'in His Majesty's name' – militia, clerics and laymen – to exert themselves 'in securing and apprehending the said Pretender's son with all his adherents' and to aid and assist his own officers 'in executing the said service'.[1] Campbell and Anderson then went ashore, hoping that the Knight's factor could provide clues about the direction the Young Pretender might have taken after landing on the island.

What the General learned at Kingsburgh astonished him, and he made haste to write to the Duke at Fort Augustus: 'The 29th of last month McAchran [MacEachen], Miss McDonald and one that went [passed] for her servant, viz the Young Pretender, lodged at Alex.r McDonald of Kingsbridge's [Kingsburgh's] house.'[2] Anderson recorded in his journal: 'On enquiring, we found the Young Pretender was in women's clothes with a hood or capuchinon [short, hooded cloak], so that little of his face was seen. The lady of the house [Mrs Macdonald of Kingsburgh] said Miss Macdonald lay [slept] in a [bed]room by herself, and that Neil and the person in women's clothes lay in another room where there was two beds.' The Kingsburghs suppressed their joyous remembrances of offering the Prince a good supper, copious liquor and their best bedchamber. 'They did not suspect who was their guest,' they affirmed, 'being acquainted with Miss Macdonald and Neil, and the 3rd person passed for Miss's Maid by the name of Betty Burk.'[3]

While Campbell was still at Kingsburgh, further sensational information about the Prince's movements on Skye came from Portree. Charles MacNab had informed one of the General's officers that Flora and Neil had spent the evening of 30 June at his public house with 'another person unknown.' The latter had 'put on clean linen and had something for supper … Then went to the door as if he was to return, but never after appeared.'[4] When this information was relayed to Campbell at Kingsburgh he was in no doubt about the identity of the 'person unknown'. He wrote to the Duke the next day: 'Thus I have traced the Young Pretender to the last day of June.'[5]

More than ever, the Major General wished to examine the 'daughter of Macdonald of Milton', whom he had named in his proclamation as the Prince's companion on the voyage to Skye. Within hours of disembarking from the *Furnace*, he had confirmation that Flora's part in shielding the Young Pretender from Hanoverian justice had not ended with that journey. Moreover, it was plain that she had all along known the true identity of Betty Burke. She had been with him when he was in petticoats at Kingsburgh and when he was in male attire at Portree.

Campbell was unaware that Talisker, ten miles north at Monkstadt, had already directed that Flora be sent north for questioning. Before leaving Kingsburgh for the Sleat seat, the General dispatched a considerable force, numbering a captain, a lieutenant, twenty-two fusiliers and fourteen Argyll militiamen, to Armadale. They had orders to take Flora prisoner – and her cousin Neil, too, if possible. In the event, upon their arrival at her mother's house, the party discovered that Milton's daughter had already left for Monkstadt under a different military escort. Neil MacEachen, their other quarry, was nowhere to be found.

When he reached Monkstadt on the evening of 10 July, Campbell learned more details of Flora's visit there after her landing on Skye: she 'would by no means accept … to stay all night'.[6] Passing over her colloquies on 29 June with Flora in the house and with Kingsburgh and Donald Roy in the garden, Lady Margaret spun a tale of innocence. Having already disposed of an earlier missive from the Prince, this Lowland earl's daughter was at her gracious best. 'Now that Gen[eral] C[ampbell] is come, her mind is at ease,' wrote the Laird, now on Skye, to Sir Alexander at Fort Augustus.[7]

While Flora was still on the road with her military escort and the General was yet at Monkstadt, he received intelligence from Kingsburgh. The Sleat factor now, Campbell was to write to the Duke on the 13th, 'frankly owned his knowing the Pretender's son whilst he was in his house'.[8] Moreover Kingsburgh had 'intelligence of moment' for the General: after proceeding to Raasay, the Prince had returned to Skye and was lurking at a house within eleven miles of Portree.[9] Brought a prisoner on board the *Furnace*, the factor declared that 'the young Chevalier' was 'in John Mackinnon's house in Aird in Mackinnon country'.[10]

As General Campbell was to tell a correspondent in the south, he acted this summer, in concert with Commodore Smith, as 'a kind of Admiral' on board the *Furnace*.[11] While Fergusson, Captain of that vessel, and other officers and men departed to the Aird in search of the Prince, the General instructed other ships of war on the station to 'cruise about this island [Skye] to prevent his getting from hence in any boats of the country' or any French vessel. He

also begged the Duke at Fort Augustus to line the west coast of
the mainland with troops: 'I think, as we have now fixed him on
Skye, he cannot escape, if we can but prevent his getting to the
continent.'[12] He himself embarked again on the *Furnace*, to guard
the north coast of the island, taking Kingsburgh with him as his
prisoner.

The search for the Prince on Skye – which had begun upon
Fergusson's arrival on 8 July and which continued after Campbell
sailed north on the 11th – was to prove fruitless. Accompanied by
Old Mackinnon, the Prince, as Old Kingsburgh may have known,
had left the island on the 4th for the mainland. On the 10th, a day
before a search was ordered in the Aird of Strath, the Prince was
in fact in hiding on the Arisaig peninsula with a rebel Macdonald
laird in a remote bothy, close to where he had landed on his arrival
from France a year earlier.

In the first week of July militia and Marines had combed the
Long Island before discovering, on the 6th, that Betty Burke had
escaped to Skye at the end of June. So now fusiliers, militia and
Marines searched Skye, and ships of the line patrolled its seas
without result. As before, the local militia and other inhabitants
of Skye knew more than they told, or told what they knew only
after that intelligence would no longer endanger the life of the
Prince. Castleton was to write privately to the Knight on the 11th
of the 'general report' that 'that person' had left the island: 'By what
passage I have not yet learned with any certainty, tho' it is said to
be by the Aird of Strath.'[13]

On the evening of that same day, following the General's removal
to the *Furnace*, Flora was consigned to the care of Fergusson, still
on Skye, and brought on board that vessel, which was guarding the
north of the island. Once Fergusson had conveyed Flora in a cutter
to the ship, however, he returned to the search for the Prince on
dry land. General Campbell, heir to the Duke of Argyll, was Flora's
captor now.

Old Kingsburgh, her fellow prisoner, expected that Sir
Alexander at Fort Augustus would plead his case and soon secure
his release. Flora, however, had no such patron. Although her

stepfather's part in the Prince's masquerade was not as yet known, he was in hiding, fearing its discovery. The Clanranalds were both soon to be prisoners. She had originally called the Knight 'too much [my] friend' for her to think of aiding the Prince. Lady Margaret, however, was to write to Duncan Forbes of Culloden later this month, when seeking his intercession on behalf of Kingsburgh, 'Your Lordship can't yet be a stranger to the trouble which has lately been brought upon this island by the indiscretion of a foolish girl [Flora], with whom the unhappy disturber of this Kingdom [the Prince] landed at this place …' With grave duplicity she added, 'I cannot but look on myself and family as peculiarly favoured by heaven in drawing that unlucky visitant [the Prince] so quickly away from the place of his landing, that there was no room for considering him as a person in disguise, far less my knowing anything of it.'[14]

Formally examined the following day, 12 July, by Campbell, Flora was careful in what she said. 'Miss Macdonald of Milton in Skye', Campbell's secretary George Anderson recorded, 'declares that about six weeks ago she left her [step]father's house in Skye and went to South Uist to see some friends.' Being asked by the General if she had had 'an invitation from those who engaged her in what she afterwards did', she 'answered in the negative' and said, in addition, that she had not known then the whereabouts of the Pretender's eldest son. When alluding to the midnight request made of her on the hillside at Unasary above Loch Eynort, she omitted all reference to her cousin Neil. The Irishman O'Neill, who was soon to be discovered and secured on the Long Island, was, in Flora's declaration, the Prince's only companion. She admitted that her brother, Milton, had accompanied her and Lady Clanranald to Rossinish. (John Maclean, the Nunton cook, had already testified to these two being of that party.) She could not deny either that Neil had been on the boat. She was made aware by the Major General, that 'the boatmen had babbled everything' about the voyage to Skye.[15] When giving the details of her visit to Monkstadt, however, she declared that she, rather than Lady Margaret, had sent for Donald Roy. Moreover, she, in her account, rather than the mistress of Monkstadt and Old Kingsburgh, had told that officer to find a boat to carry the Prince over to Raasay.

In her further narrative, Flora made out that Kingsburgh had played little part in the drama, alleging that he had merely acted as host when she was 'taken sick' at his house, upon which he had offered beds to her, Betty Burke and Neil. She rebuffed her examiners' question '[i]f any of the Family [at Kingsburgh] enquired who the disguised person was'. Flora answered that 'they did not ask her or MacEachen, but ... she observed the people of the family whispering ... From the servants Miss found they suspected him to be [the Macleod of] Bernera, a person that had been in rebellion.'

Parrying further enquiries, she stated: 'She thinks the Pretender went to Rasa [Raasay], but after leaving him at Portree Miss Macdonald does not know what became of him.' She added that 'Her father in law [her stepfather Armadale] hearing of her having engaged to go along with the Pretender advised her very much against it.' She asked him, nevertheless, 'for a pass[port]', she recounted, 'which he gave, specifying it was for his [step] daughter and an Irish girl, her servant.' George Anderson, who took Flora's testimony, noted that Ranald Macdonald, 'Baillie [constable] of Benbecula', could testify to its existence. This official had previously deposed that he saw this document – presumably on that June morning when Armadale released his stepdaughter from the guardroom on that island.[16] Although Flora had admitted to having been given this document, two witnesses at least were required for the prosecution of treason cases, and the baillie was indeed to be later named in the case against her.

There were both truth and lies to be discovered in Flora's declaration. She appears to have been determined not to incriminate her stepfather, Lady Margaret and the Kingsburgh household, although she was ignorant whether the General had other evidence of their having taken part in the recent royal adventure. Campbell may have surmised that his young prisoner was not entirely frank in her declaration. Nevertheless, he took a keen interest in her welfare. Flora was always to acknowledge that he treated her exceptionally well. Old Kingsburgh's daughter, Anne, was to write: 'She [Flora] got an apartment [cabin] for herself.' Twenty years Flora's senior, Campbell was the father, in Argyllshire on the mainland, of a daughter Flora's age. According to Anne of Kingsburgh, 'When he saw her any way distressed, he used to comfort her as his own child.'[17]

Notwithstanding Flora's efforts to deceive, the General soon learned of the Prince's successful passage to the mainland, when Old Mackinnon and his nephew Elgol, the royal fugitive's companions on the voyage there, were discovered by search parties. Brought prisoners on board the *Furnace*, they confessed their crime and, on 12 July, the search for the Prince on Skye was at last called off.[18]

The arrival, this same day, of Sir Alexander and one of the Duke of Cumberland's aides de camp on board the *Furnace* was hardly opportune. Captain Hodgson brought with him a letter from Cumberland, written two days earlier, and congratulating the Major General on having 'drove him [the Young Pretender] into the Isle of Skye'. The Duke expressed his confidence that 'by your vigilance and endeavours you will not let him escape'.[19] The Knight had accompanied the aide de camp in the hope that his local knowledge might aid the endeavour.

Campbell sent Hodgson and Sir Alexander straightaway back to Fort Augustus with Old Kingsburgh, whose fate the General wished the Duke to decide, and with dispatches. These disclosed the royal fugitive's escape from Skye and counselled an intensive search of the area where he had last been seen on the mainland. The Duke's aide carried, too, copies of Flora's declaration and that of Elgol.[20]

Further correspondence came from Fort Augustus to discomfit Campbell even before Hodgson reached that headquarters on Loch Ness. Cumberland, still imagining that the Prince was in hiding on Skye, gave details of measures to prevent the royal fugitive landing from that island on the Scottish west coast.[21] Safely concealed still in the hills there, Charles Edward heard that 'the whole coast [was] surrounded by ships of war and tenders, as also the country by other military forces'.[22]

Cumberland also ordered Campbell to broadcast a new proclamation 'as far as you can'.[23] Among its provisions, detailed by Sir Everard Fawkener, the Duke's military secretary, was: 'Whosoever shall harbour, conceal, resort to or keep company with any person or persons who have notoriously been engaged in the rebellion or with any persons in disguise, without giving immediate notice of such persons to the nearest officer of His Majesty or party of the King's Troops, shall be treated as rebels, by burning their houses, seizing or destroying their effects, driving their cattle and the utmost rigour exercised against their persons.'[24] The Duke was eager 'that people may know and feel that it is not now altogether indifferent whether they support and assist the rebels or not'.[25]

While Flora had no home or many effects to burn and destroy, nor cattle to drive away, it was now plain that 'the utmost rigour' would be 'exercised' in her case. She and the Mackinnons were joined on the *Furnace* by other captives from the Long Island, Skye and Raasay over the course of the next week. Many of them, it appeared, had been seized so that they could act as witnesses to the assistance that Flora and her fellow prisoners had afforded the Prince. In what court of law, however, would they be called upon and at what bar would Flora stand? Though Cumberland, as Commander-in-Chief of the army in Scotland, might issue any number of proclamations, government law officers, whether there or in England, must pronounce Flora's crime and a judge determine her sentence, should she be found guilty.

Cumberland had been writing to his father's Secretary of State, the Duke of Newcastle, in London, when the *Furnace* party arrived at headquarters. Livid to find that he had the Prince still 'left to hunt' – and further incensed that Old Kingsburgh, Hodgson's prisoner, was not 'sent in irons [shackles]'[26] – he added to his letter, 'I hope to God that they [government forces] may take him, for else this Country [the Highlands] never will be quiet, and whether it will be so then, is what I much doubt.' The disgruntled Duke enclosed, for Newcastle, Campbell's latest letter with the 'deposition of the girl [Flora] who accompanied him [the Prince],

and another person's [that of Elgol] which will give the best light
into the affair'.[27] Flora Macdonald, till a few weeks before a young
Highland gentlewoman of no great account, was now being
treated as a 'rebel', in accordance with the Duke's proclamation.
Her duplicitous shipboard declaration was engaging the attention
of the King's son in Scotland and would soon reach George II's
ministers at Westminster.

Cumberland now thankfully delegated the further pursuit
of the Prince to the Earl of Albemarle, his reluctant successor as
Commander-in-Chief in Scotland. The young Duke departed
south, to be hailed in London as the Hero of Culloden. Handel
composed 'See the Conquering Hero Comes' in his honour. Lauded
in Parliament, upon his arrival he was made Ranger of Windsor
Great Park and secured a considerable grant with which to build a
home there. He had, however, failed to capture the Young Pretender,
with all the might of his royal father's fleet and army at his disposal.

In the Highlands the unwelcome task of searching for the elusive
Prince continued. That large reward for his capture, which had
earlier spurred on many, no longer shone so bright. Officers
combing the hills and glens complained that their men were
suffering 'much by fatigue and the heat of the weather'.[28] An
English colonel who spent a fortnight in July tracking the royal prey
without success wrote caustically to a friend in London: '[As] for
the country through which I passed, I can only say that it was one
continued scene of rocks, bogs and mountains ... with little more
variety than one would see in the Western Ocean.'[29] Dispirited,
a government official in Edinburgh was to write in August to Sir
Everard Fawkener, Cumberland's secretary in London, 'We have,
I think, lost scent of the Pretender's son since His Royal Highness
left us which makes me fancy that he is either got off or died in a
ditch.'[30] Charles Edward was, however, still on the west coast of
the mainland eluding pursuit, thanks to the wiles of Highlander
supporters while he waited for transport to France.

Meanwhile, the *Furnace*, off Skye, became ever more crowded
with state prisoners, including O'Neill, and 'King's Evidences',

or witnesses for the Crown. Upon the arrival of the Irish Colonel on board, he was to relate, Flora greeted him with a 'gentle slap' and the words, 'To that black face do I owe my misfortune.'[31] One of Campbell's Argyll militiamen, stationed on the Long Island, told his commanding officer, 'I find the country [the inhabitants of Benbecula and South Uist] in general has been either with the Pretender or, underhand, aiding him.' Lady Clanranald, he reported, was now under house arrest at Nunton. 'I find it is agreed by everybody in the country', the officer reported, 'that the Pretender's son', when on the Long Island, 'was often seen' by her 'and her children … He gave a little fuzee [fusil, or gun], that he carried in his hand, to one of Clanranald's sons.' As retribution, the officer added, he had 'taken some black cattle of Young Clanranald … for provisions' for his men, and nineteen or twenty dairy cows. 'Should we go on to take up the cattle of every one that is less or more concerned [in efforts to aid the Prince] I am afraid we should not leave any in the country.'[32]

The complement of prisoners on board the *Furnace*, bound for prosecution and judgment in the south, was now complete. At the end of July Campbell directed Fergusson to sail for Kerrera off the west coast of the mainland. There the General was to rendezvous with Commodore Smith on the *Eltham*, his flagship.

On the cruise south, Flora later affirmed, the sloop passed near the bay where her stepfather and mother lived on the Sleat peninsula. 'The General permitted her to go ashore and take leave of her friends [family].' A guard of two officers and a party of soldiers, however, went with her. Furthermore, she was under 'strict orders … not to speak anything in Erse [Gaelic], or anything at all but in the presence and in the hearing of the officers', while on this visit.[33] No account survives of such conversation as she did have with those at home at Armadale or with any neighbours.

If Campbell had hoped to seize Flora's stepfather, a militia officer whom he had recently castigated as 'this villain',[34] he was disappointed. During her visit, Armadale remained skulking in the hills. She 'stayed only about two hours, and then returned again to the ship,' Flora recounted. With her went a very few clothes, a prayer book and little else. Previously without any female companion on board, she was now accompanied by an adventurous local girl, Kate Macdonald. Speaking only Gaelic, she had volunteered to serve as Flora's 'woman [maid]', when the prisoner 'could get not one that would venture to go with her'.[35]

The *Furnace* reached Kerrera, the island off the coast of Argyll where the *Eltham* and other ships of the line lay at anchor, on 1 August. All the prisoners on board the sloop, bar Flora, were transferred to the custody of Commodore Smith on the flagship, in accordance with orders that Albemarle had issued in mid-July. Campbell had a scheme for Flora's greater comfort during the coming days before she was dispatched south. He wrote to a kinsman, the Governor of a castle once the haunt of Scottish kings on a rocky promontory nearby. The General hoped that David Campbell and his wife would extend their hospitality at Dunstaffnage for some days to 'a very pretty young rebel … Her [Flora's] zeal, and the persuasion of those who ought to have given her better advice, has drawn her into a most unhappy scrape,' he wrote, 'by assisting the Young Pretender to make his escape …' In a postscript he added, 'I suppose you have heard of Miss Flora Macdonald.'[36]

Flora, alone of those seized, now enjoyed some respite on dry land as the Governor's guest. Ahead of her, however, lay a long sea voyage south to London. Only then, after further examination, and if convicted of 'treasonable activities', would her punishment be determined.

7

'The Famous Miss Flora Macdonald'
August–December 1746

Flora's fame was spreading southward. The *Scots Magazine* had informed its readers in Edinburgh and elsewhere in the Lowlands in its July edition that the Prince had crossed to Skye in 'Lady Clanranald's clothes' and in the guise of maid to an unnamed 'young lady'.[1] On the 22nd of that month, while Flora was still a prisoner on the *Furnace* off Skye, a friend at the War Office in London wrote to Horace Walpole that 'the pretender's son [had] escaped from Sir Alexander Macdonald's house in Skye in woman's clothes'.[2] If not wholly accurate, this news awoke an appetite for more in Walpole, a young politician later to be feted as an author. His cousin, officer Henry Conway, wrote further in mid-August from Fort Augustus:

> He [the Prince] put on women's clothes and put himself under the care of a Miss Flora Macdonald, a young girl who is since taken. She would not let O'Neill go with 'em, so they went alone into the Isle of Skye, where he [the Prince] changed his clothes again and went alone to one Macdonald [Kingsburgh], a factor of Sir Alexander's …[3]

On that hill in South Uist, Flora had dwelt on 'the risk she would run of losing her character in a malicious and ill-natured world' should she adopt Charles Edward as her 'maid'.[4] Now the truth was being mangled in O'Neill's declaration, which was Conway's source: 'They [the Prince and Flora] went alone into the Isle of Skye.' From jealousy rather than from a protective urge, the Irish officer made no mention of Neil, who had chaperoned his cousin. Over the course of the next several months, many Scottish and English newspapers and magazines, carrying reports of the Prince's escapades with Flora, also omitted to mention that Neil had been their companion. Some contained fictitious, and scandalous, accounts of her curing the Prince of 'the itch' – a genital infection – while they stayed alone together for a period of days in a Hebridean cottage.[5] It remained to be seen whether Flora's 'character' would survive these slurs.

While Campbell of Mamore, her former protector and captor, departed for home to dismiss his militia, Flora gained a new mentor upon quitting Dunstaffnage and going on board the *Eltham*. Observers were later to report that Commodore Thomas Smith, like Campbell before him, 'behaved like a father to her'.[6] Smith, an officer long in the navy and now in his forties, enjoyed, according to one contemporary, a 'universal good character ... both as a seaman and an officer'.[7] He had collaborated with a good grace with Campbell in joint operations to hunt the Prince. Now, under his direction, the flagship, in convoy with the *Loo*, the vessel to which Old Clan, among others, was consigned, embarked on what would prove a long and stormy passage round the northern coast of Scotland to Leith. This harbour town, on the south-east coast of Scotland, served Edinburgh, a few miles inland, as a port. While Smith would remain in Scotland, Flora and her fellow prisoners would be found other transport at Leith to carry them on to London.

Old Clan begged instead to travel overland south, pleading seasickness. Else, he told General Campbell, 'I must soon end my days at Sea.'[8] His request was not granted, nor did he expire, though he travelled all the way to London by sea.

Some of the prisoners on board the several other ships which left the north-west station in July and August were bound for Edinburgh

Castle. Old Kingsburgh already languished 'in irons' in a cell in that fortress, where he awaited trial. Fergusson, in the *Furnace*, ferried others, who were to be vociferous in their complaints of their ill-usage at his hands, to London. Lady Clan and Boisdale were aboard yet another vessel destined for the metropolis.

Old Clan's wife and brother, like Flora and Old Clan himself, were to be further interrogated there. Recent legislation, entitled the Juries Act, had enacted that those who 'carried arms against the Crown' could be tried in any county of the United Kingdom.[9] Highland juries, in the government's estimation, might be either too favourable to those accused or too open to threats by the prisoners' friends and families. It was also convenient, given the large numbers of rebels taken after Culloden and in its aftermath, to commit them for trial in only two or three locations – London, Carlisle and York.

Flora, and most of those now cruising south who had aided the Prince, had not carried arms against the Crown. The Juries Act did not apply to them, and the Duke of Cumberland and his subordinates had erred in sending them south. The Long Island, Skye and Raasay lay in Inverness-shire. Charges against these particular rebels should have been laid against them in the sheriff's court of that county, where they were deemed to have transgressed, or alternatively in the High Court of Justiciary, Scotland's most senior court, in Edinburgh. The Duke was furious that Charles Edward still evaded him. He was determined that those who had aided the royal fugitive should suffer. No one at Fort Augustus, in consequence, gainsaid their Commander-in-Chief's decision to send these prisoners south to London. Law officers in Edinburgh and in London, however, were well aware that there was no justification for sending Flora and her fellow islanders out of Scotland.

While the *Eltham*, having withstood gales in the Orkney Islands off the northern coast of Scotland, cruised down the kingdom's eastern coast, passing Inverness and Aberdeen, Commodore Smith was beguiled by Flora. He 'tendered her many good advices as to her behaviours [conduct] in her ticklish situation', she afterwards recounted.[10] Fond of good living himself, as his ample girth attested, the naval officer made every effort to provide Flora with such comforts as were available on board and render tolerable to her the voyage of over a month.

Flora's earlier patron and former captor continued to be intrigued by her even after they had parted at Kerrera. Six weeks later Campbell of Mamore, writing from Argyllshire to a friend in London, mentioned that Flora was being sent, a captive, to London. The General added, 'I cannot but say I have a good deal of compassion for the young lady. She told me that she would have, in like manner, assisted me or anyone in distress.'[11]

Nothing in any account of Flora's wanderings with the Prince so struck London society as this remark that she made to Campbell, and which Lady Townshend, his correspondent, repeated. Few who heard it were sure that they would have courted danger in the place of Flora, who was no Jacobite rebel, from motives of compassion alone. In the course of time, numerous pretty fictions, based on Flora's remark to Campbell, would appear in print. In one later anecdote, Frederick, Prince of Wales, Cumberland's elder brother, replaced the Major General as Miss Macdonald's interlocutor. Visiting Flora in captivity in the Tower of London – where she never was – His Royal Highness wondered at Miss Macdonald's magnanimity: 'That such a young girl as you should have joined in this headstrong scheme, seems almost incredible. And for what purpose?' The fictional Flora solemnly replied, 'I simply followed the dictates of common humanity, in endeavouring to save a human being from misery …'[12]

Flora's fame preceded her to Edinburgh and Leith. In his cell in the Castle, Old Kingsburgh regaled visitors with spirited accounts of that June night when Betty Burke and Flora had been his guests. The *Caledonian Mercury*, meanwhile, informed its readers on 8 September 1746: 'We hear Captain Clanranald [Old Clan] is Prisoner on board the *Loo* Man of War of 40 Guns, and Miss Florence [Flora] Macdonald, on board the *Eltham*, both at Stromness [in the Orkney Islands].'[13] Later that month the same newspaper announced the arrival of the flagship bearing Commodore Smith in the Roads – outer harbour – of Leith.

In that town a coterie of Jacobite women were accustomed to assemble at the home of Dame Magdalene Bruce, a formidable if elderly widow, in the Citadel, a former Cromwellian fortification. Young and old, noblewomen and merchants' wives and daughters, all shared their hostess's Stuart sympathies and all thrilled to know that Flora was accessible, albeit out at sea. Although Flora was not allowed ashore, Commodore Smith took pains to soften her captivity now that the resources of Edinburgh and Leith were available and positively encouraged these ladies, previously unknown to his passenger, to visit her on the *Eltham*. In early October she was transferred with her fellow prisoners to the *Bridgewater*, a vessel in which they would continue their voyage to London. Thomas Knowler, the captain of this ship, was, like Smith, remarkably 'civil and complaisant [obliging]' to his notable captive and to those who braved the waves to pay court to her. Robert Forbes, an Episcopalian minister who lodged at the Citadel, was to record that both officers placed a state room at Flora's disposal and 'took it exceedingly well when any persons came to visit her'. She 'was indulged the privilege ... to call for anything on board, as if she had been at her own fireside'. The cabin servants 'were obliged to give her all manner of attendance' and she was at liberty to 'invite any of her friends' – her Leith admirers – 'to dine with her when she pleased'.[14]

Soon Flora would be regularly named in the English press 'the famous Miss Flora Macdonald'.[15] Meanwhile she was feted and celebrated in her native land, while the *Bridgewater* underwent repairs. Among those who came on board were daughters of the earls of Galloway and Dundonald, the daughters of Hugh Clerk, a prominent wine merchant in Leith, and ladies of the Rattray of Craighall family in Perthshire. Having expected to find a raw Highland lass, they were much struck by Flora's elegant manners and the pure English or Scots she spoke. Forbes was afterwards to write of her serving tea to these shipboard guests, that 'no lady, Edinburgh bred', could have acquitted herself better.[16] In short, Flora resembled a gentlewoman of the kind who inhabited the Scottish capital and its environs.

Over and over again, Flora told the story of her adventures with the Prince to these female admirers. Avid for every detail, when they learned of his lulling her to slumber with 'several pretty songs' on the voyage to Skye and of her awakening subsequently to find 'his hands spread about her head' to keep her from harm, they were overcome: 'Oh Miss, what a happy creature are you who had that dear Prince ... to take such care of you ... when you was sleeping! You are surely the happiest woman in the world!' One visitor, Miss Mally Clerk of Leith, said, 'I could ... wipe your shoes with pleasure, and think it my honour so to do, when I reflect that you had the honour to have the Prince for your handmaid. We all envy you greatly.'[17] Flora, a prisoner since July, as yet ignorant of what her fate would be in the south, may have been less convinced that she was indeed a 'happy creature', or anyone to envy.

In her captivity Miss Macdonald conversed, she entertained and she sang. 'She has a sweet voice, and sings well,' wrote Forbes.[18] This accomplishment, much prized in polite society, came naturally to Flora. In the Long Island and on Skye, song was an integral part of the ceilidhs, or entertainments, that marked high days and holidays. She numbered noted bards, composers of eulogies and laments among her relations. Dance, however, she would not. Her visitors 'pressed Flora much to share with them in the diversion' when they performed in the cabin with a select number of officers. 'They could not prevail with her to take a trip [step].' She told the ladies 'that at present her dancing days were done, and she would not readily entertain a thought of that diversion till she should be assured of her Prince's safety, and perhaps not till she should be blessed with the happiness of seeing him again.'[19] On one occasion, word came that the Prince had been taken prisoner. 'Alas, I am afraid that now all is in vain that I have done,' Flora said 'with tears in her eyes'. Though the rumour proved false, such fears continued to afflict her.[20]

For some time, Albemarle, following the Duke of Cumberland, his predecessor as Commander-in-Chief in Scotland, had pursued the Prince with ardour on the west coast of that country. He told Newcastle that he would 'with infinite pleasure walk bare foot from Pole to Pole', in order to seize the Young Pretender. 'But we have no sort of intelligence about him,' he continued. He held out the hope that his royal prey might have 'died in misery in some of his hidden places'.[21]

Such was not the case. Charles Edward had fallen in with a band of Highland brigands, who had an intimate knowledge of this western terrain. While waiting for a French ship to come in, he moved for some time at night with these companions from shelter to shelter. Albemarle, despairing of ever locating the Prince, left only a skeleton force on the west coast and headed for Edinburgh. Commodore Smith, meanwhile, when leaving Kerrera, had deployed only three vessels on the north-west station. The diminution of both fleet and troops on the west coast acted greatly in the Prince's favour. At the beginning of September he found a refuge in Cluny's Cage, a camouflaged structure built among trees on a precipitous hillside by a rebel Macpherson chief. With others including the Lochiel, chief of Clan Cameron and himself a wanted man after Culloden, the Prince remained here for a week, and later that month succeeded in secretly boarding *L'Heureux*, a French ship. With him went, among others, the Cameron chief, Young Clan and Neil, Flora's cousin, who had made his way to the mainland. They landed at Roscoff, on the coast of north-west France, on 30 September.

Flora, however, knew none of this. She believed that any day might bear news of the royal fugitive's capture. The authorities in Edinburgh, meanwhile, made a search of Dame Magdalene's home in Leith in October, believing the Prince to be secreted there.[22] It was to be weeks before they learned of the Prince's escape and of the rapturous welcome later afforded him in Paris.

At times Flora had much to bear from her enthusiastic new friends, although they were 'of rank and dignity'. Lady Mary Cochrane was visiting her out on the *Bridgewater* when 'a brisk gale began to blow and make the sea rough'. This earl's daughter told Flora that she 'would with pleasure stay on board all night'. She anticipated boasting thereafter, she confided, that she had 'had the honour of lying in the same bed with that person who had been so happy as to be guardian to her Prince'. Accordingly,

Flora and Lady Mary did 'sleep in one bed that night'.[23] Commodore Smith on the *Eltham*, and Captain Knowler on the *Bridgewater*, and their officers were punctilious in denying access to those who 'came out of curiosity and not out of respect' to visit Miss Macdonald.[24] The Citadel coterie was certainly respectful to Flora. There was, however, a large dollop of curiosity mixed in with their reverence.

When Flora was still on the *Eltham* in the roads of Leith, Commodore Smith had 'made her a present ... of a handsome sute [suit] of riding-cloaths [clothes] ... with plain mounting ... some fine linen for riding shirts, as also a gown to her [waiting] woman', Kate Macdonald. The Citadel ladies followed the naval officer and made valuable offerings too. Dame Magdalene bestowed on Flora practical gifts, so that she could further enlarge her wardrobe: 'a thimble, needles, white thread of different sorts, etc., with some linen and cambric cut and shaped according to the newest fashions'.[25] Others of the coterie gave 'gowns, skirts, headsutes [headdresses], shoes, stockings, etc.', and also 'some linen to be shirts' for Kate.[26] Moreover, when Flora 'regretted much the want of a bible', having with her only that prayer book brought from home, she was presented with 'two pretty pocket volumes, handsomely bound'.[27] She also wrote to her younger half-brother, James, soon to pass through Edinburgh on his way to enlist in the Dutch service, where a Scots Brigade of foreign mercenaries was long established. Confident that she would return from whatever ordeal awaited her in London, she instructed him to bring those velvet and silk garters which the Prince had given her, and deposit them with Dame Magdalene in Leith.[28]

During October the *Caledonian Mercury*, in Edinburgh, published an account, drawn from O'Neill's declaration, of the Prince's wanderings after Culloden. It featured Flora's adventures on the Long Island with the Prince and her embarkation with Betty Burke.[29] Ladies and gentlemen all over the United Kingdom read with fascination of Miss Macdonald's humanity, steadfastness and remarkable powers of deception. Her arrival in London and her trial there were the more eagerly anticipated.

Thomas Smith continued assiduous for Flora's welfare, as did John Campbell of Mamore. 'Miss Flora Macdonald sailed this morning on board the Bridgewater under the care of Captain Knowles [sic],' Lord Albemarle wrote to Newcastle on 27 October. He was misinformed, and the vessel weighed anchor only on 7 November. The concern for Flora's well-being on the part of her former captors, however, is undeniable. 'Her behaviour has been such, during her Confinement,' wrote the Earl, 'that Commodore Smith and General Campbell beg of your Grace, that when she arrives she may rather be put into the hands of a [King's] Messenger, than into any common Prison.' King's Messengers, although in the pay of the Royal Household, also boarded state prisoners 'of quality' in their town houses. 'This favour the poor Girl deserves,' Albemarle agreed, 'her modest behaviour having gained her many friends.'[30]

Unlike her former voyage on the *Eltham*, the journey to London was short and uneventful. Late in November, Yarmouth Steeple and Lowestoft Church, landmarks in southern England, came into view. The *Bridgewater* reached the Nore, the anchorage at the mouth of the Thames estuary, on the 29th.[31]

Five months earlier, Flora's acquaintance had been limited to those who inhabited the Long Island or Skye. Now she thought nothing of troubling the heads of government departments. Knowler wrote to Campbell of Mamore, whom Flora thought to be now in the south: 'As she esteems you her best friend she has in the world, she should be much obliged if you would be pleased to let her know what is to become of her ... Miss joins with me in respects.' He begged the General to write to the Admiralty and ask their lordships to transfer Flora to a King's Messenger.[32] Knowler was understandably reluctant to commit Flora, with the other prisoners he carried, to the *Royal Sovereign*, a prison ship moored near Gravesend in the Thames, as he had been bidden to do (these were Royal Navy ships used as holding pens for prisoners awaiting trial).[33] Typhus and other diseases raged among the hundreds of Jacobite rebels committed to these vessels. No word came from the Admiralty. Flora was duly transferred to the designated ship on

4 December.[34] Two days later, however, William Dick, the senior King's Messenger, arrived with an Admiralty warrant to remove 'the body of Flora Macdonald' from the transport.[35] Past the arsenal of Woolwich and the royal palace of Greenwich, into the metropolis of London, with a population of a quarter of a million, she and her escort plunged.

It was a city this winter choked with Jacobite prisoners who had been out in the Rising and were now paying the price. Some noblemen, who had raised their clans for the Prince, had already ascended the scaffold. Others were in the Tower of London, awaiting trial in the Palace of Westminster. A Special Court convened in Southwark, across the Thames, condemned hundreds of lesser rank, lingering in London's jails or on the river, to death by hanging or transportation to the West Indies. Jubilant crowds gathered for every execution and hanging. Other rebels were quietly dispatched home to the Highlands, under oath never to bear arms against the Crown again.

Passing the Tower and churches and public edifices rebuilt after the Great Fire eighty years before, Flora and Dick came to the tall brick home of the latter on Dartmouth Street, close to fashionable St James's Park. Here Flora would remain in the custody of her companion until called for examination. It had been determined that the Privy Council, a body including members of Newcastle's government which sat in Whitehall, would hear her case, as they would consider those of Old Clan, Boisdale and numerous others from the Long Island, Skye and Raasay, whom Dick already lodged.[36]

As the only female prisoner in the house, Flora may have slept in a chamber with Dick's wife and daughter. Later during her residence in Dartmouth Street, she was on friendly terms with Miss Dick. Her fellow prisoners were more importunate. Accustomed to fine living within their Highland homes and to moor and glen without, they carped at the conditions of their imprisonment. Another captive, Aeneas Macdonald, was used to a sumptuous existence in Paris, where for decades he had owned a banking house. 'We are four to a room, and no opportunity for a fire,' he complained, asking that he and Old Clan be moved to less crowded quarters elsewhere.[37] The government did not comply. The banker and his fellow Highlanders then addressed a querulous letter to Newcastle's secretary, Andrew Stone, begging 'permission now and then' to breathe 'a little fresh air in the Park, having a [King's] Messenger with us [as warder]'.[38]

Although there is no evidence that the requested promenades took place, Dick and some of the other King's Messengers and their families proved kindly jailers to their charges, obstreperous though they might be. At one point there was an official order to send Lady Clan, who was in the custody of a John Money, another Messenger, 'to Bedlam [Bethlem, the then disreputable London hospital for the insane]. Were it not for Mrs Money', her husband learned, 'Lady Clan would be there now.' The Messenger's wife 'would not allow it, until she would have your answer. Ten days ago, your lady was very ill, but Saturday night turned raving mad, more than ever you did see ...'[39] The strain now of being separated from her husband, and a prisoner far from home, might have affected a woman with a stronger constitution. Requesting that the government allow a Clanranald servant in custody elsewhere in London to care for his wife, Old Clan was sanguine: 'such misfortunes ... generally do not last long'.[40]

Dr John Burton, a rebel 'man-midwife', or obstetrician, from York confined with Flora at Dick's house, took advantage of the 'many opportunities' he had there 'of conversing with the chief of the parties who were instrumental' in the Prince's outwitting his would-be captors.[41] Later satirised as 'Dr Slop' in Laurence Sterne's novel *Tristram Shandy*,[42] he himself published anonymously, after further conversations with other, earlier prisoners in Scotland, *A Genuine and True Journal of the Most Miraculous Escape of the Young Chevalier, from the Battle of Culloden to his Landing in France* by an 'English gentleman'. It was in part, the author maintained, 'taken ... from the mouths of Kingsburgh, his lady, and Miss Flora Macdonald'.[43] He there comments on the 'great sprightliness in [Flora's] looks', on her 'very pretty agreeable person' and on her abundance of 'good sense, modesty, good nature and humanity'.[44]

The *Journal* was not published till 1749, but a pamphlet entitled *The Female Rebels* appeared to gratify the public appetite for intelligence about Flora while she was yet a prisoner in London. The author, also anonymous, began by disparaging two Highland noblewomen who had been 'female Furies' and active in the Rising. When the writer turned to the subject of 'Miss Florence [Flora] Macdonald, now in custody of one of His Majesty's messengers in London', however, his tone changed:

> We now enter upon a character more amiable, more feminine and less shocking to the imagination … If she is a criminal, it is only against political Justice that she is supposed to have erred. The crimes … leave her still the character of a woman … She has carried those social and endearing virtues of mercy and compassion that she is charged with to an unseasonable height … How would she wish to be divested of humanity?… A surly plodding statesman may be possessed of such adamantine hearts … Woman, while she remains woman, must still be under a temptation to act as Miss Macdonald has done, or is supposed to have done.

Though it would have been 'more politic for that unfortunate young lady to have acted another part', they continued, they hoped that 'the plea that she is a woman and subject to the frailty of her sex, will have some weight with her judges and jury when admitted to trial'.[45]

The civil war in Scotland and the north of England in which the Prince had led out in battle those whom good Hanoverians termed 'rabble', 'vermin' and 'animals' was still fresh in men's minds. Justice had not as yet been fully meted out to all the Jacobite renegades. For those who wished to look forward to more peaceful times, Flora was presented in *The Female Rebels* as a heroine, exhibiting, instead of partisan spirit, benevolence and charity, both qualities then much esteemed in women. While Old Clan, Boisdale and the other chiefs and lairds at Dick's were of greater rank than Flora in their native Hebrides, in the metropolis her star shone bright.

Alexis, or The Young Adventurer, that allegorical novel, probably written by Neil MacEachen and sophisticated in its use of pseudonyms, also enhanced Flora's reputation this autumn. As already noted, the titular character, though a shepherd, represents the Prince, and Sanguinarius (the Duke of Cumberland) is described in the key as 'Some butchering fellow'. Culloden is 'Lachrymana, or Vale of Tears', and Fort Augustus 'Voluptuaria, or A Voluptuary's Palace'. Flora features as Heroica, a young shepherdess, whose 'breast', we are told, 'glowed with desire to preserve the gallant Alexis'. She is promoted, with good reason, as 'possessed with a greatness of soul and happiness of invention far superior to most of her tender years'. Once resolved to take Alexis 'in a female dress' as her maid to her mother's house 'in the island Aetheria [Skye]', Heroica affirms, 'The trusty stout Honorius [Armadale] will frankly give me a passport.' The account of the voyage to Aetheria, as given in *Alexis*, includes these lines: 'Upon their setting out, a thick mist descends, by which means they get safely through the Sea Monsters [Royal Navy vessels] who would have been ready to devour them.'[46]

The *St James's Evening Post* informed its London readers on 30 December 1746: 'The famous Miss Flora Macdonald … was last week very particularly examined as to her conduct, in relation to her harbouring the Young Pretender after the battle of Culloden, and recommitted into the custody of a messenger.'[47] The Privy Council held its judicial sessions in the Cockpit, a small octagonal building, once a royal theatre, on the edge of St James's Park. Flora's fellow prisoner Dr Burton had been examined there earlier in the year, 'From eight o'clock in the evening to near one o'clock in the [next] morning'.[48] In November, Lord Lovat, imprisoned in the Tower since the summer, was led there one night under strong guard and under protest. Not having himself carried arms against the King, he declared that he should have been tried in Inverness, if at all, or in Edinburgh. In this bid he failed. The Laird, then in London, told Duncan Forbes of Culloden that all London was vying for tickets for Lovat's trial in Westminster Hall, to come on in the spring.[49]

Meanwhile, the *St James's Evening Post*, carrying intelligence of Flora's examination in the Cockpit and return to Dick's in December, affirmed, 'She is a young person of some fortune in the Highlands.'[50] Although this was then wishful thinking, within a very few years she would, remarkably, acquire undreamed-of wealth.

8

High Treason
January–July 1747

Flora had aided the Prince when he was 'in distress'. Did the long confinement on board ship and the conditions at William Dick's, at which her fellow Highlanders jibbed, affect her? Lady Clan had gone 'raving mad'.[1] Other women apprehended on the Long Island and Skye suffered in other ways, and were vocal to the government. Old Mackinnon's wife, living at the home of King's Messenger John Money, begged for an 'order' in January 1747 so that she could 'go now and then out to get the air'.[2] The following month, announcing that Money's house was 'overcrowded', she petitioned for another residence.[3] Meanwhile, Ann Stewart, a gentlewoman from Orkney, petitioned to be released, declaring that 'her estate and effects' in the north were left 'prey to the enemies of her family'.[4] The King's Messengers had much to bear from their imperious Highland guests, and only a few government shillings a week per prisoner as recompense.[5] Flora's name, however, does not appear in any of the addresses that these northerners addressed to the Prime Minister, his secretary and numerous law officers.

It seemed, shortly after her examination in the Cockpit, as though the Crown, in its turn, was about to extend executive clemency to her. The minutes for a Cabinet meeting, held on 21 January 1747 at the Duke of Newcastle's home, note: 'Miss Flora Macdonald to be released.'[6] In October of the previous year, Lord President Forbes had suggested that a general pardon might be afforded to all those who had been out in the Rising. While this was as yet a matter for discussion in London, the government had tired of sustaining over 1,000 rebels in England and Scotland, held these many months without trial, in castle keeps, jails and prison ships.

In these same January minutes, Newcastle directed John Sharpe, the Treasury Solicitor, to obtain a pardon for all officers who had fought in the Rising and were in foreign employ. Captain O'Neill, held in Edinburgh Castle, was among those released to find his way home. The Treasury Solicitor, moreover, was directed to 'get all the common Highlanders who are pardoned on condition of transportation transported forthwith'.[7] Eight hundred were now turned over to shipping agents in London and Liverpool and were sent off to be found indentured labour – unsalaried work for a specific period of time – in the British colonies. A number of 'common Highlanders' were pardoned and allowed to return home, on condition they give up all their arms to the authorities there. Slowly the jails and prison ships emptied. Were Flora now to join these rebels journeying north, she could be home on Skye within weeks.

She may not have viewed the prospect of returning home with unalloyed pleasure. Patronage was, in the eighteenth century, the wheel on which personal fortunes turned. Those of rank commonly interested themselves on behalf of lesser relatives. Flora, although new to the wider world, was well versed in such matters. The Clanranalds and the Macdonalds of Sleat, in different ways, had both previously been good to Flora's family on the Long Island and on Skye. Now, however, Old Clan, Lady Clan and Boisdale, who managed the family lands, were in custody in London. Moreover, on Skye, Lady Margaret blamed Flora for the hospitality the Sleat factor had offered the Prince, resulting in Old Kingsburgh's long absence from duty while incarcerated in Edinburgh.[8] Compounding the disorder in the Trotternish and Sleat peninsulas, Sir Alexander himself had died unexpectedly at the age of thirty-five, following a fever and chills, in November of that year. James, the elder of his young sons, inherited the baronetcy and became head of the Sleat Macdonalds. Old

Kingsburgh's son-in-law wrote from Skye to the estate's lawyer in Edinburgh: 'This is a weak family [clan] the day.'⁹ The factor's elder son, Allan, concurred. 'Alas, we have lost our happiness on earth,' he wrote to the Lord President. Referring to the new widow Lady Margaret, the young man continued, 'I cannot express her sorrow ...'¹⁰ The Sleat estates, with neither the Knight nor Old Kingsburgh, still 'in irons' in Edinburgh Castle, at their helm, suffered accordingly. However, Flora's stepfather, soon to emerge from hiding, and her mother continued to farm at Armadale. Unlike many who were burned out of their houses in the aftermath of Culloden, Milton's daughter at least had a home to go to.

No reason is given in the January Cabinet minutes for the order to release Flora, alone of all those held in London. Had Flora's examination by the Privy Council in December inspired confidence that she was no rebel? Had the earlier representations of such men of standing as Lord Albemarle, Commodore Smith and Major General Campbell carried weight? She was as culpable as any held in custody. Did the claims made in *Alexis* and *The Female Rebels* that Flora acted out of pity move the Cabinet to mercy?

The government law officers were well aware that Flora, not being subject to the provisions of the Juries Act, could be tried only in Scotland. In this same minute, the Cabinet ordered various ladies who had entertained the Prince at their homes during the Rising to be prosecuted there. Their stories belonged to the annals of Jacobite failure. The future trial of Lord Lovat, who had armed his Fraser clan at Culloden, would remind the public anew of Cumberland's triumph in that battle. Flora, however, had helped the Prince to hoodwink government regiments and militias and had facilitated his escape to the Continent. In short, her story was that of Jacobite success. The newspapers and magazines which these past months had carried accounts of her adventures with Betty Burke did not condone her 'treasonable activities'. They emphasised, rather, her quick thinking and powers of deception in the Stuart cause.

A new pamphlet, entitled *Ascanius, or The Young Adventurer*, embroidered details already given in *Alexis*. Aeneas, who went on to found Rome, had carried Anchises, his father, on his back and his infant son, Ascanius, in his arms when he fled burning Troy, his native city. Parallels with the three generations of Stuarts were not exact, but they were sufficient to entertain the public. The former James III, now deceased, had been driven out of England with his son, James Edward, then an infant. Charles Edward, a modern Ascanius, had sought, though he failed, to found a new Stuart kingdom in the name of his father, a latter-day Aeneas.

In this publication, the hero Ascanius meets, by good fortune, 'a lady on horseback' – Flora – 'attended by only one servant ... on the mountain of Currada [Corradale].' The 'Young Adventurer', according to *Ascanius*, immediately recognised her, 'Mr Macdonald of South Uist having formerly brought her to pay her court to him at Inverness'.[11] A broadsheet entitled *The Pretender's Flight* owes much to this pamphlet's embroidered tale. In one of the former's vignettes, the Prince, fashionably dressed and on foot, converses with Flora, plainly a lady of quality, who is on horseback. In another of the images the Prince is visible, dressed as Betty Burke, while Flora, in a bedchamber, occupies the foreground.[12]

Ascanius further spread Flora's fame, and prints and engravings circulated also which purported to give her likeness, though Flora had as yet sat for no artist. One print of 'Miss Macdonald', around whose neck hung a miniature of the Prince, was inscribed 'Let pomp and grandeur meaner beauties grace, / They are but foils, Macdonald, to thy face.'[13] The frontispiece of one edition of the *London Magazine, or Gentleman's Intelligencer* bore an image of the Prince next to Flora, she in chip bonnet and tartan dress. Jenny Cameron, one of those featured in the *Female Rebels* and also in custody in London, is on his other side. 'How happy could I be with either / Were t'other dear charmer away,' ran the motto beneath, taken from John Gay's musical satire *The Beggar's Opera*.[14]

Throughout 1747, the Duke of Newcastle received news of landings of French forces projected or effected on the Scottish west coast. Although in each case the information was afterwards deemed false, the government remained vigilant. The Act of Proscription 1747 provided that, with effect from 1 August the previous year, clan chiefs, lairds and clansmen were to surrender all their 'warlike weapons', on penalty of transportation. The tartan dress in which Flora appeared, in the *London Magazine* and in a plethora of other prints and mezzotints, was also controversial. The Act further decreed that, from 1 August 1747, 'No man or boy, within that part of Great Britain called Scotland … shall on any pretence whatsoever, wear or put on the clothes commonly called Highland Clothes,' and enumerated 'the plaid, philibeg, or little kilt, trowse [trews or trousers]' and other elements of 'highland garb'.[15] It was declared 'a dress fit only for war, theft and idleness'.[16] Those serving in Scottish regiments, whose uniforms incorporated Highland dress, were accordingly exempt.

Though the dress of women was not covered in the Act, on at least one occasion 'tartan gowns and white ribbands [signifying Stuart sympathy]' were designated 'rebellious dress'. Having heard, in December 1746, that some in Leith were to 'have a ball or dancing' thus attired to mark the Prince's birthday, the authorities dispatched a party of soldiers to stop the gathering. One lieutenant, searching Dame Magdalene's home in the Citadel for examples of the seditious dress, grumbled, 'Never was an officer sent upon any such duty before, as to enquire into the particular dress of ladies, and to hinder them to take a trip of dancing, etc.'[17]

Farce it may have been. It was also proof that the authorities remained nervous about any gathering in Scotland tending 'to promote and stir up rebellion' once again. Although the scant details of Flora's dress in 1746 include no 'partly coloured [tartan] plaid or stuff', the printmakers liberally decked her image with such cloth, as well as with the Stuart rose and ribbons.[18]

Despite the previous order for Flora's release, minutes of a meeting between Newcastle and government law officers on 13 February reveal that she was still at that time an inmate of William Dick's house in Dartmouth Street. Just why she had not been freed is a mystery, but Sharpe, the Treasury Solicitor, was now instructed 'to attend the Attorney and Solicitor General' – Sir Dudley Ryder and William Murray – and refer to them 'the case of the prisoners in the custody of Messengers'.[19] With a few exceptions, these 'prisoners' were those who had been apprehended in the Long Island, Skye and Raasay. Fifth in the list that Sharpe furnished to the law officers later that month was Flora's name.[20]

Miss Flora Macdonald, the Treasury Solicitor affirmed, had been 'made prisoner for having carried off the Pretender's son in women's apparel. Her declaration [made to Campbell, on board the *Furnace* the previous July] was sent to HRH the duke, which Mr Sharpe has not [does not have].' Since then, Sharpe continued, Flora had stated 'that her father-in-law [stepfather], Hugh Macdonald of Armadale, gave her a pass to protect her and her pretended servant from the King's troops and that he wrote a note to his wife recommending his daughter-in-law's [stepdaughter's] pretended servant to her favour and protection'. The Treasury Solicitor added, 'Persons were sent to take up this Hugh Macdonald, but he had made his escape.'[21]

Sharpe, stating the case against Flora, noted: 'There are three witnesses who speak to her being with, and assisting, the young Pretender to make his escape.' The Benbecula baillie, who had seen Armadale give her the passport, was one of them, John Maclean, Lady Clan's cook, who had dressed the lochside supper before the passage to Skye, the second, and Rory Macdonald, crew member, the third.

Sharpe, laying out the 'state of the evidence against' Flora and her fellow prisoners, had this question for the Attorney General and Solicitor General: 'Whether there be sufficient evidence against any and which of them, and in what manner and against which of them will it be proper to proceed?'[22] Ryder and Murray did not keep the Treasury Solicitor waiting long. On 23 March, they gave their opinion 'upon the state of the cases of the following prisoners laid before us.' Some of these latter, having been out in the Rising, were, they determined, 'triable here under the late [Juries] act and special commission [at Southwark]'. Flora, however, was included among those who had, the law officers judged, committed high treason for which they were 'only triable in Scotland'. The Clanranalds and Boisdale were also of this number.[23]

The Cabinet acted swiftly on the advice of the Attorney General and Solicitor General. A minute dated 31 March notes that the

Clanranalds and Boisdale were in due course to be prosecuted in the High Court of Justiciary in Edinburgh. In the case of 'Miss Macdonald', however, the government ignored their law officers' opinion. For all the wealth of witnesses who proved her 'high treason', the Cabinet, reverting to their earlier decision in January, decreed that Flora was to be released.²⁴ A few days later, the *Derby Mercury*, a provincial weekly newspaper, published intelligence from London: 'Several ladies who were taken up on account of the late rebellion, are ordered to be discharged, among which are, we hear, the Duchess of Perth, Miss Jenny Cameron, Miss Flora Macdonald, &c.'²⁵

Mere days after Londoners had learned of Flora's reprieve, multitudes gathered on Tower Hill to see the Old Fox beheaded. Squinting for lack of sight, crippled by gout, the notorious Lord Lovat had argued passionately that spring, in a packed Westminster Hall, that the proceedings against him were unjust. The production of correspondence in which he had engaged with the Stuart court proved his undoing. Stands built to provide spectators with a good view of the scaffold filled up on 9 April, and 1,200 troops were on hand to quell disturbances. When the aged rebel's head was severed from his body, the London mob's bloodlust, fed by the public hangings and executions of other Jacobite rebels over the past year, at last began to abate.

Unlike Lovat, Flora Macdonald had sought no personal or political advantage in the 1745 Rising. Her quiet life had been disrupted and endangered by her week's adventure with the Prince. Would she now return home and fade back into the obscurity from which she had so recently emerged?

In the event, Flora was not to leave London until the high summer of 1747.²⁶ Although she was 'discharged', she appears to have remained at Dartmouth Street for the most part until that time, while now being free to visit where she liked. She was 'very much noticed by her own party' – English Jacobites – 'as she was smart and lively', Flora's future sister-in-law was to aver. 'A Lady Primrose was her patron and adviser' and 'introduced her to many good families'. The Skye matron added that on these forays into

London society 'Miss Macdonald' was 'always attended by the Messenger's daughter [Miss Dick]'.[27]

Some of the English Tories mentioned had secretly favoured a Stuart restoration. Their party had been out of office ever since the Hanoverian accession in 1714, yet none of them had come out or proffered funds when the Prince marched south. For all that, these clandestine Jacobite circles south of the Scottish border did not splinter but pressed for a further Rising. Anne, Lady Primrose, the wealthy widow of a viscount, was among the most ardent of these southern Tories for the Stuart cause. Only Sir Watkin Williams Wynn, an enormously rich baronet and the peeress's near neighbour during her youth in Wales, was more fervent. This summer the old Jacobite had the pleasure of hosting Flora at one of his sumptuous residences.[28]

Leading a comfortable and monied existence at her London town house in Essex Street off the Strand when not at a villa in Windsor, Lady Primrose moved with ease between gatherings where literature was celebrated and where she was held to be 'very sensible [cultured]' and 'good-natured' and more discreet conclaves where Jacobite plotting was the order of the day.[29] In a portrait made at about this time, when she was in her thirties, the widowed Viscountess appears fair of face and blooming with health.[30] Her beneficence already extended to endowing charity schools in Wales and Ireland, where her father had been a dean, and lately to aiding Jacobite fugitives in hiding in London. Now Flora Macdonald became the object of Lady Primrose's kindness.

Sir Walter Scott was to write in his *Tales of a Grandfather*, destined for a junior audience,

> Flora Macdonald found refuge, or rather a scene of triumph,
> in the house of Lady Primrose, a determined Jacobite, where
> the Prince's Highland guardian was visited by all persons of
> rank who entertained any bias to that unhappy cause ... Many
> ... who, perhaps, secretly regretted they had not given more
> effectual instances of their faith to the exiled [Stuart] family,
> were desirous to make some amends, by loading with kind

attentions and valuable presents, the heroine who had played such a dauntless part in the drama.[31]

Lady Primrose's patronage of Flora was in time to extend to her protégée's children and only ended with the Viscountess's death. The wealth that she was soon to bestow on this young Highland gentlewoman spoke to the strong attachment that came to bind the two.

Robert Chambers, in his *History of the Rebellion*, did not restrain his imagination:

> Instances have been known, according to the report of her [Flora's] descendants, of eighteen carriages belonging to persons of quality, ranking up before the house in which she was spending the evening. Throughout the whole of these scenes, she conducted herself with admirable propriety, never failing to express surprise at the curiosity which had been excited regarding her conduct – conduct, which, she used to say, never appeared extraordinary to herself, till she saw the notice taken of it by the rest of the world.[32]

Chambers was steeped in Jacobite lore, but he wrote in 1827, long after these fabled scenes had taken place. Later still, one of Flora's granddaughters would delight Victorian readers with an *Autobiography of Flora Macdonald: Being the Home Life of a Heroine*, which she 'edited'. In this inventive narrative, Miss Macdonald visited a 'fashionable warehouse' with Lady Primrose, where the Viscountess selected a 'complete outfit of every article' that her guest could possibly require. The *Autobiography*'s author, who was born over twenty years after her grandmother died, wrote in the character of 'Miss Macdonald' as follows: 'One piece chosen for a company [best] gown was the sweetest thing I ever saw; a silk so thick and rich, it would stand [up] alone. It was a pale rose-colour, with alternate stripes of green shaded with brown. Oh! I loved that pretty gown beyond all the others, and have kept the remnants; they are in my boxes somewhere.'[33]

It is possible that Flora's granddaughter did indeed possess such 'remnants' associated with her grandmother when she penned the *Autobiography* in the 1870s. A souvenir from Flora's London season in 1747 which survives is a sandalwood fan, painted with figures of fur-clad Turks. She was to treasure this modish accessory until her old age and bestow it, only then, on a great-niece in the Hebrides. A Highland folklorist, long afterwards, acting upon information from that lady, was to give it this label: 'Presented to her [Flora], while she was a prisoner on parole in the house of Lady Primrose in London, Nov[embe]r 1746'. Flora was in that month still in transit on shipboard to Dartmouth Street. While Flora is said to have received the fan at the house in Essex Street, it is unclear from the label whether Lady Primrose or another was its donor. It remains, however, an item of delicate beauty to which its recipient was long attached and which perhaps in hard times to come recalled former days of glory.[34]

Flora sat for two leading portrait painters this summer, Lady Primrose and others of her admirers having the riches to pay these artists. Richard Wilson, who had earlier painted a fine likeness of Commodore Smith, depicted the Highland gentlewoman in a blue dress with a shadowy boat on water in the background. A small tartan bow and a letter in her hand, alluding to Armadale's passport, hint also at her time with the Prince.[35] In a bolder portrait by the same artist, now in the Scottish National Portrait Gallery, Flora wears a costly tartan dress with white Stuart ribbons.[36] Nigel Gresley, a volunteer lieutenant on the *Bridgewater*, later a wealthy baronet, appears to have received this lavish gift as a token of Flora's gratitude for kindness shown her when on Knowler's ship.[37] She had no money at this point to pay Wilson for either portrait, nor for her likeness by Thomas Hudson, of which mezzotints were taken this summer.[38] Rich patrons, wishing to record her appearance before she left London, she had in number.

While Flora was still in London and after she left it, in her lifetime and later, many observers, including Scott, were to ascribe to George II's 'good-natured and generous' son, Frederick, Prince of Wales, and others of the royal family a warm appreciation of 'what was due to the worth of Flora Macdonald, though exerted for the safety of so dangerous a rival'. The Hanoverian heir was held to have admired 'the simplicity and dignity of her character'. While Frederick's expression of any such view is only anecdotal, the persistence of this legend reveals a public wish to afford 'Miss Macdonald' the ultimate compliment of royal – Hanoverian – approval. 'The applause due to her noble conduct, was not rendered by Jacobites alone,' wrote Scott.[39]

A General Amnesty passed into law on 4 July 1747 and extending a pardon, in the King's name, to 'all who have been artfully misled into treasonable practices against his person and government' caused little demur in London.[40] There were exceptions from this Act of Grace, as the legislation was known in Scotland. Old Clan was among those still deemed triable there. Embracing his new freedom, however, Aeneas Macdonald, the Paris financier at William Dick's, proposed to Miss Macdonald 'a jaunt to Windsor', where Lady Primrose's villa was situated.[41] Before the outing could take place, however, he was transported to a jail south of the river where, he later declared, he was 'almost eaten up with vermin of all kinds'.[42] Trial and conviction were in store for him later in the year, although he was afterwards reprieved.

No such dark future awaited Flora. Lady Primrose offered a coach and four horses to take her north and, from those many at Dartmouth Street now freed, the Viscountess's protégée selected Malcolm Macleod as an escort. This Raasay man, pleasantly surprised by the change in his fortunes, was later to say, 'I went to London to be hanged, and returned in a post-chaise with Miss Flora Macdonald.'[43] Breaking their journey at York, where they stayed with Dr Burton, their former fellow at William Dick's, the companions reached Edinburgh in early August.

9

A Jacobite Dowry
August 1747–April 1751

In London, in the summer of 1747, Flora had attracted the patronage of many who, though they hankered for a Stuart restoration, had not joined the recent Rising. In Edinburgh she was among Jacobites who had been active in that rebellion. At the ancient market cross in the autumn of 1745 David Beatt, 'writing-master', had proclaimed the Prince to be Regent, and his father King. Now in September two years later this tutor, as he informed a friend in the Borders, had 'entered with [been engaged by] Miss Flory Macdonald'. She had, Beatt told his correspondent, 'waited five weeks for my return to Town' and desired 'very much to be advanced in her writing'. This would confine him to 'daily attendance, and must do so, till she is brought some length in it [her course of writing]'.[1]

There is no clue here who supplied Flora with the funds for this intensive course of lessons. However, Lady Primrose would soon provide her with a substantial endowment, to which other Jacobite patrons contributed. It is reasonable to suppose that they also furnished her with the means to pay Beatt and also to lodge in Edinburgh for what would prove to be a prolonged stay. At any rate, the weeks that she spent with the writing-master were to bear bounteous fruit. Not only did Flora learn to write an 'advanced', or businesslike, letter, a tool which would soon prove invaluable, but – literate before – she now became confident with her pen.

Whenever she or members of her family were in need of 'interest' or patronage, she would boldly petition members of the nobility and gentry of her acquaintance.

Edinburgh and Leith were crowded this summer with former rebel prisoners, now released following the Act of Grace and pausing on their way home to the Highlands. Dame Magdalene Bruce's lodger Robert Forbes conceived the idea of collecting their oral and written accounts of 'that extraordinary historical episode' – the Prince's wanderings in the islands and on the west coast of Scotland. Chief among those whose testimony the Episcopalian minister wished to capture was Flora. By good fortune, a close relative of her stepfather who had come south and set up as a joiner was a frequent guest at the Citadel. This 'Skye man' agreed, in August, to 'do all that lay in his power' to effect an encounter between the cleric and the young woman.[2] Busy at her books with Beatt, Flora was not free to meet for some time, but when she at last submitted to an interview, Forbes was delighted in equal measure by her testimony and by the haberdashery items associated with the Prince which she brought. The cleric later affixed a segment of ordinary tape inside one of the boards of the octavo volumes where he inscribed witness statements. It was, he recorded, 'a piece of that identical apron-string which the prince wore about him when in the female dress' and he received it 'out of Flora Macdonald's own hands on Thursday, November 5, 1747'. 'I saw the apron', he exulted, 'and had it about [tied around] me.'[3]

Forbes was to become one of the most assiduous and idolatrous of those who, early on, hunted after memorabilia of the Prince's evasion of the redcoats after Culloden. Chips of wood from the boat that took the Prince to the Long Island, as much as tattered tartan from a waistcoat he had worn, delighted Forbes. Flora and Lady Clan at Nunton had sewn the gown, the 'white apron' and other articles of female dress, which Betty Burke wore, a matter of deadly earnest.[4] Now, while Flora looked on, the Edinburgh minister reverently tied the apron about his middle and prized the piece of apron-string tape as though it were a Stuart jewel.

The minister had also written to Old Kingsburgh, now released from the Castle and returned to Skye: 'If you would send me a bit off one of the lugs [flaps] of the brogues, you would do me a very great favour.'[5] These were the shoes which Betty Burke had worn on that island. The Sleat factor, who guarded jealously mementoes of the Prince's visit to Kingsburgh, replied, 'I have ill will to mangle my favourite shoes.'[6] Nevertheless, in due course he sent off the leather trophy that the Leith cleric desired. In time to come the brogues themselves, minus one flap, would be bartered by Flora for hard cash.

She was well aware even now of the currency which items associated with the Prince represented. Recovering those buckled French velvet garters, 'covered upon one side with white silk', which the Prince had worn under his female dress, and which had been earlier deposited by her younger half-brother at the Citadel, she bestowed a small strip of the costly stuff upon Forbes.[7] When she had been a prisoner on the *Eltham* and the *Bridgewater* in the Roads of Leith, she had not known if the Prince was safe. Now she was enjoying a kind of triumph in Edinburgh among friends. Her new friend, the Reverend Robert Forbes, was to inscribe in his octavo volumes:

A SONG in praise of Miss FLORA MACDONALD, to the tune of 'My Dearie an' thou die':

...

Wreckt was our hope, thy charge and thee,
　　And cruel death the fate;
Had not a powerful hand sent down
　　Protection to thy boat.

...

The mist which blinded William's fleet
　　To you gave safety there.
A ray directive shone for you
　　And led you where to steer.
O happy nymph! Thou sav'dst the Prince;

Thy fame be handed down.
Thy name shall shine in annals fair
    And live from sire to son.[8]

Among the keepsakes that Forbes stuck inside the boards of his volumes of testimony is: 'A small square piece of printed linen, (the figures [pattern] being in lilac on a white ground)'.[9] Old Kingsburgh had been prevailed upon to send south a swatch from 'the Irish maid's' gown which he and his wife had kept all this time. Stewart Carmichael, a habitué of the Citadel and a prosperous Leith linen merchant, wished to use it 'as a pattern to stamp other gowns from'.[10] In due course, Betty Burke dresses, emanating from Carmichael's works, were to adorn ladies far beyond Edinburgh and Leith. 'The printed cloth,' Forbes was to write to one correspondent, 'I hope, will please the worthy ladies … I can assure you it is done [printed, by Carmichael] exactly according to the original, there being not one ace of difference in the figure.'[11]

The orders poured in, and were fulfilled with celerity. In York, Dr Burton's wife was headed for fashionable Harrogate Spa, in Yorkshire. She had a person 'sit up all night to finish her gown, that she might show it there'.[12] The Citadel had earlier been searched when rumours spread that ladies, dressed in 'that rebellious dress [tartan]', were to celebrate the Prince's birthday. This alternative, subversive costume, evoking memories of the Prince's desperate evasion of redcoats with Flora at his side, further spread his companion's fame.

Over the coming months Flora was to become a frequent visitor to the Bruce household in the Citadel, to Forbes's delight. In the particulars she revealed of her adventures with the Prince, there was no detail too small to edify the minister. She, like Old Kingsburgh before her, read and commented on the accuracy of the 'Journal' that Burton in London had written and since confided to the Edinburgh cleric. In March 1748, Forbes noted, 'Miss Flora Macdonald being in my room in the Citadel of Leith, I took an opportunity of reading to her Armadale's letter to his wife [Flora's mother] … and of asking her whether or not it was exact enough.'

Donald Roy, on an earlier visit to the Citadel, had given the minister
the gist of the missive. Flora answered that the Captain was 'right
enough as to the substance of the letter', but had forgotten to add
Armadale's words, 'I have sent Neil MacEachen along with your
daughter and Betty Burke to take care of them.' Forbes continued,
'At the same time Miss Macdonald assured me that her brother,
Macdonald of Milton, was the person who delivered the Prince's
pistols into Armadale's hands.'[13]

When in Edinburgh in 1747 or 1748, Flora was apparently
reunited with her cousin Neil, who seems to have paid a visit
to Scotland, undetected by the authorities.[14] He had earlier left
for France with the Prince and others in the autumn of 1746 on
L'Heureux. Remaining in Paris thereafter, he and Young Clanranald,
Old Clan's heir, were often with Charles Edward in the French
capital. When the Prince appeared at the theatre, once more
powdered and exquisitely dressed, he was greeted, for all the failure
of his enterprise, as a hero. His popularity in France kept hopes of
that country's aid for a Stuart restoration alive in British Jacobite
breasts, and possibly Neil was the Prince's emissary to some of
those supporters when he and Flora met in the Scottish capital.
In January 1748 Forbes wrote to Kingsburgh with heavy-handed
humour, 'I am glad it is in my power to inform you from good
authority that Bettie Burke [the Prince] frequently makes mention
in her conversing with friends of Macdonald of Kingsburgh with
great respect and warm affection. But you must not let Mrs.
Macdonald know this, lest jealousy should arise in her breast.'[15]

In the summer of 1748, Flora left her new friends in the Scottish
capital and set out overland for home, not without adventure.
She almost drowned when a vessel carrying her across a stretch
of Argyllshire water foundered. A 'clever Highlander saved her',
Forbes informed Burton in York.[16] Though she reached Armadale,
and her family, in July, Flora had no intention of settling there at
present. Even before she left Edinburgh for Skye, she had informed
Burton that she would favour him with her company at York in
September, when she would be on her way to London. The affable
doctor wrote to Forbes, 'the longer she makes the visit, the more

she'll oblige my wife, myself, and friends. For I would have her see our country a little, and not hurry away too soon.' If he had wished to display his famous friend in York society, however, the doctor was disappointed. Flora was on the wing. She stayed only two nights with Burton in November, and he heard later that month that she had 'got well up to London'.[17]

She was still in that metropolis when her cousin Neil wrote to her from Paris, on 28 February 1749: 'Dear Florry, I've often had it in my head to write you since I parted with you at Edinburgh, but as I did not know how long you stayed there, I was at a loss for a direction.' He added: 'as yr. welfare is always agreeable to me, it gives me pleasure to hear the reason that has brought you back to London. I hope you will make it your endeavour to deserve, as much as in you lies, the protection of those worthy people that has took you by the hand.'[18] Neil does not name those in the south who interested themselves in Flora, nor indeed does he expound on the 'reason' for her return to London. Within two years, however, Lady Primrose was to pay a vast dowry to her protégée, part of which the Viscountess funded and part of which appears to have come from other English Jacobites. In March of this year she sent a receipt for £20 to Innes and Clerk, a London merchant house with whom donations appear to have been lodged before being transferred to the Viscountess's account.[19] Furthermore, an Edinburgh lawyer was to write in 1751 of money of Flora's 'intrusted to ... her [Lady Primrose's] hands'.[20]

Neil further wrote in his letter of February 1749: '[Young] Clanranald ... and I dined with somebody [the Prince] the very day they were took. Good God, what a fright we got!'[21] By the terms of the 1748 treaty of Aix-la-Chapelle, and at the behest of the British Crown, France had agreed to eject Charles Edward from its borders. The Prince, however, refused to depart. Finally, guards seized the unwelcome guest as he was about to enter a Paris theatre. Bound with silken ties, he was bundled off in a coach to a fortress in Vincennes and subsequently dispatched across the border to Avignon, then part of the papal lands. French support for any further Stuart assault on the United Kingdom was at an end.

Even so, the Prince continued to keep up a correspondence in cipher with Jacobites in England, though their number was dwindling. Stubbornly clinging to hopes of a restoration, he was to steal into the country at least once under an assumed name in September 1750 and surprise Lady Primrose at her house. Persuaded to return to the Continent, he afterwards declared that he had embraced the Anglican faith at a church in the Strand.[22] While the Prince for whose sake she had braved so much twisted and turned in the wind, Flora's fame remained constant. In 1747 Thomas Hudson had been an artist in 'vast vogue' when mezzotints were published of a painting he made in London of Flora, 'ad vivum [from life]' and in a billowing gown, embellished with tartan ribbons.[23] Allan Ramsay, a Scottish artist who was later to enjoy great Hanoverian favour, painted her now in 1749. The portrait entered the celebrated collection of the physician Dr Richard Mead and, the subject of a fine contemporary mezzotint and a good later engraving, has since generated countless other representations.[24]

In the original painting, now in the Ashmolean Museum in Oxford, a Stuart rose is in Flora's curled, dark hair, a corsage of further blooms embellishes her blue bodice and a tartan stole is pinned to one shoulder.[25] Over a hundred years later this painting was to hang among other 'national portraits' at the new South Kensington, afterwards Victoria and Albert, Museum in 1866. Frederick G. Stephens, a contemporary art critic, judged that the Duke of Cumberland, also represented there, looked 'like a great squab of flesh, and fat, and blood'. The critic was, however, taken aback by Ramsay's portrait of Flora. While, as an admirer of Pre-Raphaelite art, he did not admire Flora's dark Celtic looks, hers was, he declared, 'a most striking face'. He noted the 'intensity' of the sitter's gaze and 'the expression of an extraordinarily resolute will'.[26]

Neil MacEachen asked a favour of his cousin in his letter of February: 'The gentleman who delivers this is a friend of mine, and I hope that is enough to make you exert yourself, among the honest and worthy [her patrons], to help him to dispose of [sell] some valuable toys [Stuart relics] he has upon hand.' Neil concluded: 'I am sure it must give you a sensible joy to hear, the person [the Prince] you once had the honour to Conduct is in perfect good health.'[27] Charles Edward, expelled from France, also lacked funds, and over the following years would consign a plethora of these 'toys' to Jacobite markets. Flora's descendants were to treasure an enamelled pearl and diamond brooch in the shape of a key. The words 'J'ouvre [I open]' were engraved on its shaft, which terminated in a locket. They were convinced that Flora had received this as a gift from the Prince once he had returned to the Continent. This costly item may, instead, represent one of these 'toys' which one of Flora's London patrons acquired and gave to her.[28]

The relics more often associated with that week in the Hebrides were motley and, without Jacobite connection, of little monetary value – apron strings, brogue flaps, tattered tartan cloth, linen swatches, chips of wood.[29] In the course of the nineteenth century, further items, including china cups, silver needle cases, a bodkin, or darning needle, 'a pair of Scots pebble earrings' and even a tablespoon, all purportedly once the possessions of the Heroine, were exhibited or sold.[30] Many women had aided Charles Edward during the Rising and after Culloden. However, at the 1889 London 'Exhibition of the Royal House of Stuart' where mementoes of the exiled House were gathered, the 'Personal Relics of Flora Macdonald' alone had an honoured place.[31] The fascination with her 'treasonable activities' and captivity has not dissipated, and her sandalwood fan is now among other Jacobite treasures associated with her name in the West Highland Museum at Fort William.[32]

In 1750 Flora was sometimes in London, sometimes in Edinburgh and sometimes in Skye.[33] In the closing months of the year, she settled in the last of those places. Now twenty-eight years old, she had fixed on a partner for life. The husband whom she married on 6 November 1750 was Allan Macdonald, Old Kingsburgh's elder son, and the place of their union her mother's house in Sleat, according to the *Scots Magazine* issue for that month, rather than the Sleat parish church.[34] A branch of her descendants in Vancouver long maintained that Flora wore a black silk dress at her wedding.[35] The

Edouard en Ecosse (Edward in Scotland) by Hippolyte (Paul) Delaroche, 19th century.
Oil on canvas

Rouled, o'er Hills the young *Adventurer flies*,
And in a Cottage sinks to this *Disguise.*
Fled his gay *Hopes* defeated his fond *Scheme,*
His *Throne* is vanish'd like a golden *Dream.*
By manly *Thoughts* He'd charm His *Woes* to rest;
In vain! *Culloden* still distracts His *Breast.*

J. Williams fecit

Prince Charles Edward Stuart as Betty Burke by J. Williams, c.1746. Mezzotint

Tableau vivant at Balmoral Castle, showing Princess Victoria of Wales as Flora Macdonald and Prince Albert Victor of Wales as Charles Edward Stuart by Charles Albert Wilson, 1888. Albumen print

Flora Macdonald, embarked for Skye, with Oarsmen from W. E. Aytoun, *Lays of the Scottish Cavaliers and other Poems,* illustrated by J. N. and W. H. Paton (Edinburgh, 1863)

During the Wandering of Charles Edward Stuart by Robert Alexander Hillingford, 19th century. Oil on canvas

The Baptism of Prince Charles Edward Stuart by Antonio David, 1725. Oil on canvas

Bonnie Prince Charlie Entering the Ballroom at Holyroodhouse by John Pettie, 1891-92. Oil on canvas

Charles Edward Stuart by Hugh Douglas Hamilton, c.1785. Oil on canvas

Flora Macdonald by Richard Wilson, 1747. Oil on canvas

William Augustus, Duke of Cumberland from the studio of David Morier, c.1760. Oil on canvas

Anne Drelincourt, Lady Primrose by a follower of Allan Ramsay, 18th century. Oil on canvas

Johnson and Boswell with Flora Macdonald by an unknown artist, 19th century.
Oil on canvas

'Home of Flora Macdonald', Flodigarry, Skye. Postcard, c.1920s

Boswell and the Ghost of Samuel Johnson by an unknown artist, 1803. Engraving

Flora Macdonald on Way to Barbeque Church, North Carolina by
Elenore Plaisted Abbott, *c.*1900. Oil on canvas

May Day at Flora MacDonald College, Red Springs, North Carolina c.1916. From James Alexander Macdonald, *Flora Macdonald; a history and a message* (Washington D.C., 1916)

Historical marker on site where Flora waved off Highland army, 1776. Placed by the Cumberland County Historical Society, Fayetteville, North Carolina

Flora Macdonald's Monument, Kilmuir, Skye from *Illustrated London News*, 27 January 1872.
Engraving

A still from the film *Bonnie Prince Charlie*, 1948. David Niven as Prince Charles Edward Stuart and Margaret Leighton as Flora Macdonald

recent deaths of her two younger half-brothers in circumstances now unknown would account for this sombre choice. Others, perhaps influenced by the glorious hues of her portrait by Richard Wilson in the Scottish National Portrait Gallery, and following the Reverend Alexander Macgregor, Flora's early biographer, have claimed that she wore for the ceremony a robe of Stuart tartan, an earlier present from a 'lady friend' in London.[36] An earasaid or plaid stole was traditionally worn over one shoulder of their dress by women in the Highlands, an example of which may be seen in Ramsay's portrait of Flora now at the Ashmolean. Indeed, an enterprising woollen manufacturer in the 1820s was to offer, among other fancy designs, a 'plaid worn by Flora Macdonald', based on the Macdonald tartan in that painting.[37] It is not inconceivable that Flora wore both silk and earasaid, rather than a tartan wedding robe, on 6 November, adopting mourning dress for the exchange of vows and Highland dress for a ceilidh, or dance, later that same day.

Allan of Kingsburgh appeared an excellent choice of spouse. Now aged thirty, he had been previously educated in the Borders, at the expense of the late Knight, and the widowed Lady Margaret continued to show the factor and his family every favour.[38] As lieutenant of a Skye militia, the young man had been on garrison duty at Fort Augustus when Flora and his father had so fatefully become embroiled in the Prince's Hebridean adventures.[39] Hopes of preferment in the military sphere had faded after the death of Sir Alexander, his patron. It was intended, however, that in due course Allan would succeed his father, now aged sixty-three, as factor to the Sleat estate. To render him still more appealing to his bride, Allan was, as a North Uist bard would one day relate, stalwart in build, dark haired and with a red and white complexion.[40]

The large man, the little woman, appeared ideally suited when they wed. Robert Forbes wrote from Leith to Old Kingsburgh the following January, 'The welfare of the happy pair I heartily rejoice at … [A]ll friends and well-wishers … agree in affirming it to be one of the best judged events of life that could be devised by any set of honest folks.'[41] Dr Burton, in York, was also delighted by the news. 'I heartily wish my worthy Flora as happy as it is possible to be on this side the grave,' he averred, 'and that she may live to see her children's children so too.'[42]

Forsaking the more sophisticated circles in which she had recently moved, Flora had returned to her roots. Moreover, the finances of the young couple were on a very secure footing, as the contract of marriage, witnessed by Flora's stepfather and others at Kingsburgh in early December, attests: 'The said Mrs Flory Macdonald assigns, transfers and dispones [disposes]', ran the document, 'to the said Allan Macdonald, her husband, his heirs and assignees ... the sum of seven hundred pounds sterling ...' Under common law, married women's property and assets passed to their husbands. Only widows like Lady Primrose were free to dispose of their money as they chose. Bonds and securities for this sum lay 'in the hands of certain Trustees and friends of hers [Flora's] in England', the document ran.[43] Among these was Lady Primrose, who had spearheaded the earlier fundraising for Flora, and who was to engage, the following year, in correspondence with merchant house Innes and Clerk about 'Miss Macdonald's money'.[44] The new bride must hope that her husband showed the financial acumen that had distinguished his father, Kingsburgh, in his role as Sleat factor.

Flora's various embassies to London, her courting of Lady Primrose and other patrons there, had reaped this remarkable harvest, and her study with writing-master Beatt in Edinburgh had rendered her competent in business correspondence. In April 1751 she wrote from her new father-in-law's home to London merchants William Innes and Thomas Clerk: 'Yours of the 26th March came to [my] hand ... I understand my Lady Primrose hath Lodged in your hands for my behoof [behalf] £627 Sterling, but that her Ladyship had in view, to add more, of which you would acquaint me.' She begged that the sum lodged with the merchant house should be paid in May to John Mackenzie of Delvine, writer to the signet, or senior solicitor, in Edinburgh. Delvine was lawyer for several Highland estates, including that of Lady Margaret's son James (Sir James since his baronet father's death).[45] Delvine himself wrote to Innes and Clerk on 11 May: 'the money is wanted [needed]'.[46] It is probable, then, although no documentary evidence survives, that this £627 went to pay the Sleat estates in part or in full for the lease of Flodigarry, a tack on the Sleat estates which fell vacant at Whitsun that year and which the young Kingsburghs were to occupy for a number of years.[47] Although it is unclear what happened to the balance of the £700 stated in Flora's marriage contract to be lodged in the South, there was more to come.

Delvine wrote from Edinburgh to Innes and Clerk in London in June 1751:

> Sir, Agreeable to yours of the 18th of May, I have value on you, of this date, to the order of Messrs Thomas and Adam Fairholm [Edinburgh bankers], for the £800 of Mrs Flora Macdonald's money, which Lady Primrose lodged in your hands. The discharge my lady proposed … shall be transmitted as soon as in course of post it can return from the Isle of Skye.[48]

The receipt sought for this further sum, however, although duly penned by Flora, went astray. The Edinburgh lawyer apologised profusely, dispatching another to London in November: 'Mrs Macdonald's obligations to good Lady Primrose's generosity are such that both she and her friends would be to blame if dilatory in anything that may give my lady the least satisfaction.'[49] In total, then, Flora appears to have received and turned over to her husband between £1,427 and £1,500. Even after leasing Flodigarry, purchasing livestock and making repairs and improvements to the tack, it seems likely that there remained some cash in hand.

In 1746, when the Prince made Flora's acquaintance in that sheiling at midnight, she had no dowry to offer a suitor. Now, thanks to her quiet determination to take advantage of her fame, she and Allan had a comfortable married home in the far north-east of the Trotternish peninsula on Skye. Above their tack reared the Quiraing, a massive landslip which had created high cliffs, hidden plateaus and pinnacles of rock. A little further north lay Duntulm, the ancient seat of the Macdonalds of Sleat, now in ruins. Across the peninsula, on its western coast, lay Monkstadt, home to the widowed Lady Margaret and her children. Further south on that shore, Allan's parents' home, Kingsburgh House, stood on the banks of Loch Snizort. Flora's stepfather and mother, meanwhile, were sixty miles distant at Armadale, on the southern coast of the island.

If the farm at Flodigarry should fail, it would be in no way attributable to lack of generosity on the part of Flora's English patrons. There seemed no reason why she should ever stir far again from Skye. A life as a farmer's wife and as a mother, too, if God smiled, looked to be her lot all her days.

PART TWO

Loyalist

10

Married Life
April 1751–1770

Flora had grown up at close quarters with the Clanranald family and other inhabitants of the Long Island, that low-lying archipelago far out to sea which felt the full force of Atlantic gales on its beaches and watery plains. The Isle of Skye, in shape a large, outstretched hand, had a far greater land mass and a milder climate. Flodigarry, the tack above the shore that now became Flora's home, lay in the wild north-east. Portree, however, that harbour where Flora had once parted from the Prince, lay only thirty miles down the coast; further south, at low tide, fords connected island and mainland. Lady Margaret and her children, the Laird, Old Mackinnon and their fellow islanders were of Flora's own faith. While there was only one church of this denomination in Catholic South Uist and Benbecula – where, in about 1755, there were 2,040 'Papists' and 169 'Protestants' – Presbyterian ministers served five parishes in the larger island with congregations totalling 6,777.[1]

Flora's fortunes were now bound up with those of her husband and his family on Skye. In numerous ways, after the 'Forty-five those like Flora and Allan, who inhabited the Sleat lands in Skye, lived a relatively blessed existence. Other estates of rebel chiefs had been forfeited to the Crown; the Clanranald lands escaped that fate through a legal loophole. Even so, Hanoverian troops had seized 500 of Old Clan's cattle in that turbulent summer of

1746 and burned entire villages elsewhere. The Knight and the Laird on Skye had incurred no such penalties, professing loyalty to the Crown and raising government militia. Monkstadt, the Sleat residence, and Dunvegan Castle, the Macleod seat, stood untouched. Secure in their leaseholds for the moment, Macdonald and Macleod tacksmen farmed, and reared cattle and horses for sale at Portree and on the mainland, as they had before the Rising.

In the first years of Flora's and Allan's married life at Flodigarry, the Sleat family was absent from the Isle of Skye. Lady Margaret had taken her young sons – Sir James, Alexander and Archibald – south to be educated in Edinburgh. She and Sir James's tutors – trustees – in Edinburgh had every confidence in Old Kingsburgh's ability, in the meantime, to manage her eldest son's inheritance in the north.

For decades, the factor had driven his master's cattle and horses to market on the mainland and secured good prices for that livestock. He had, however, been weakened by his year-long captivity in Edinburgh Castle, and often now looked to his elder son for assistance in the management of the Sleat lands. Allan acted as his father's emissary to John Mackenzie of Delvine, the Sleat lawyer in Edinburgh, when once Old Kingsburgh himself would have made the journey.

Flora, meanwhile, gave birth at Flodigarry in October 1751 to a son whom she and Allan named Charles. In the Highlands, it was then usual to name the eldest son after his paternal grandfather, if not his father, and the next after his maternal grandfather. Old Kingsburgh and Flora's deceased father were in due course to have their own namesakes among the family of seven children whom the young Kingsburghs raised. Their eldest son's appellation, however, proudly announced his mother's link to Stuart royalty. Flora was a woman characterised by foresight. She may well have judged that coupling the illustrious forename with her own would, in time to come, be of service. It would remind others of the aid she had once given the Royal House of Stuart and encourage them to find a place for her son in the great world.

The Prince himself, however, whose name Flora's eldest son bore, proved no benefactor from afar. Five years after he had persuaded Flora to risk all on his behalf, Charles Edward was living a will-o'-the-wisp life on the Continent. Once, in the Western Isles, his masquerade had been a matter of life and death. Now he took pleasure in posing as an *abbé* or priest, or assuming an alias. Brandy and whisky had sustained him when he lived on the hill and endured rain, wind and midges in the summer of 1746. Now, disappointed and increasingly dissolute, he drank still deeper, as his hopes of a Stuart restoration seeped away.[2]

Upon his return to Paris in 1746 Charles Edward, though he had failed in his expedition, had been hailed a hero by Frederick the Great among others. Only four years later, however, Voltaire ended a spirited narrative of the 'Forty-five in these cool terms in a work later published in English as *The Age of Louis XIV and Louis XV*: 'Thus ended an adventure which, in times of knight-errantry, might have proved fortunate; but could not be expected to succeed in an age when military discipline, artillery, and above all money, in the end decides everything.'[3]

The celebrated writer was kinder about Flora's part in the Prince's escape. Voltaire drew on an account that he declared had been given to him by 'a person who accompanied the Prince a considerable time, both in his prosperities and adversities'.[4] If, as seems likely, this was Colonel Felix O'Neill, who was then on the Continent, either he or the eminent author himself took great liberties with the truth: 'At break of day they [the Prince, O'Neill, and Neil MacEachen] met with a lady on horseback, followed by a young domestic, and ventured to speak to her. This lady was of the family of the Macdonalds, which was strongly attached to the interest of the Stuart line. The Prince, who had seen her in his prosperity, knew her again, and discovered [revealed] himself, when she immediately threw herself at his feet …' The Prince, his companions and Flora were all, according to Voltaire, 'drowned in tears', and 'those which Miss Macdonald shed in this extraordinary and affecting interview, were redoubled by the peril in which she saw the Prince.'[5] What follows is also often imaginary. Voltaire's fame throughout Europe, however, ensured that Flora's story gained an audience far beyond the United Kingdom. While respect for the Prince ebbed, the good name of his 'preserver' was only burnished with time.

Flora herself was always to cherish memories of the Prince as he had been in the Hebrides – gallant, courtly and intrepid. She owed him a measure of gratitude, having gained a fortune following Lady Primrose's enthusiasm for her assistance to him. She had, however, suffered as a state prisoner for nearly a year. Moreover, she never received any tangible reward from the House of Stuart. Her cousin Neil appears to have been more successful. When indigent in France in 1764, following the disbandment of a Continental regiment in which he had served, he begged that his 'miserable situation' in Saint-Omer might be made known to 'His Majesty'. Neil had now reverted to the earlier family name of Macdonald. Addressing, in turn, an outgoing and an incoming secretary in James Edward Stuart's household in Rome, he announced himself as 'one of the chief instruments ... in making his [the Prince's] escape'. His hopes that the royal father would look 'with an eye of pity' on his plight were realised, and he was promised a grant of 300 livres.[6]

When a daughter was born at Flodigarry in the spring of 1754, Flora and Allan honoured the former's patron, Anne, Lady Primrose, as well as his sister, with their choice of her name. The Viscountess had by now cut her ties with the Prince. Two years earlier, the moment had seemed opportune to some Jacobites for a renewed Stuart attack on the throne. Frederick, Prince of Wales had died unexpectedly in 1751, his father George II was aged, and the heir apparent, Frederick's son Prince George, was only thirteen. Lady Primrose travelled to the Continent to consult in secret with Charles Edward in 1752. There she found the Prince a debauched and drunken host, and at his side Clementina Walkinshaw, whom he had made his mistress in the 'Forty-five and who was soon to bear her love an illegitimate daughter, Charlotte Stuart, later to be known as the Duchess of Albany. Dismayed and affronted, upon her return to London the Viscountess withdrew support for this and any future Jacobite project.[7] Her kindness to Flora continued, however, and in due course she would interest herself in the Macdonald children, too.

In the summer of 1754, while Flora's son and daughter were still infants, Sir James, now in his teens, returned with his mother and younger brothers to Skye. Lady Margaret and Old Kingsburgh had work to do, executing a new 'sett' of leases (parcelling them out anew) on the island. General Humphrey Bland, the officious Commander-in-Chief of forces in Scotland, objected. The widow's residence on Skye, he wrote to Lord Holdernesse, Secretary of State in London, would 'tend towards her keeping up the spirit of disaffection amongst the people there, and inspire her son with the high notions of clanship'. Bland was resolved to let the young Sleat baronet know that he was 'not king of the isles, as that family vainly imagined themselves but … as liable to the law as the meanest of his tenants'.[8]

Having served the Crown in both the 'Forty-five and an earlier Rising, Bland was determined to enforce the legislation designed to ensure that chiefs and clansmen alike owed allegiance only to the Crown. He also saw rebel plots everywhere. Convinced that Lady Margaret remained a fervent Jacobite, Bland extended his suspicions to Allan's father. Bland had, he told Holdernesse, 'set some engines to work which, I hope, will fix some crimes on her governor and favourite [Old Kingsburgh]'.[9] Bland had learned that the Act of Proscription, which called for Highland dress and weapons to be laid aside, was being widely ignored in Skye. He sent, in consequence, a party of soldiers to Skye to arrest Flora's father-in-law and other Sleat tacksmen who countenanced these crimes.

Although Old Kingsburgh evaded the redcoats, others were seized. When their prosecution was threatened, Bland reported grimly, Lady Margaret 'lost all her usual courage'[10] and left the island herself with Sir James. The officer insisted he would have the islanders tried unless she agreed to educate her sons in England; in that case, he would, he stated, 'endeavour to get His Majesty's permission to pardon the offenders'.[11]

Sir James was enrolled at Eton College. His mother softened when he proved a brilliant scholar there. Her life in London proved agreeable. No further thought was given to Sir James's education, or that of his younger brothers, in Scotland. Within a few years, the young baronet took up a place at Oxford University. Bland was to be disappointed, however, in his hope that a man of good government principles would replace Kingsburgh as factor on Skye. Indeed, upon attaining his majority in 1756, Sir James rewarded his kinsman who had stewarded the estates so long with an annuity of £50.[12] Lady Margaret in London relied on Old Kingsburgh, as before, but now he acted in a supervisory role. In recognition of the former steward's advancing years Armadale was appointed factor for the Sleat peninsula and Allan for the Trotternish peninsula and the baronet's estates in North Uist.[13]

Meanwhile, the Macdonald family at Flodigarry grew. When Charles and Anne were four and one, in 1755, Flora gave birth to a second son, Alexander, or Sandy. The next year Ranald followed. These two boys were named after their paternal and maternal grandfathers, respectively. James, meanwhile, who greeted the world in the winter of 1757, was called after Allan's younger brother and the young Sleat chief. His was also a fine Stuart name, now borne by Charles Edward's elderly and ailing father in Rome and previously by seven kings of Scotland. Any restoration now of that Royal House in the United Kingdom, however, was unlikely, for all Bland's belief that every Highlander was a secret Jacobite. When a fifth son swelled the number of Flora's and Allan's children in 1759, he was given the name of John, in tribute to John Mackenzie of Delvine, and was affectionately known as Johnny.[14]

The provision for such a large family of children and their education constituted a considerable call on the family purse. A woman whose first act upon being released from custody in 1747 had been to immure herself with a writing-master in Edinburgh for many weeks, Flora made sure that her sons, in their turn, acquired 'good handwriting' and a solid grounding in 'most of the classics and the common rules of arithmetic'.[15] In the Catholic Clanranald lands, some of those dominies who taught tacksmen's children had, like Neil MacEachen, trained for the priesthood. On Skye one at least of Flora's sons attended the grammar school in Portree,[16] while an education was also to be had at the hands of various learned Presbyterian ministers in different parishes.

Allan, a fond husband and father, incurred 'a good deal of trouble and expense' making 'the principal house lodgable [inhabitable]' at Flodigarry.[17] He was ever ambitious for change and innovation. Eager to introduce 'enlightened' farming practices to Skye, he was later to take pride in having 'brought three different sorts of potatoes' to the island in 1761. Before that time, only 'the small red Scotch sort' had been sown.[18] Three years later, importing a 'large brood [breed] of sheep', Allan gave 'to every gentleman and a good many of the tenants [smallholders] a tup [ram] and ewe'. These were crossed with small Skye sheep. As a result, he declared, 'the country had a very fine appearance of having one hardy strong good brood of sheep'.[19] The master of Flodigarry also 'brought home' from the mainland 'six swine and two boars' so that a species of hog, which, he remarked, had been 'quite worn out [nearly extinct] for this forty years past', would once again thrive on the island.[20]

Unfortunately, Allan's enthusiasm for innovation on his tack and elsewhere was not matched by the strength of mind and cool judgement that distinguished his spouse. Nor did he possess the good head for figures and understanding of profit margins that characterised his father. That sage, however, who might have offered advice, was struggling at Kingsburgh after the death of Allan's mother in 1759.[21] She had been buried, at her request, wrapped in the linen on which the Prince had once slept. Only one of his bedsheets, however, had served as her shroud. The other passed into the keeping of her daughter-in-law, and, when her time came, Flora would also have a royal winding sheet.[22]

Weakened by age, Old Kingsburgh was no longer the careful guardian of the Sleat estates that he had once been, and was inattentive to his son's management of the 'factory' entrusted to him. Allan was later to say that he had acted 'with integrity and an honest heart' in all his financial doings. 'I had no dishonest plan at heart.'[23] Nevertheless, twelve years after Flora had brought him a dowry of at least £1,427, Allan was substantially in debt to the Sleat estate in 1763, following losses incurred after droving Sleat cattle to market at Crieff on the mainland.

He was to report that he then 'proposed to give up the factory' and 'pay off the arrears I was then due my master [Sir James] ... about £360'. He 'plainly saw [that] the droving of that year have [had] but a gloomy aspect'.[24] Drought on the island affecting pasturage, or some cattle disease, in 1763 may have occasioned these reflections. Had Sir James consented, the Kingsburgh family at Flodigarry might not have faced ruin a few years later. Unfortunately, the Trotternish factory was kept in Allan's hands.[25]

That summer Sir James, while still an Oxford undergraduate, came north for the first time in many years with his mother. It was time once more to sett the estate. Lady Margaret reported to John Mackenzie of Delvine, the Sleat lawyer in Edinburgh, on 3 November her horror at what they found. 'Almost everything in this country [the Sleat estate]' was 'in confusion', she wrote. She blamed 'the falling off of Kings[burgh]'s resolution and activity'.[26] After some weeks' residence on the island, her wrath against the factor only increased. Some of the houses at Portree, she told the lawyer, had 'fallen to the ground, since we came to the country ... I never saw greater dissolution, for so much money.' Kingsburgh had not, Lady Margaret judged, 'given himself any sort of trouble for years past.' The factor seemed, she wrote, 'as perfectly ignorant of many things [estate business] I've mentioned to him, as I was myself, that was not within a thousand miles of the country'. Castigating Allan as well, the noblewoman declared, 'He [Kingsburgh] has been, in short, blinded by his son and the indolence of old age ...'[27]

Sir James was no less irate. 'Notwithstanding the favour that has been shewed to Allan and the generosity to his father,' he wrote to Delvine on 6 October, 'I find that Kingsburgh's family are much disappointed that the whole country [Sleat estate] is not divided among [leased out to] themselves.' The baronet had just endured a most 'impertinent' conversation with Allan's brother, James.[28] Their sister, Anne McAllister, was meanwhile resentful when her husband's lease of some land was not renewed.[29] Sir James continued in his letter of the 6th: 'That [Kingsburgh] family possess [leases] at present near one third of [the] Trotternish [peninsula] ... If they had the whole, they would not be more thankful.' He told Delvine that he would 'always behave with delicacy where Kingsburgh is concerned ... [but] I must be excused for not complying with many unreasonable expectations of his children ...'[30]

Allan, too, confided in Delvine. He feared, he told the Edinburgh lawyer on 18 November, that Sir James was 'angry at me through the ill will and envy that others bear to me and my father'. He swore, 'I never with my will or knowledge wronged him in a sixpence.'[31] He and Flora were now giving up the Flodigarry tack and taking over the lease of Kingsburgh, where his father would continue to live with them. Relentlessly optimistic, ignoring the woeful state of his finances, Allan wrote, 'I am determined to begin immediately to enclose, plant and ... build all my office houses [outbuildings]' at Kingsburgh 'with stone and lime. I mean, barns, byres and kiln.'[32]

Disaster followed the following year. In his father's place, Allan supervised the summer drove, swimming 2,800 head of Sleat cattle across the shallow Sound of Skye to the mainland and driving them to market 150 miles south at Crieff. Upon his return to the island, he settled up with those tacksmen whose livestock he had sold. As he subsequently told Delvine with dismay, however, his 'list of buying, including the driving [droving] expense', that year exceeded his 'list of selling' by £1,354 13s. Notwithstanding this evidence of his mismanagement, Allan believed that he 'had a fair chance of making up a good part of my loss' in a subsequent summer.[33] Flora and his father at Kingsburgh may well have doubted this assertion.

In any event, Allan soon ceased to be in charge of the Sleat drove. Sir James deprived him of the factory in 1765 and appointed a cattle dealer in his place. There were 'proclamations at the church doors', furthermore, to give Flora's husband, he wrote, 'no cattle on my credit' as his own was worthless.[34] The humiliation of the family into which Flora had married, once so powerful on Skye, was complete. And still that family grew. In late March 1766, amid 'a very deep fall of snow', the island surgeon made 'a short excursion' to Armadale to visit Flora. Now in her mid-forties, she was 'lying in [recovering]' at her mother's house, 'after the birth of a daughter'.[35] This seventh child, named Frances and known as Fanny, was to be the last of Allan and Flora's children.[36]

Allan was conscious that he was failing Flora and their offspring. He wrote to Delvine, 'Was there anything in the world [in the way of employment] thrown in my way, which would help their own and [their] mother's support, I would cheerfully submit to any slavery to better them.'[37] The Edinburgh lawyer had no solution to offer. Nor could Flora look to her brother Milton. Though farming on the Long Island with modest success, he had fathered a large family and did not have the means to offer financial aid to his sister. Armadale, Flora's stepfather, ensured that Flora's younger half-sisters, Annabella and Florence Macdonald, married men of consequence on Skye, but again he had no funds to spare.

The year of Fanny's birth sounded, if it were needed, a death knell for Jacobite hopes. Pope Clement XIII broke with the tradition of his predecessors when James Edward Stuart died in Rome. That Prince had always been acknowledged by the Vatican as rightful monarch of the United Kingdom. Now, nearly eighty years after James II had fled to the Continent, Clement gave the Hanoverian dynasty its due. George III, who had come to the throne six years earlier, was recognised by the Papacy as British sovereign. Meanwhile, the Hanoverian dynasty continued to strengthen a growing empire, having gained new territory at a peace treaty in 1763, following the cessation of the Seven Years' War fought principally against France.

Shocking news reached Skye later in 1766. While touring the Continent, Sir James had sickened and died that August in Rome. His younger brother, Alexander, now assumed the baronetcy and possession of the Sleat lands. Allan wrote to Delvine in alarm the following January. 'It is true', he admitted, 'and I own that my conduct hath been foolish in many steps of my by passed [bygone] life.' But, he lamented, 'the loss is entirely to myself and family. Therefore, it would be greater charity in any man who professes friendship for me, my poor wife and seven children to recommend me to the man [Sir Alexander] on whom all my dependence is.' Allan implored Delvine to 'fix him so, my friend, that the groundless backbitings of my evil wishers may not gain ground on him to my disadvantage'.[38]

Some months later, Delvine received another importunate missive from the same correspondent. 'A man of my family', wrote Allan, 'who hath but a slender hold of his only support – I mean my tack of Kingsburgh – must always be fashious [troublesome] to the friends whom he is convinced can be of service to him.' Allan hoped, with the lawyer's assistance, to secure a long lease – forty years or more – when Sir Alexander came to sett the estate that summer. 'I make one who, my neighbours will attest, is as useful a member of society as any of themselves,' he claimed.

He and his father before him, Allan asserted, had 'improved our tack and laid out on building, planting and enclosing, etc., more than the whole estate put together'. He had that very year sown twenty-four bushels of rye grass and six of red clover. He dwelt on his earlier importation to the island of superior species of potatoes and sheep.[39] But Sir Alexander was to prove no more receptive to Allan's overtures than had his elder brother. The Kingsburgh lease was renewed in September 1769 for nineteen years.[40] Flora, meanwhile, turned her capable mind to securing a future for her sons far from the tack, where she and their father lived in increasingly straitened circumstances. Over the next few years she would energetically court former benefactors in London and Edinburgh with the aim of placing her five sons in the army, the navy and the law. She had no control over the family's finances, brought to such a parlous state by Allan, but she had dominion over her good name, and could be sure she would obtain a hearing from these sponsors.

'We Have Hardly What Will Pay our Creditors'
1771–1774

The first of her sons whose prospects Flora took pains to improve was Johnny, youngest of the five. His elder brothers' education was confined to tuition in Skye. Flora, however, in alliance with her father-in-law, had other plans for Johnny, a promising pupil at Portree grammar school. That academy's dominie, a hard taskmaster, testified in 1771 that the twelve-year-old was 'busy at the Latin. He reads Eutropius [author of a short history of the Roman Empire, commonly then used as a school text], and gets [learns] the grammar [therein]. His genius [intellect] is tolerably good ... I am pretty well satisfied with the progress he has made.'[1]

Flora was eager that Johnny should be enrolled in the high school in Edinburgh, as a preliminary to his entering upon the law. In the Scottish capital that spring she begged Delvine, the Sleat lawyer, to consider taking her son 'off his parents' hands, and putting him in a way of doing for himself [prospering in a career], if he deserves it'. The lawyer agreed to lodge the boy, and Old Kingsburgh wrote to his old friend from Skye, 'Heaven will reward you for this, though it's out of my power or any of his relations so to do.'[2]

The following year, 1772, Johnny duly became a pupil at the high school in Edinburgh. His mother wrote to Delvine on 12 August,

'Johnny … is happy in his having so good a friend as you are to take him under his [your] protection … Make of him what you please …' Flora believed her son to be 'good natured, biddable … without any kind of vices'. A mother of seven, she was, however, without illusions. She added, 'If you see anything amiss in the boy's conduct … let me know of it … Some children will stand in awe of their parents more than anybody else.'[3] Flora was the disciplinarian in the family. Later, Allan was to write weakly to Delvine, 'It will add to the happiness of his mother to hear of his being tractable and obedient, without bad pranks, and submissive.'[4]

Hopeful that Johnny would prosper under Delvine's protection, Flora next turned her attention to her eldest son, Charles, who turned twenty-one in 1772. She invoked the aid of Lady Margaret in London on his behalf as well as that of Delvine. Together, noblewoman and lawyer obtained a cadetship for Charles in the Bengal army, which the East India Company maintained in Bombay. 'My Lady Dowager Primrose', meanwhile, Flora's earlier patron, 'rigged out', or equipped, the young man with uniform and arms, 'and paid for his passage'.[5]

Flora turned to a distinguished naval captain, Charles Douglas, then at the helm of HMS *St Albans*, when seeking occupation for Ranald, her third son. What former connection she or the Kingsburgh family had to this officer cannot be established, but he duly used 'his interest [influence]' at her request with officials in the Admiralty. The boy was accorded a lieutenancy in the 'marine service', a branch of the Royal Navy, consisting of amphibious light infantry.[6] 'God reward the good Gentleman [Captain, later Sir Charles, Douglas],' Allan wrote piously to Delvine when Ranald left Skye, in the spring of 1773, to join his ship. 'He acts the part of a friend to me and my wife.'[7]

Allan, reckless both as factor, or 'doer', for the late Sir James and as Sleat tacksman, had brought the family to indigence. His wife made good his failure to provide for the family. It was no mean achievement to have secured, from the fastness of her Skye home, patronage and places, or positions, for Charles, Ranald and Johnny in Bombay, at sea and in Edinburgh, respectively. Flora had proved herself as adept a doer for her sons as Allan was inept in managing their finances.

One child at least needed no providing for, after Flora's elder daughter, Annie, while still in her teens, made a good marriage in about 1770 to Skye man Alexander Macleod of Lochbay. Considerably older than his bride, Lochbay was a tacksman with cosmopolitan experience, having served as an officer in the Marines for twenty-two years. Though now on half-pay, he had seen action in the 1760s in Quebec and had also suffered 'the unwholesome climate of Pondicherry [in India], and Manila [in the Philippines]'.[8] An illegitimate son of the Laird, Lochbay was much favoured by that chief before his death in 1771 and was a man of standing on the island. Moreover, he was comparatively wealthy, having in 1774 an estate of £3,000.[9]

Flora's son-in-law was to do much in future years to aid the penurious Kingsburgh family. Now she battled on further, invoking her past fame to secure places for her two sons still at home. Addressing the Duke of Atholl in 1774, she represented herself as a 'poor distressed woman (once known to the world)'. The Duke's father having been one of Charles Edward's senior field commanders in the 1745 Rising, her words were a coded appeal to the common Stuart history she shared with her correspondent. Her husband, Flora noted, had 'once had the honour of a little of your Grace's acquaintance', but 'could not be prevailed upon to put pen to paper'. Although personally unknown to the Duke, she declared, 'with the assistance of what remained of the old resolution [former spirit]' she took upon herself 'this bold task'.

'I would wish', she affirmed, 'to have one of two boys I have still unprovided for, in some shape or other, off my hands,' she told Atholl. Sandy, or Alexander, the elder of the two, was, she said, 'bordering on 19 years of age' and had studied both 'the classics' and 'arithmetic'. He had 'a pretty good hand writing, as this letter', which her son had penned, at his mother's dictation, 'may attest'. She concluded, 'Your Grace's doing something for him would be the giving of real relief to my perplexed mind ...'[10] In the event Flora's plea went unheeded after the Duke was stricken by apoplexy and died later that year. Sandy and his younger brother, James, remained at home, as did Fanny, their younger sister, just eight.

Flora had pursued her project to settle her sons with all the more dedication given a momentous decision that she and her husband had taken, as early as 1772. She told Delvine, in her letter that August, that she and Allan could anticipate only 'poverty and oppression' at home. Terming Skye 'this poor miserable Island', she wrote, 'the best of its inhabitants are making ready to follow their friends to America, while they have anything to bring them. And among the rest we are to go …' Their care of Allan's father, which might have kept them at home, had ended earlier that year with his death. She added sombrely, 'We have hardly what will pay our Creditors, which we are to let them have, and begin the world again anew, in another Corner of it.'[11]

The Kingsburghs' destination was North Carolina, one of the most southerly of the thirteen colonies then ruled by George III, who had succeeded his grandfather George II in 1760. The territory was vast and wooded, and its longleaf pines were an important source of tar, pitch and turpentine for Royal Navy and merchant vessels. An intrepid group of Highlanders from Argyllshire had crossed the Atlantic thirty years earlier and founded a new home way up the mighty Cape Fear River in this colony. River traffic burgeoned between Cross Creek, this Scots town in Cumberland County, and Wilmington, a hundred miles to the south, the colony's principal harbour. Merchants in the former settlement sent downriver, among other commodities, 'flaxseed … Indian corn, barrelled beef and pork' and 'square timber of different sorts, deals [planks], staves, and all kind of lumber'.[12] Upriver came purchases for the Highland community.

Since the 1740s North Carolina had seen a steady trickle of Scots immigrate and join family and friends. As the 1770s dawned, however, there was a new urgency about the departures. The *Caledonian Mercury*, in September 1771, informed its readers, 'We hear from the isle of Skye, that no less than 370 persons have lately embarked from that island, in order to settle in North Carolina,'[13] and the following year the Board of Trade in London computed that since 1770 1,600 Highlanders had emigrated from islands lying off the Argyllshire coast.[14]

Armadale, in Skye, was, if elderly, as enterprising as ever. The *Caledonian Mercury* remarked, 'Several of them [the emigrants] are people of property, who intend making purchases of land in America.'[15] Flora's stepfather was among the first of those on the island who 'had in view to form a settlement to themselves and Families in ... North Carolina'. It would seem that Flora's mother did not go with her husband. If she had died before this time, Armadale was a free agent. Having been 'for some time ... making Dispositions [arrangements], by engaging Servants, and disposing of their effects in this Country [Skye]', they were ready, he and other Skye men reported in June 1771, 'to embark and carry their intention into Execution'. Two of their number petitioned the government for a grant of forty thousand acres in the colony.[16]

Although this request was denied,[17] the Skye emigrants were not deterred. 'Five hundred souls' crossed the Atlantic that autumn and made their way to Cross Creek.[18] Among them were Armadale and Flora's half-sister Annabella with her husband, Alexander Macdonald of Cuidreach and their children.[19] Flora's other half-sister, Florence, had married one Archibald MacQueen, and that family appears to have emigrated shortly thereafter. Allan, still on Skye, recorded, 'there shipped and arrived safe in said place [North Carolina] four hundred and fifty souls' a year later, in the autumn of 1772.[20]

Dr Samuel Johnson, the famous lexicographer, who visited Skye in September 1773, commented on the 'epidemick desire of wandering, which spreads its contagion from valley to valley'.[21] Bearing this out, Allan had commented six months earlier, 'The only news in this Island is Emigration ... They have already signed [with shipping agents] and [are] preparing to go above 800 souls, and all those from [the Sleat lands on] Skye & North Uist ...'[22] Sir Alexander Macdonald conceded that summer, writing from the island to James Boswell in Edinburgh, 'America is still in people's mouths.' He was confident, however, he informed the young lawyer, a protégé when in London of Lady Margaret, that none but 'a few bankrupts and adventurers' would leave his estates that autumn.[23] Into the former category, Allan could arguably be said to fall, although he and Flora would not leave Skye for a further year.

The 'poverty' on Skye, of which Flora was to write, was in part responsible for this wholesale emigration. Islanders were accustomed to the deluges of rain, which assailed Skye from September to March and left the October harvest sodden in the fields. Snow, however, rarely lay long on the ground. The 'Black Spring' of 1771 was, in consequence, long remembered. In this severe season, snow bound the earth for two full months. Many of the black cattle perished from exposure or for want of forage. Those that survived, emaciated, were unfit for sale on the mainland. Other beasts succumbed to numerous murrains, or cattle diseases. The Kingsburgh family were among many who suffered. 'We lost, within these three years, three hundred and twenty-seven heads [of cattle],' Flora was to tell Delvine the following year.[24]

The 'oppression' which Flora had mentioned to Delvine was a second factor in the emigration of Sleat tacksmen and their families to America. The *Caledonian Mercury* informed its readers in 1771, 'The late great rise of the rents in the western islands of Scotland is said to be the reason of this emigration.'[25] British customs officials, interviewing emigrant Highlanders at various Scottish ports in 1773, told the same story: 'The reason they alleged for coming [going] to America was that the Rents of their Lands were so raised, that they could not live upon them.'[26]

Sir Alexander Macdonald, Sleat clan chief since 1766, had decided ideas on how to ameliorate the income of his estates. First, he took as a bride an English heiress, whereas his forebears had married into other Scottish families. Next, he made a new sett of the estate, and, as Flora was to declare, 'prodigiously augmented [raised]' the leases he proffered to islanders.[27] 'The rents have been too low,' Sir Alexander believed. 'When that is the case, no tenant will give himself the least trouble [to work the land].'[28] The Sleat tacksmen, however, struggling after the Black Spring and after several bad harvests, procrastinated in paying, or failed entirely to pay, the new sums due. Sir Alexander was later to record, with ire, that the master of Kingsburgh 'had not paid rent for some years' before Flora and Allan took the decision to emigrate.[29]

Encouragement from those with knowledge of conditions in North Carolina was a third factor in emigration. Indeed, the Skye departures had approval on high. Josiah Martin, Governor of the colony in question, observed in March 1772 that its 'prosperity and strength' would be greatly increased 'by the accession of such a number of hardy, laborious [hard-working] and thrifty people'.[30] Allan's sister Anne, recently widowed, had remarried Lachlan Mackinnon of Corriechatachan, another Skye man and a widower himself. The couple, who had numerous children between them, meditated emigration, and Corry, as Anne's new husband was known, elicited from Campbell of Balole, an Argyll man who knew North Carolina well, the following information:

> The town of Wilmington, which is now the principal one in the province, is a fine thriving pretty place. It had but 3 huts in it, when my Uncle [a founder of Cross Creek] went over. It is 24 Miles from the Sea on a river larger than the Thames, and has a considerable trade with most parts of England; 100 Miles above this town lies Cross Creek on the same River, a very thriving place, the Highlanders are mostly settled about this last, each has a plantation of his own on the river Side & live as happy as princes, they have liberty & property & no Excise, no dread of their being turned out of their lands by Tyrants, each has as good a Charter as a D. of Argyle, or a Sir A. Macdonald, and only pay half a Crown a year [quitrent] for 100 Acres they possess …[31]

Such intelligence repaid scrutiny and added to the Kingsburghs' growing store of knowledge about the colony for which they were bound.

Flora was to write later, with regret, of the need to leave her home. James Boswell, who visited the island in September 1773, was told of scenes at Portree the previous year when a ship had left for America: 'The people on shore were almost distracted when they saw their relations go off. They lay down on the ground, tumbled, and tore the grass with their teeth.' He added, 'This year there was not a tear shed: the people on shore seemed to think that they would soon follow.'[32] Boswell was the companion on the island of Dr Samuel Johnson. 'I had desired to visit the Hebrides, or Western islands of Scotland, so long', the lexicographer was to write, 'that I scarcely remember how the wish was originally excited.'[33] As a boy, he had read Martin Martin's *Description of the Western Islands of Scotland* (1703). The recent publication of *A Tour in Scotland*, chronicling a journey undertaken in 1769 by Thomas Pennant, a pioneering naturalist, had further piqued Johnson's interest in the Highlands.[34] With the aid of a stout stick and with Boswell at his side, the elderly savant did manful battle with the terrain and the elements on Skye and Raasay for nearly a month.

Dr Johnson came expecting to see 'a people of peculiar appearance, and a system of antiquated life'.[35] He was greeted, instead, by Sir Alexander Macdonald, a chief devoid of patriarchal sentiment and by a tenantry apparently all intent on departure. He and his companion lodged with Anne and Corry at Corriechatachan. Boswell was to publish in 1785 *The Journal of a Tour to the Hebrides with Samuel Johnson, LlD.*, which was afterwards incorporated into the third edition of his *Life of Johnson* (1799). He wrote there that their hostess 'talked as if her husband and family would emigrate, rather than be oppressed by their landlord [Sir Alexander]'. She also remarked, 'How agreeable would it be, if these gentlemen should come in upon us when we are in America.'[36]

The largest ship on the Clyde was then lying at Portree, ready to take on board passengers bound for America. Even when at leisure, the islanders did not forget their preoccupation with emigration and gave the name 'America' to a new dance, in which each couple successively whirled round in a circle till all were in motion. Boswell observed that the performance 'seems intended to show how emigration catches, till a whole neighbourhood is set afloat'.[37]

Johnson had been disappointed by the modest hospitality that Sir Alexander afforded the travellers on their arrival in the bay of

Armadale at a 'small house on the shore'.[38] The baronet had been on his way from Monkstadt to the mainland when surprised by his visitors. This dwelling, 'built by a tenant' with 'two storeys and garrets', was in all probability the home so recently vacated by Flora's stepfather and that to which she had returned from the *Furnace* to bid farewell before embarking on the voyage south to London in the summer of 1746.[39] The doctor declaimed, 'Were I in your place, sir, in seven years I would make this an independent island. I would roast oxen whole, and hang out a flag as a signal to the Macdonalds to come and get beef and whisky ...' Anciently all clansmen were welcome at their clan chief's table. Johnson continued, 'I would have a magazine of arms.' His host was laconic in response: 'They would rust.'[40] The baronet was, however, indignant when gauchely informed by Boswell that the lawyer's 'only errand into Skye was to visit the Pretender's conductress [Flora]' and was long to remember his guest's assertion that he 'deemed every moment as lost which was not spent in her company'.[41]

Sir Alexander had been far from pleased, some years earlier, when his English wife's uncle went off in 1769 to dine with 'the famous Flora' at Kingsburgh.[42] He was not on the island, however, to condemn Thomas Pennant in 1772. On a second tour of Scotland, in which he voyaged to the Hebrides, the naturalist left aside investigations of rocks and minerals on Skye to visit 'Kingsburgh; immortalized by its mistress, the celebrated Flora Macdonald'. Pennant hoped to renew an acquaintance formed thirty years earlier, during her residence in London, at the home of the Jacobite baronet Sir Watkin Williams Wynn. The author found when he arrived at the Macdonald house on 22 July that Flora was 'unfortunately ... absent on a visit'. Allan, however, obligingly lodged his guest in the same upper chamber and, as Pennant wrote, in 'the same bed that formerly received the unfortunate Charles Stuart'.[43] An observant visitor the following year was to note that among the 'great variety of maps and prints' decorating this room was a celebrated 1763 engraving by Hogarth of John Wilkes, MP, holding the cap of Liberty.[44] Presumably the politician's attack on George III in issue no. 45 of his newspaper, the *North Briton*, that

April, which earned him arrest for seditious libel, struck a chord with the mistress of Kingsburgh, though Wilkes was no lover of the Scottish premier Lord Bute or of her nation. If so, this print, recalling the popular radical cry of 1763, 'Wilkes, Liberty and Number 45', is tangible, if discreet, proof that Flora remained at heart 'a firm Jacobite', as Robert Chambers, in his well-informed *History of the Rebellion of 1745*, was to declare. 'Such is said to have been the virulence of this spirit in her composition', the author wrote in 1827, 'that she would have struck any man with her fist, who presumed, in her hearing, to call Charles by his ordinary epithet, the Pretender.'[45] According to a granddaughter, whose father was Flora's youngest son, 'Flora Macdonald retained to the last a great dislike to hear allusions made to the reigning monarch of England. Nor would she ever name George III and on one occasion not only very sharply reprimanded her son John for styling the latter His Majesty but actually slapped the boy's face, saying "she would hear nothing of Soft Geordie".'[46] Flora would not have been the only Scot of her time who was privately contemptuous of this Hanoverian sovereign but looked to the Crown for protection and for preferment for their family.

When Pennant left the august chamber next morning and departed on his way, he was later to write, he took with him the 'pair of gloves' worn when the Prince 'appeared in the character of the tender sex' – as Betty Burke.[47] Allan's sister Anne McAllister, now Corry's wife, according to Kingsburgh family records, had taken possession of the gloves when Charles Edward resumed male dress on the way to Portree in 1746.[48] Allan also bestowed on his guest the 1765 edition of a Jacobite pamphlet detailing particulars of the Prince's escape in that year wherein, as the traveller later wrote, his absent hostess was 'the Heroine of the Piece'.[49] Whether or not Anne and Flora approved of their brother's and husband's liberality, Pennant valued his acquisitions. He preserved the pamphlet in his library and was to write in 1790 of the gloves, 'They are kept as a memorial of a daring adventure, most unequally supported.'[50]

Now Johnson and Boswell, in their turn, were received at Kingsburgh 'most courteously' by the master of the house and, together with their travelling companions from Portree, the local minister and doctor, ushered inside. Large and stately, wrote Boswell at the time, Allan was 'quite the figure of a gallant Highlander'. Defying the Act of Proscription, as many did in these remote parts, Allan 'had his tartan plaid thrown about him' and his 'jet-black hair tied behind [in a queue or pigtail] and with screwed ringlets on each side', surmounted by 'a large blue bonnet with a knot of black ribbon like a cockade'. A 'tartan vest with gold buttons and gold button-holes' was visible beneath a 'brown short coat [jacket]'. His filibeg (kilt) was 'bluish' and his stockings also tartan. Once the travellers were established in what Boswell described as a 'comfortable parlour with a good fire', a dram of 'admirable Hollands [Dutch] gin went round' the company, which now included two members of Allan's brother James's family. The Edinburgh lawyer was distressed to learn that Allan 'had fallen sorely back in his affairs, was under a load of debt, and intended to go to America'. However, ever optimistic, if not necessarily a good judge of character, Boswell opined that 'so fine a fellow would be well everywhere'.[51]

When supper was served, Boswell was to note, 'there appeared the lady of the house, the celebrated Miss Flora Macdonald'. The diarist was elated. 'To see Mr. Samuel Johnson, the great champion of the English Tories, salute Miss Flora Macdonald', he recorded, 'was a wonderful romantic scene to me.'[52] Johnson was to inform his readers in 1775, 'She is a woman of middle stature [medium height], soft features, gentle manners, and elegant presence.'[53] The lexicographer had arrived very deaf, and in a bad temper, after riding through a rainstorm from Portree. A droll conversation that ensued between him and his hostess now enlivened his mood, as much as a meal that Boswell described thus: 'We had as genteel a supper as one would wish to see, in particular, a fine roasted turkey, porter to drink at table and, after supper, claret and punch.'[54] Flora informed the diarist that 'she heard upon the mainland, as she was returning to Skye about a fortnight before this, that Mr. Boswell was coming to Skye, and one Mr. Johnson, a young English buck [man of fashion], with him'. The doctor was, the young lawyer wrote, 'highly entertained with this event'.[55]

The travellers spent the night in the upper chamber, where the Prince had once slept so soundly. Johnson took the 'neat bed, with Tartan curtains [bed hangings]', his companion its pair.[56] Like Pennant before him, however, the doctor did not lie in 'The sheets which he [the Prince] used'. They 'were never put to any meaner offices', Johnson was to inform a friend, 'but were wrapped up' by Allan's mother 'and at last, according to her desire, were laid round her in her grave'.[57] Flora appears to have kept from both Johnson and Boswell, who repeats this information, that her mother-in-law had, before her death in 1759, given one of the sheets to her daughter-in-law to be used for her own royal shroud in time to come.

In the morning Boswell found 'a slip of paper' on the table in the chamber on which the doctor had written in pencil, 'Quantum cedat virtutibus aurum'.[58] The Pindaric quotation – 'And how much brighter virtue was [is] than gold', in the original – came from an early eighteenth-century ode rendered into Latin.[59] Boswell was to suggest that, as seems likely, Johnson meant by this to express his admiration of all those Highlanders who had resisted the 'golden temptation' of £30,000, proffered in 1745 to any who should 'seize and secure' the Prince.[60] Flora, however, rather than the Highland race in general, may have been uppermost in the doctor's mind.

The doctor said at breakfast the next morning that 'he would have given a good deal rather than not have lain there'. His travelling companion owned that his friend was 'the lucky man', and observed that 'without doubt it had been contrived between Mrs Macdonald and him [Dr Johnson]'. Flora 'appeared to acquiesce; adding, "You know young *bucks* are always favourites of the ladies"'.[61] Both plainly relished their meeting. Flora told the doctor that she 'thought herself honoured' by his visit. 'I am sure', he was to write to a friend later in the month from Skye, 'that whatever regard she bestowed on me, was liberally repaid.'[62]

Dr Johnson spoke at breakfast 'of Prince Charles being here' at Kingsburgh, and addressed his hostess archly, '*Who* was with him? We were told, madam, in England, there was one Miss Flora Macdonald with him.' She replied, Boswell reported, 'They were very right.' Perceiving that the doctor had much curiosity but 'delicacy enough not to question her', Flora then recited all 'the particulars which she herself knew of that escape'.[63] When telling of sitting at table at Monkstadt with 'an officer of the army [Skye militia]' stationed there 'with a party of soldiers, to watch for the Prince', she said that she 'afterwards often laughed in good humour' with the Lieutenant 'on her having so well deceived him'.[64]

In his later published narrative of the Prince's summer in the heather, Boswell was to describe Flora as having been 'animated' in 1746 'by what she thought the sacred principle of loyalty' and imbued with 'the magnanimity of a heroine'.[65] More immediately, when she fell silent, Dr Johnson, who had been listening to her 'with placid attention', said, 'All this should be written down.' His hostess, in answer, said that Robert Forbes at Leith 'had it' – that is, her testimony.[66] The doctor's admiration for his hostess is plain in the summary he wrote of her narrative to his friend Mrs Thrale on 30 September: 'the farfamed Miss Flora Macdonald ... conducted the Prince dressed as her maid through the English forces from the Island of Lewis [the Long Island], and when she came to Skye, dined with the English officers and left her Maid below. She must then have been a young lady, she is now not old, of a pleasing person and elegant behaviour.'[67] Meditating further upon Flora's character and story, Johnson was to write in *A Journey to the Western Isles of Scotland*, which he published in 1775, that hers was 'a name that will be mentioned in history, and if courage and fidelity be virtues, mentioned with honour'.[68]

Having feasted on Jacobite history at Kingsburgh, Johnson and Boswell went on to Dunvegan, which offered the feudal hospitality they craved. Johnson likened the Macleod seat to 'a Castle in Gothick romances'[69] and wrote appreciatively, 'There were two [dead] Stags in the house, and venison came to the table every day in its various forms.'[70] After his departure, he reflected, 'At Dunvegan I had tasted lotus.'[71] The new Macleod chief, who had succeeded his grandfather, the Laird, in 1771, had vowed to live among his people and deter emigration. His efforts to extinguish the bright light which the very name of America conjured up among his clan were, however, not notably successful. Among those who dined with the visitors from the south at Dunvegan was Lochbay, the old chief's illegitimate son and Flora's son-in-law. The following morning, he and others departed at an early hour, so as to bid farewell to friends departing for America.[72]

The 1773 journey to the Western Isles was, for Johnson, an ambition achieved, and material for a book. Boswell, however, was pursued, the following year, by an importunate Allan. He reminded the Edinburgh lawyer, 'when in the [this] country', of his promise to James, the writer's brother and a Sleat tenant, to 'be his friend' in a rent dispute with the baronet. Kingsburgh wrote, 'I am sorry necessity obliges me to be so very troublesome. This is surely bold and over forward in both him and me, but he [James] hath not a single sixpence.'[73]

Boswell, fortunately, was spared further correspondence with Allan about indigent relations. Flora and Allan, she told the Duke of Atholl in her letter of 23 April 1774, were no longer 'able to keep this possession [the Kingsburgh tack]'. Another took over the lease. The time had now come for the Kingsburgh family to leave Skye. Contrary to 'their inclinations [wishes]', Flora wrote, they were following 'the rest of our friends, who have gone this three years past to America ... I leave (with reluctance) my native land ...'[74] Flora left not only her home of fifty years, but also her near relations and two of her children. Allan's sister Anne Mackinnon and her husband had, in the end, resisted the lure of emigration. The decision was made to consign Fanny, Flora's younger daughter, to the care of relatives on Raasay. Meanwhile Johnny, aged fifteen and now studying for the law, was to continue as Delvine's ward in Edinburgh.

Mustering money where she could, Flora obtained twenty guineas from a 'well-wisher' for those brogues, missing a lug, which the Prince had once worn and which her father-in-law had preserved. Souvenirs and memorabilia of her part in the 'Forty-five were now a means for Flora to finance life in the New World.

In preparation for the voyage west, Kingsburgh had 'engaged a knot of his friends, followers and dynasties [family groups]', as Sir Alexander was later to recall. These partners subscribed their names to 'a paper, whereby they bound themselves by certain sums' to the Captain of a merchant vessel for their passage to America.[75] Flora's younger sons Sandy and James, both still without a profession, accompanied their parents. Their elder sister, Annie, her husband and their three young children were also of the seafaring party. Lochbay had taken note of which farming implements and household goods would be most valuable in North Carolina. 'He went to settle in America, very amply supplied with everything necessary to that purpose,' a Highland army colleague was to relate, 'having laid out his fortune' – some £3,000 – 'in that way.'[76]

Flora and Allan could expect a warm welcome among her maternal relations already in the colony. They could, moreover, practise their religion there with ease. Three Presbyterian churches and two ministers served the Highland community in and around Cross Creek. Family and faith notwithstanding, Flora and Allan looked to life in America for economic stability above all. 'You will bless the day you left that country [Scotland],' wrote one of the Cross Creek community to his brother, still in the Old World, 'where the face of the poor is kept to the grinding stone ... This is the best poor man's country I have heard [of] in this age.'[77]

12

Cheek's Creek, North Carolina
1774–April 1775

'Four hundred friends and dependents' accompanied the Kingsburgh party when Flora, a mother of seven and grandmother of three, and her husband quitted Skye.[1] Among other emigrants was Flora's nephew, Kenneth Macdonald, Annabella and Cuidreach's son. He was to retain vivid memories of a French privateer menacing the merchant ship on which they travelled.[2] Had the corsairs prevailed, their haul, in cash, would have been considerable. Campbell of Balole had strongly advised Flora's brother-in-law, Lachlan Mackinnon, to prospect for a plantation on arrival in North Carolina rather than commit to one beforehand. 'If a person takes £500 sterling with him, and employ[s] it in any rational manner,' the Argyll man had declared, 'he may live equal to any laird [on an income] of £500 per annum in any part of Great Britain.'[3] Even if the majority of the families on board had scraped together considerably less, the privateer would still have secured a considerable sum in cash.

On board too were chests packed with '[silver] plate', china, books, linens, 'bedcurtains and window curtains', blankets and apparel which had long served the emigrants at home in Skye.[4] Many openly flouted the Act of Proscription and wore full Highland dress when embarking. Though still proscribed, Highland arms – broadswords, holstered pistols, *skhian dubhs* (daggers) and muskets, or rifles – would serve for personal defence and for bringing down game. Two years later, Allan was to assess the value of the 'books, plate and furniture' that he and Flora owned in their colonial home at £500.[5] With their future domicile as yet in question, however, the Kingsburghs may have temporarily left in Scotland those 'Jacobite relics' recalling Flora's exploits with the Stuart Prince.

The Kingsburgh family and their fellow passengers brought with them, too, implements suitable for clearing and working the wooded acres they intended to purchase. In 1772 Campbell of Balole had sent a would-be emigrant a precise list of tools and other items required for pioneer life in North Carolina. 'Strong spades, hoes, hatchets, adzes, handsaws, crosscut and whip saws' featured there, as did 'augers, gimlets, nails of different kinds', hammers, chisels and 'window glass putty'.[6]

After weeks at sea, land at last came into sight. The white sandhills and tall pines that distinguished the vast coastline of North Carolina heralded new beginnings for Flora and her fellow emigrants. They had left behind in Skye jagged eminences, green pastures and icy burns flowing over stones and rocks into lochs below. Now they entered the sluggish mouth of the great Cape Fear River. The ship's passengers first gazed on Fort Johnston, where a garrison defended the colony from attack by sea. Here all male passengers on board aged sixteen and over and not invalid swore an oath of allegiance to King George III. They vowed, too, to be 'faithful against all traitorous Conspiracies & attempts whatsoever, which shall be made against his [the King's] Person, Crown, and Dignity'.[7]

As the ship ventured further north towards safe harbour in Wilmington, it passed, on the Cape Fear's western bank, Brunswick, a fine seaport, although one sparsely populated. After this hint of civilisation, trees and bushes, vines and brambles overhung the black river for miles, sometimes reflected in creek waters and swamp. Further off, forests of pine, walnut and oak stretched back miles into the hinterland.

Vessels of size could not proceed upriver past Wilmington, and the Kingsburghs' transatlantic crossing ended here. Some Scots, long established in the colony, occupied prominent positions in this mercantile town where, as a visitor had earlier observed, 'the regularity of the streets are [is] equal to those of Philadelphia and the buildings in general very good. Many of brick, two and three storeys high with double piazzas, which make a good appearance.'[8]

Accounts of Flora's arrival in the colony were, as the years passed, to grow fanciful: 'A crowd had gathered to greet her, famed and beloved Scotswoman that she was, and welcoming shouts and banners went up: "Welcome Flora Macdonald, Preserver of Bonnie Prince Charlie!" ... They were greeted and feted not only in Wilmington but at the Royal Governor's Palace in New Bern as well ...'[9] There is no evidence, however, that the Macdonald party lingered in the former town. Josiah Martin, Royal Governor of North Carolina since 1771, was only to make the acquaintance of Flora's husband, and correspond with her son-in-law, the following summer.

The Kingsburghs' and Lochbays' destination was always the so-called Scots country, a hundred miles upriver from Wilmington. Flora's son Charles was to write, late the following year, that his parents had settled in Cumberland County, 'as did his sister, Annie, and her husband, Lochbay Macleod, and their three children'. So too did the 400 friends and dependants who had been the Macdonalds' and Macleods' companions on shipboard.[10]

The journey from Wilmington to Cross Creek, up the north-west branch of the Cape Fear River, occupied the best part of a week. Commercial traffic on trading boats along the river, up which the Macdonalds now found their way, was extensive. Inhabitants of Wilmington depended on the Scots country for wheat, which grew poorly in the coastal lands, and other cereals and animal produce. Merchants in Cross Creek, for their part, imported personal attire, household items and agricultural wares from Wilmington, and sold these items on to planters and farmers in the backcountry, the less populated western reaches of the colony. On dry land, too, rough-hewn roads followed the course of the Cape Fear River. Wooden bridges surmounted creeks, and causeways – logs laid crisscross – were constructed over areas of swamp. Lachlan Mackinnon had asked Balole if the trees were 'far from one another' in North Carolina. The Islay man had responded stoutly, 'They are so much [far apart] that you can gallop a horse through all the woods I saw there, without touching a tree.'[11] This was indeed true in the lower reaches of the river, but the Macdonald party penetrated further up the river, where thick stands of longleaf pines began to oppress their view, rising above sandy soil as if growing on patches of snow.

Outside Cross Creek, states one imaginative historian,

> the party was met by a large procession, in order that Flora might be properly escorted into their midst. As they approached the capital [county town], the strains of the pibroch [bagpipes] and the martial airs [military marches] of her native land fell upon the ears of the multitude. In the vast concourse of people were some of her old neighbours and kinsfolks … Their faces, manner, and voices bore testimony to the welcome of the heart. Many families of distinction pressed upon her to make their dwellings her home, but she respectfully declined, preferring a settled abode of her own.[12]

While corroboration for the above account is wanting, Flora's arrival in Cross Creek in the autumn of 1774 undoubtedly aroused interest in a population that boasted so many immigrants from Skye and the west coast of Scotland. Members of the Argyll community, established here thirty years before, still represented the district in the colonial assembly in New Bern. Now, however, immigrants from the Hebrides were prospering also as plantation owners and merchants in the town.

Mezzotints, engravings and woodcuts bearing Flora's image were familiar from home to many of these Scots. Those prints in which she was swathed, in youth, in tartan and adorned with a white rose or white ribbons – Jacobite emblems – were especially popular. British book markets, still doing a roaring trade in tales of the 'Forty-five, supplied the preponderance of reading matter for Scots in North Carolina, as for other emigrants and those born in America too. Moreover, there had appeared in the colonial press, earlier this year, notices advertising the forthcoming publication of Dr Johnson's *Journey to the Western Isles*. 'When in the isle of Skye,' the *Virginia Gazette* informed its readers, 'he paid a visit to the celebrated lady so well known by the name of Miss Flora Macdonald, whose heroic adventures in 1745 have rendered her fame immortal with the generous of all parties.'[13] A distinguished visitor to the Hebrides in 1825 was to remark that the events of the 'Forty-five were as fresh in the minds of those he visited as were those of the previous week.[14] This was true, too, of those who had emigrated, and who now found Flora, who had once caused such a stir in the world, come among them.

Flora first took up residence in an 'abode' close to the market house and courthouse and on the brink of the creek which bisected the township. Its confluence with the Cape Fear River was a mile off, and grist (flour) mills, saw mills and tanning yards made good use of its waters. A cluster of bridges afforded passage over different stretches of this fast-flowing water to various dwellings, outbuildings and stores. Blacksmiths, wheelwrights, carpenters, and coopers exercised 'mechanic arts', as a visitor observed, and, like timber merchants, butchers and corn merchants in the settlement, dispatched a proportion of their goods to Wilmington on wagons or on rafts.[15]

Should Flora want for anything in her new colonial home, Murdoch Macleod, formerly a physician in Skye, prescribed medicine at his dispensary in the town.[16] Neill McArthur, who sold all manner of dry goods in his store, was among the town's foremost merchants.[17] Tavern keepers, saddlers and gunsmiths, likewise, did brisk business, and tailors, shoemakers and mercers prospered. Ornate fire irons, japanned tea sets, backgammon tables, decanters, glasses and china punchbowls gleamed in the hearths and homes of this far-flung Scottish outpost.[18]

Dr Johnson had observed, two years earlier, that Flora was 'of a pleasing person and elegant behaviour'.[19] In her daughter Annie's estimation, she had 'a small but neat figure';[20] but, if compact in stature, Flora had undoubted presence. Compliments in Cross Creek from those with whom she kept company came thick and fast. In the 1840s, an inhabitant of the town, by then rechristened Fayetteville, had vivid recollections of the matron at this time. Her hair was 'nearly covered with a fine lace cap and slightly streaked with white', her complexion fair, and her blue eyes 'sparkling', the elderly woman recorded. 'She was often at my mother's house when she first came,' she added, and noted for good measure that Flora possessed 'the finest teeth I ever saw'.[21] Another Fayetteville citizen, an ensign in the Cumberland County militia when young, had still more rapturous memories. He declared that, 'for grave demeanour and dignity, Flora Macdonald excelled all the women he ever beheld. That it was worth a day's ride to see her graceful manner of sitting or rising from a chair. That there was a perfection of ease and grace in that simple act, that could be felt but not described.'[22]

Those who wished to gaze on a simulacrum of Flora, as she was when young, turned to another in the Macdonald party who exhibited 'pleasing, and even polished manners'. Annie Macleod, Flora's daughter, was not yet twenty-one, though already a wife and mother of three. She had, by all accounts, inherited her mother's Celtic good looks – her likeness to her mother, when that lady was young and famous, was judged remarkable. As striking proof of this, Annie was later to narrate, she was looking at a print of her mother in a shop window in the Strand, one of London's most fashionable streets, when a military man who chanced to be passing at the time was so struck with the resemblance that he accosted her and taxed her with the relationship.[23]

Flora's fame was not the only reason for the rustle of excitement – and some envy – that these newcomers from Skye excited in the town. Highlanders, whether in America or at home, had an exact knowledge of their place in the hierarchy of their different clans. Lochbay's illustrious, if illegitimate, parentage and Flora and Allan's close ties of blood to the chiefs of Clanranald and Sleat were of service too. The Kingsburgh Macdonalds would ultimately seek a home, suiting their feeble means, on the very outskirts of the Scots country. For the moment, however, they could profit by Flora's fame and their clan claims to build relationships with merchants and planters in Cross Creek, and to secure intelligence there about land for sale.

Flora next took up residence at Cameron's Hill, some thirty miles north-west of Cross Creek, in Cumberland County. Here her sister and Cuidreach farmed 200 acres of good land and occupied a well-furnished home. Five miles away Barbecue Church, built earlier by Scots on a creek of that name, attracted good Presbyterian Highlanders from miles around and tradition holds that Flora worshipped here while in the colony. At its inception a rude log cabin, the kirk was rebuilt as a 'one-room frame building', forty-five feet in length. Minister John Macleod preached alternately in English and Gaelic, and elevated the host in silver communion cups, brought from the mother country.[24] Flora – in the words of a fellow parishioner, 'a dignified and handsome woman, to whom all paid great respect'[25] – is held to have been 'a pious member of the Barbecue congregation'.[26] The illustrator Elenore Plaisted Abbott later captured the spirit, if not the reality, of Flora's stately progress in *Flora Macdonald, On Way to Barbecue Church, NC*, a colourful oil painting now property of the Presbyterian Historical Society in Philadelphia.[27] Against a background of feathery pine trees and framed by other Scots ladies and their squires, Flora and Allan each clasp a prayer book as they eternally proceed to kirk. Allan sports a cock feather in his bonnet and is in full Highland regalia. Flora, fashionably dressed, has been given the twin gifts of youth and rouged lips.

While Allan prospected for cheaper land further west in Anson County, where the Cuidreachs also had a house and land, Flora absorbed the familiar and exotic details of agrarian life on her half-sister's plantation. In the two years that Annabella and her family had lived at Cameron's Hill, Cuidreach had cleared many of the pine trees which abounded there, planted corn and acquired a herd of seventy-eight cattle.[28] The Scots in the backcountry took a keen interest in each other's plantations and husbandry. Alexander Morrison, a neighbouring planter, 'out of mere curiosity ... happened to number [count] the ... stock of milch [milk, or dairy]-cows' then on the Cuidreach plantation, 'which he is certain was in number above twenty'. This Cumberland County farmer also noted a proportionate 'stock of young [beef] cattle'.[29] Lochbay was later to observe that Cuidreach also had a 'very considerable stock of horses, cows and hogs'[30] – thirteen horses and a hundred hogs in all[31] – and 'such furniture [wagons and ploughs] and utensils [farming implements] as a planter required'.[32]

Flora might well hope, though she and Allan had to look to less fertile land further off, that they could 'improve' their investment and see a good return for their expenditure. Hard by the Cameron's Hill homestead was a spring where the Cuidreach family drew their water. Here, according to later Cumberland County lore, Flora sat on a rock, smoking a clay pipe, while she waited for Allan to return with news that he had purchased a property.[33]

Annie and Lochbay and their young children, meanwhile, had settled twenty miles from the Cuidreachs, on land that they rented from another Scots settler, Kenneth Black. Six men and six women, all indentured for four years, served these new planters' needs and took care of a herd of sixty cattle.[34] Some among the Highlanders entrusted the cultivation of their plantations to enslaved field hands and the care of their houses to enslaved servants. In this, they followed the example of wealthy landowners and merchants in the coastal counties. However, as Armadale had done in 1771,[35] many engaged servants before leaving Scotland. The latter contracted to work without salary in America for a stated number of years. In return their masters bore the cost of these dependants' passage to the New World and provided them with board and lodging there and a small sum at the end of the period of indenture. In common with those of other Skye emigrants, Lochbay's accounts do not reveal whether the farm's workforce was Scottish born or whether he had entered into contracts with impecunious Americans.

In keeping with their comparative wealth, the Lochbays had brought plate and china, bed and table linens and furniture 'from Britain' later valued at nearly £500. A separate catalogue of their books, listing works of ancient history, Gaelic and Latin texts, novels and numerous treatises on farming and animal husbandry, had an estimated worth in 1784 of £56 1 shilling and 6 pence.[36] While they remained in the rented 'log house', however, they did not unpack a good portion of their furniture which was, as a neighbour was later to observe, 'fit for a larger House'. Another planter agreed: 'His [Lochbay's] House was very well furnished but the whole of his furniture was not displayed. He had some in Chests,' and there was 'no Library put up but … books scatter'd in the House'.[37]

Armadale, meanwhile, was farming 500 acres on Mountain Creek in Anson County, around forty miles west of his daughter Annabella's home and around twenty west of the plantation where the Lochbay Macleods now settled.[38] While his sons by Flora's mother had died young, and he was now in his seventies at least, Armadale remained spry and had the aid of his other son-in-law, who had settled nearby. Moreover, Flora's son James was to write that these Anson County lands were 'made over' to Annabella and Cuidreach's son, Donald, by the young man's grandfather around this time.[39] While this junior Macdonald took up residence with Armadale at Mountain Creek, Donald's younger brother, Kenneth, remained farming with his father at Cameron's Hill.

All Flora's maternal relations and her daughter and son-in-law were now established in the colony, and Allan's prospecting bore fruit about four miles from the Armadale farm, at Cheek's Creek, also in Anson County. This stream was a tributary of waters which debouched eventually into the ocean in South Carolina. The Kingsburghs' eyes, however, were firmly set on Cross Creek, about fifty-five miles east, as a trading centre. Flora's 1789 Memorial records that 'Her husband purchased a plantation, with the stock of different cattle thereon …'[40] One of the farms which made up the Kingsburgh holdings was 'some four hundred and seventy-five acres in extent', Allan later noted, of which eighty acres were already 'cleared [of pine forest and brushwood], and in cultivation', before his purchase. The new American landowner could call on the labour of five male servants, all indentured for five years, as well as on the aid of Sandy and James, in his bid to make the land profitable. Three 'good orchards' provided 'peach, apple and other fruits', while a grist mill on a 'good run of water' was soon 'in excellent order'. The smaller farm of fifty acres was some five miles off and no less productive. 'Thirty [acres] were cleared land and in cultivation' two years later. The master of Cheek's Creek raised cattle and other livestock, and the farms had the usual outbuildings and barns in which to store 'Indian corn [maize]' and other crops when harvested.[41]

This woodland complex was in many ways unpropitious. It was remote from any other plantation, hamlet or village. Dense forest dominated the uncleared land, and the hills either side of the winding creek were precipitous. As was the custom of the country, the stumps of pine trees were left in the ground on the acres which Allan and previous owners 'cleared'. Crops were laboriously sown, tended and harvested among these intractable timber remains. A lesser woman of fifty-odd, aiming to make a new life in a foreign territory with a husband who had little head for business, might have been cast down. Allan was, however, for all his faults, a good judge of cattle and might hope to sell their livestock, in due course, at a profit. Moreover, the premium he was paid for milling local farmers' wheat at his grist mill provided an income which, he declared, 'kept the whole family in bread'.[42] Flora was to write that she and her immediate family 'lived comfortably for near a year' on the plantation in Anson County.[43]

Her words signal her pride in now owning her own home and no longer being 'oppressed' by 'augmented' rents in Skye. The Kingsburghs lived among familiar possessions, brought from Scotland. Flora oversaw the work of their three female servants in the dwelling house and adjacent outbuildings, including a 'keeping house [meat and dairy larder]' and kitchen.[44] Allan employed their male counterparts in the stables and as field hands. She, no doubt, fervently hoped that they would now live within their income.

Others in the Scots country in North Carolina echoed this refrain of living comfortably. These emigrant Highlanders believed themselves to be in a kind of Eden. While those who lived near the colony's coast, where stagnant water and swampland abounded, suffered from typhus and malaria in the summer months, the climate in the Upper Cape Fear Valley was healthy and the winters temperate. The sandy, forested uplands there, if difficult to farm, were well drained. Balole, who had so lauded the advantages of the colony the previous year, appeared justified.

In the space of only two or three years, Flora and her maternal relations and closer family had successfully executed a plan of emigration and were, moreover, settled within a day or two's ride of each other in the colony. Lochbay had an income on which he could have settled, with Annie, in the south of Scotland, or even in England. Flora and Allan, however, had no such option available to them. Their recent outlay, which had secured more than 500 acres and two dwelling houses on Cheek's Creek, would have bought them little in the British Isles. In America – that 'best poor man's country' – the family, rich and poor, could thrive together.

While still in Skye, Flora had described herself to the Duke of Atholl as a 'poor distressed woman (once known to the world)'.[45] Her earlier fame, however, had never been wholly eclipsed. Dr Johnson, Boswell and Thomas Pennant, among others, had come calling in recent years, eager to cast eyes upon her. Now, no longer distressed, she was considered a venerable ornament to society by the Highland community that centred on Cross Creek. The recent bleak years at home in Skye promised to recede now that she and Allan were making a new life with her relations in America. Those days when warnings to give Allan no credit were affixed to the church doors in Skye were now only a painful memory. Sandy and James were helping their father work the farms. Charles was with the Bengal army in Bombay, while Ranald was in the Marines. Johnny looked to have a bright future in the law in Edinburgh, and Fanny was safe on Raasay. For all the upheaval, for all Flora's reluctance to leave Skye, she had reason to hope that she had escaped 'poverty and oppression' for good.[46] Such hopes, however, were to prove short-lived.

13

'King and Country'
April–June 1775

What Flora and her relations had not expected was to find that the colony where they now made their home was in political turmoil. Much later, Lochbay was to be asked, 'How he could think of going to settle in a Country, which was at that moment in flame.' Flora's son-in-law replied that 'he did not know, at that time, that the troubles had grown to such a height.'[1] In this he was not alone in Scotland or even England at the time. News travelled slowly. Furthermore, it had not been in the interests of those who sought to entice their fellow Highlanders westward to dwell on 'troubles' in the thirteen British colonies. While the Kingsburghs and Macleods were crossing the Atlantic in the summer of 1774, however, the territory had come alive with disaffection.

Earlier in the year, in retaliation for the Boston Tea Party, Parliament in London had passed legislation – the Boston Port Act, the Massachusetts Government Act, the Administration of Justice Act and the Quartering Act – designed to splinter resistance and damage the economy in Massachusetts Bay and to serve as a warning to other American territories of the consequences of insubordination. These Coercive Acts, however, had the effect of stimulating colonists in North Carolina and elsewhere to spring to the defence of Boston and to condemn the legislation as an attack on American liberty. An irregular assembly in Wilmington declared in July that the cause of that distant town was 'the common cause of British America'.[2] Josiah Martin, Governor of North Carolina, censured such resolves and other 'plans derogatory to' the Crown as 'inflammatory, disloyal and indecent' and intended to 'excite clamour and discontent'.[3] The Governor, however, failed to prevent irregular county Committees of Safety electing delegates to an extra-legal Provincial Congress which convened in August and itself elected delegates to a Continental Congress which met in Philadelphia that September. In a modest guildhall representatives of all Thirteen Colonies, bar Georgia, gathered at this historic convention and 'associated and agreed for themselves and their constituents' back home to ban all imports from Britain, Ireland and the British West Indies.[4] The aim of this Continental Association, which took effect on 1 December 1774, was to force Parliament to repeal the Coercive Acts. It also provided for a ban on exports to these same territories a year later, if the Acts were still in force then.

Martin, in his early thirties, the indulged son of a wealthy Antigua planter, was strong in his disapprobation of the Congress and of its measures. He described those who attended the 'unconstitutional' gathering in Philadelphia to the Earl of Dartmouth, Secretary of State for the Colonies, as 'men selected out of the several colonies for their democratical principles' and for 'their known averseness and opposition to Government'.[5] Martin hoped that he could rely on 'Scotch merchants' in Wilmington, long established in the colony and engaged in trade with the mother country, not to sign the Association. 'Democratical' merchants and tradesmen, however, were forceful in argument with any unwilling to sign and adhere to the Association in this and other towns in the coastal plain, as were each of the county Committees of Safety.

The existence of a Committee of Safety in Anson County did not deter Flora and Allan from purchasing land there. Lochbay, however, was later to recall that he and his wife and the Kingsburghs found on their arrival in North Carolina that 'enemies of the country [rebel colonists] had poisoned the minds of many'.[6] Some Scots served on the Cumberland County Committee of Safety and aimed to temper what they saw as the violence of their fellow representatives, but

Flora's son-in-law was still disturbed by commotion in the colony. Meditating a possible return to Scotland, for which he had ample means, he and Annie made no move to purchase a property, and a good part of their possessions continued to languish in packing cases in the plantation home they rented.[7]

Flora and her extended family had no spur to champion the cause of American liberty. Far from having a quarrel with London, the Kingsburghs, the Macleods and her maternal relatives had fled a capricious landlord and hoped for financial advantage to ensue from their ownership of land in the New World. They were eager for the Crown's protection, wanting only to farm and trade with others in peace.

It was inconceivable to Flora, who had good reason to regard the Hanoverian government as all powerful, that rebels in America would prosper in any clash with the state. She and other Highlanders remembered only too well the debacle at Culloden thirty years earlier when redcoats had destroyed the Jacobite army. Since then, moreover, her son-in-law and others from Skye had been among those mighty British forces which gained victory across the globe in the Seven Years' War.

However, if Flora hoped that she and her family could remain aloof from a quarrel in which she wanted no part, she was not to get her wish. Her menfolk, with other Scots in the 'midland counties', had demonstrated 'their attachment to Government', Martin wrote to the British Commander-in-Chief, General Thomas Gage, then in Boston. Gage could, the Governor declared, depend on their 'zeal and steadfast loyalty'.[8] Lochbay later recorded that it was 'impossible for him not to feel himself called by Duty and Inclination, to resume His Military Character again'.[9] Allan was now in his fifties, and had no experience of warfare beyond serving in the Skye militia during the Rising. No less eager, nonetheless, than his son-in-law to take up arms in defence of the colony, he later declared himself one 'whose principles were always steady to his King and country'.[10]

Should the need arise, and should the King see fit to authorise it, the Governor informed Dartmouth, he could 'raise a Battalion' of Highlanders that 'would do credit to the service'.[11] The Scots, however, as Flora was later to stress, had only 'old, bad firelocks [muskets], and ... broadswords'.[12] Martin begged both the Secretary of State and the military command in Boston for arms and ammunition.

Some of these Scots who offered their aid were, like Armadale and Allan, of an age to have carried government or rebel arms in the 'Forty-five. Others, like Lochbay, had served in Scottish regiments raised for the Crown in the Seven Years' War, where they won a reputation as courageous and well-disciplined officers. In consequence, Dartmouth in London paid careful attention to Martin's declaration. No authority as yet, however, was sent to issue beating orders for a Highland regiment.

A community with a less martial history might have contrived, at least initially, to negotiate a less partisan path through the colony's travails. Caution might have deterred the Scots from declaring for a governor who was patently failing to contain revolt. Fatally, however, having long paid fealty to Highland overlords, they now as blindly deferred to the government. Lochbay later recalled that he, 'without delay, gave his attention to encouraging and keeping the Spirit of Loyalty in his Countrymen [Highlanders] there' in the Scots country.[13]

Within two months, neutrality ceased to be an option. Martin told Dartmouth in May 1775 that colonists near the ocean were 'infected with the ill spirit that prevails in the adjacent provinces [colonies]'. They were 'arming men, electing officers and so forth ... Civil government becomes more and more prostrate every day.'[14] The warlike reputation of the Scots in North Carolina had not escaped the attention of these rebels. Cuidreach was offered the rank of major in a militia, which, he later declared, his 'principles' would not allow him to accept.[15] Flora was to write of the North Carolina Provincial Congress 'forcing her husband to join them [in a militia], he being a leading man among the Highlanders'. She added that Allan saw that 'he would be obliged to join either party'.[16] He plumped for 'King and country'.[17]

The colony was in tumult, the patriots – the name increasingly used, among militant colonists, for those who opposed parliamentary encroachment on American liberties – ever in the ascendant, and loyalists – those who adhered to the Crown – ever more outraged. Towards the end of May, Martin was harassed at his palace in New Bern by a 'motley mob' and took refuge in rickety Fort Johnson, thirty miles south-west of Wilmington, at the mouth of the Cape Fear on the coast. Although the *Cruizer*, a sloop of war moored there, offered the Governor protection, communicating with those in the Scots country was now extremely difficult. All messengers had to pass through the harbour town to the north-east and ran the risk of being seized with such dispatches as they carried.[18]

News from the northern colonies reached the Carolinas slowly. In early summer, however, Flora and Allan at Cheek's Creek had reason to know that the fight between Crown and rebel colonists was in deadly earnest. Since the previous December their third son, Ranald, a second lieutenant in the Marines, had done duty in Boston. After clashes outside that town on 19 April in the villages of Lexington and Concord, a return of British officers and men killed and wounded by patriots was published in the colonial press. Ranald was listed among the latter.[19] Three months later, now promoted first lieutenant, he was still in Boston when a rebel Continental Army, comprising regiments from all thirteen colonies, besieged the town.

In North Carolina, Lochbay, meanwhile, as he was later to recall, was energetically 'establishing a train of Intelligence' and 'encouraging the conducting of secret correspondence with Governor Martin'.[20] At a meeting of the leading Highlanders that summer, it was determined that Allan should seek an audience with the Governor at Fort Johnston. Flora later recorded that her husband's mission was to 'settle the plan of rising [raising] the Highlanders in arms'.[21] He bore with him a letter from Lochbay, and was to inform Martin that they were all ready and willing to arm and obey the Governor's orders.

Allan 'went in disguise' in May or June to Fort Johnston, Flora affirmed, for fear of meeting patriot militia, a precaution that proved wise.[22] Her husband noted that his mission presented 'some danger', two parties being sent from Wilmington 'to intercept him in his way'.[23] At Fort Johnston, the impetuous Highlander and the naive administrator took an instant liking to each other. 'I part with him [Kingsburgh] more reluctantly than I can tell you,' the Governor wrote to Lochbay on 4 July in a letter he entrusted to Flora's husband. Martin had been delighted by 'the opportunity' afforded him 'of making a personal acquaintance with that worthy gentleman'.[24]

In Skye, Allan, though pursued by creditors and having failed as a factor, had struck Boswell as 'completely the figure of a gallant Highlander'.[25] The Governor of North Carolina was no less deceived. Meanwhile, Flora waited at home while her husband was 'fourteen days' away. The investment they had made in their plantation allowed for little deviation from a modest way of living. Even the £28 'travelling expenses' which Allan incurred on his journey represented a strain on their exchequer.[26]

Martin thanked Lochbay for his letter: 'I perfectly agree with your sentiments of the propriety of the good and faithful Highlanders forbearing any open declaration [of war], until there is a necessity to call them into action, and they are amply provided to take the field with dignity and effect [supplied with arms].' Martin ended by writing warmly of 'your lady and family in particular, and in general … all the good and faithful Highland people, in whom I have the firmest confidence, and for whom I have ever felt peculiar regard and attachment'.[27]

Reports reached the Wilmington Committee of Safety regarding Allan's embassy and its members questioned whether the Scot had 'an intention to raise troops to support the arbitrary measures of the ministry against the Americans in this colony'. Further, they queried 'whether he had not made an offer of his services to Governor Martin for that purpose'.[28] Allan, however, avoided detention. The intelligence he brought home of that colonial official's hearty endorsement of the scheme he had outlined at the fort may have caused Flora's spirits to sink. Her husband was grandiose in his plans, she the very reverse.

Martin, for his part, was reinvigorated by Allan's visit. He wrote to London on 30 June of his plans to raise 'a battalion of a thousand Highlanders here'. Were the King to approve this proposal, Martin would 'most humbly beg leave to recommend Mr Allan Macdonald of Kingsborough to be Major, and Captain Alexander Macleod [Lochbay] of the Marines, now on half pay, to be first Captain'. Both gentlemen, he declared, were 'of great worth, and good character'. They had, besides, 'most extensive influence over the Highlanders here, great part of which are of their own names and families'. The Governor was ever credulous.

Martin, with little basis for his belief, also asserted that he could count on 20,000 'fighting men', American born, in the western counties. All, however, lacked the means to make war. The Governor begged Lord Dartmouth to dispatch urgently from England, among much else, arms and a 'good store of Ammunition', cannon, including 'six light brass field pieces' and 'six Pounders', 'Colours, Drums, etc.' and 'such a supply of money, as might be necessary for the support of such a force'.[29]

Delighted with his new friendship with Allan, keen to pursue his acquaintance with other Highlanders too, Martin 'resolved to spend the remainder of the summer' in the Scotch country. He directed that important colonial documents should be dispatched 'to my friend Mr Macdonald of Kingsborough ... upon Cheek's Creek in Anson County'. Martin, who intended to make Allan and Flora's home his temporary residence, wished to look over the papers there. Should a guard be required for their transport, the Governor wrote to the agent who had the documents in his keeping, Kingsborough would readily 'furnish an escort of Highlanders'.[30]

As Flora's house guest, and in concert with Allan, the Governor intended to pursue his 'plan of rising the Highlanders in arms' in defence of the Crown.[31] Only a few months before, the plantation on Cheek's Creek had appeared to be an asylum where Flora and her family could be free from want and oppression. Now, although she was as yet 'living comfortably' there, the unholy alliance between her husband and the colonial official would soon imperil that peaceful existence.

14

'All Killed or Taken'
July 1775–February 1776

Flora was not, after all, to play hostess to the gregarious Governor at the Kingsborough plantation in Anson County in the summer of 1775. Days after Allan struck out for home, Martin was forced to flee Fort Johnston. Wilmington patriots made good a threat to destroy that flimsy government outpost, and the Governor retreated on board the *Cruizer*. Moreover, learning of his project to go into the backcountry, his opponents issued orders on 31 July for his arrest should he be discovered on any such journey: 'It is in all probability he intends kindling the flames of a Civil war.'[1] A month later, Martin wrote to Dartmouth from the British sloop, 'I am reduced to the deplorable and disgraceful state of being a tame Spectator of Rebellion spreading over this Country.'[2]

A wiser man than Kingsburgh might have considered it now inopportune to pursue the plan that he had settled with Martin of 'rising the Highlanders in arms'.[3] Still exhilarated, however, by the cordial reception afforded him at Fort Johnston, he was energetic in recruiting officers and men that summer and autumn. Various Scots wives were to inform Flora later that they held her spouse responsible for enticing their husbands to rise for the Crown.[4] Lochbay, Cuidreach and their fellow 'leading men' in the Scots country were later to document their own efforts to engage others.[5] Two officers, arrived in August from Boston to recruit for a Highland regiment in the north, were pressed into service as commander and senior officer of the corps.[6] These emigrant Scots' enthusiasm for the House of Hanover and their faith in Martin were soon to prove as fatal as once had been the adherence of those in the 'Forty-five to the cause of Charles Edward Stuart.

The Lochbays' home served the Highland army as an informal headquarters and Major Donald Macdonald, one of the officers from Boston, later commented that he was 'a great part of his time there' when in North Carolina.[7] How did Flora view the military ambitions of her husband, who received the rank of colonel in this as yet untried and unorthodox provincial regiment? No rash romantic, she was a woman of quiet good sense. All her married life, in the wake of her great adventure with the Prince, she had endeavoured to turn events to her advantage and to that of her sons, when they required places in the world. Now it was unclear where the advantage lay.

There were those, hoping to survive the troubles unmolested, who held back from declaring themselves for either the Crown or the patriots. Armadale, ever the careful politician, was conspicuously absent from the various meetings in late 1775 which Highlanders held with Americans in the western counties on whom Martin believed he could count.[8] Had Flora lived longer in the colony, in the interest of escaping reprisals from patriots she might have made efforts to deter her husband from blazoning forth his loyalism when the troubles flared. In time she was to consider that he and her sons had a poor return for their service to the Crown. She never, however, voiced any regret that her menfolk had not joined the rebels, though they would have reaped much benefit. Flora Macdonald, so adept at extracting patronage from power in Hanoverian Britain, while nursing an attachment to the former Stuart line, had no appetite for a revolution conducted on 'democratical principles'. The Declaration of Independence, signed in Philadelphia later in the year, said of George III, 'A prince, whose character is thus marked by every act which may define a Tyrant, is unfit to be the ruler of a free people.'[9] Flora and those others who emigrated from the Highlands were fleeing other despots and looked to the British Crown to safeguard what they perceived as liberty across the Atlantic. Above all else, Flora wished to continue to live 'comfortably' as a Carolina farmer's wife in the home on Cheek's Creek in which she and Allan had invested their all, and where the grist mill and their black cattle provided an income, while other livestock, the orchards and the fields were a source of provisions and liquor.

In October 1775 Lochbay made his way by circuitous means to the *Cruizer* and informed Martin that he and Allan had 'each raised a company of Highlanders'.[10] There was encouraging intelligence, moreover, of the recruiting efforts of other Scots. The Governor, still awaiting a reply from the government to his many requests for arms and ammunition, resolved to wrest back control of the colony with such resources as he had. He advised the Highlanders that he would soon give them the signal to muster and march to the coast.

The patriots, however, obtained intelligence of Martin's intentions. They too began to arm. Flora now had every reason to fear the future. An action between Scots and American militia was likely to be a very bloody affair, the fighting haphazard and the gunfire erratic. Furthermore, she and Annie, who was now 'far advanced in pregnancy' with a fourth child,[11] would have little protection if rebels or robbers came calling.

In early January 1776 the Governor, who had now transferred to the *Scorpion*, another sloop of war,[12] received momentous news in a letter from Lord Dartmouth in London. The previous year much of South Carolina had been under the control of patriots. Its Royal Governor was living in ignominious safety on a naval vessel in the harbour of Charleston, the colony's capital. The British government was determined to recover this southern city, and Martin learned from the Secretary of State's letter that an expedition was being dispatched across the Atlantic for that purpose. Seven regiments and 'two companies of Artillery, and a proper number of Battalion Guns, Howitzers, etc.' were set to embark from Ireland, Dartmouth wrote in October 1775. Before proceeding to Charleston, he further informed Martin, this force would make landfall in North Carolina with the aim of restoring order in that colony. The Secretary granted his correspondent authority to raise and command a 'corps of Provincials' to assist these regulars in their task.[13]

Calculating that the expeditionary fleet, bearing arms for the 'provincials', would arrive at Cape Fear in mid- to late February, Martin sent an emissary to the Scots country with orders for Highlanders to begin their march to the coast on the 15th of that month. This envoy also carried powers for 'commissioners', including Allan, Lochbay and Cuidreach, and Neill McArthur, the wealthy Cross Creek merchant. These Highlanders were to 'raise, levy, muster, and array in arms, all His Majesty's loyal and faithful subjects … who are willing and ready to repair to the Royal banner'.[14] Those addressed agreed among themselves to rendezvous with other commissioners from the western counties on 5 February at Cross Hill, Alexander Morrison's home in Cumberland County.[15]

The historian Benson Lossing, passing through Fayetteville (formerly Cross Creek) in 1849, was shown a letter dingy with age and written in Scots. Its eighty-seven-year-old owner assured him that the missive had been addressed to her elder sister, a young woman of twenty in 1776, and penned by Flora Macdonald, days before the rendezvous at Cross Hill. The historian copied the text exactly: 'February 1, 1776. Dear Maggie, Allan leaves tomorrow to join Donald's standard at Cross Creek, an' I shall be alone wi' my three bairns [children]. Canna ye com' an' stay wi' me awhile?'[16]

Many of the details in the letter, which does not survive, find corroboration elsewhere. Allan was due in Cumberland County, if not in Cross Creek, on the 5th, as were Sandy and James, who were both to serve as volunteers. Major Donald Macdonald from Boston had been placed by Martin in command of the Highland army. Flora had three Macleod grandchildren. Possibly she was minding them for her daughter. Finally, if not 'alone', Flora was left at Cheek's Creek with a very few servants, when her husband and two sons departed. They took with them five saddle horses, two packhorses, the 'family arms [muskets and broadswords]' and arms for the servants who accompanied them.[17]

The custodian of this letter in 1849 pointed out the signature to her visitor: 'You see, she wrote her name "Flory". She always did.'[18] Flora's cousin Neil addressed her as such in his missive of 1749,[19] and so she signed her marriage contract.[20] Indeed, Sir Walter Scott, who afterwards acquired the latter document, found it 'remarkable that this distinguished lady signed her name "Flory", instead of a more classical orthography'.[21] While very different from the careful letters which Flora wrote to grandees, this hurried note, whether forgery or not, reflects the drama of those times.

Meanwhile, at Cross Hill on the given day, Donald Macdonald commanded 'all loyal subjects in this Province [colony]' to 'repair to the Royal banner' in accordance with the proclamation that Martin had earlier issued.[22] Though only four of those from the western counties named as commissioners appeared, they promised that 3,000 of their number were ready to arm.[23]

While Flora remained at Cheek's Creek, her husband and two sons, Sandy and James, enjoyed the amenities of Morrison's plantation home at Cross Hill, which was equipped with fine furniture, books, backgammon tables and clocks. 'Eight new houses', one of them 'floored and lofted', adorned 500 acres of land among extensive orchards.[24] The dwellings and the grounds, however, soon became a busy encampment. Flora's son-in-law was later to record that he 'raised, in four days', and brought to the mustering ground 'four hundred and fifty Highland Emigrants'.[25] The Cross Creek merchants were kept busy, too, supplying the requirements of the different Scots captains. Lochbay paid £91 for '30 Guns [muskets] given to the Highlanders, and colours [flags] for them', and 'swords and pistols'.[26] Allan purchased 'nine stand of arms' from one storekeeper and, from another, a 'silver-mounted rifle'. A 'cask of rum for the use of the Highlanders on the expedition' and 'blankets, shoes and shirts' were among his other acquisitions.[27] Morrison was appointed quartermaster, and McArthur provisioned the expedition with 'camp kettles', 130 barrels of flour and over 1,000 bushels of rice, wheat and 'Indian corn'.[28] Murdoch Macleod, the Cross Creek physician who was to act as battalion surgeon, contributed 'two valuable chests of medicine', later valued at £300 each.[29]

Growing numbers of Highland officers and men bivouacked at Cross Hill and at Cross Creek, but they waited in vain for reinforcements from the western counties. Envoys sent in search of those who had promised so much at the earlier rendezvous discovered that these gentlemen were 'skulking and hiding themselves through swamps and such concealed places'. Nor did the 3,000 troops they had promised ever appear.[30] The Highland army must do service alone.

When the Highlanders, officers and men, assembled on 12 February at Cross Creek, they were found to number 1,600.[31] As Flora was later to report, however, they had 'no arms but six hundred old bad firelocks and about forty broadswords'.[32] In 1849 Lossing heard from his garrulous informant that Flora now 'came [to Cross Creek] with her friends [relatives]', the old lady telling the historian, 'I remember seeing her riding along the line [of troops] on a large white horse, and encouraging her countrymen to be faithful to the king. Why, she looked like a queen.'[33] Later legend would relate that Flora, mounted on her white palfrey – a second Queen Elizabeth I, addressing the troops at Tilbury – delivered her rousing speech in Gaelic. A North Carolina historian was to remark, 'Massachusetts has her Lady Arabella; Virginia her Pocahontas; and North Carolina her Flora Macdonald.'[34] When the Highlanders marched out of the town on the 18th, however, according to these tales, Flora became once more a sober grandmother. She returned to her home on Cheek's Creek. And like all other wives and mothers in the Scots country, she waited for news that their menfolk had reached the coast.

Days passed, and no word came. Much later, Flora was to give an account of what she was later told had occurred in the lower country in the early hours of 27 February: 'After marching two hundred miles and driving the Enemy from two different posts [positions] they had taken', the Highland army 'made a night attack' on the patriots eighteen miles from Wilmington.[35] Deceived into thinking that rebel militiamen, under the command of Richard Caswell, were in retreat on the far side of a bridge over miry waters known as Widow Moore's Creek, the Scots advanced before dawn.

To the beat of drums and the sound of skirling bagpipes, Captain Donald Macleod from Boston, who was in command on the day, led 500 men roaring out 'King George and Broadswords' in a charge towards the bridge.[36] Unbeknown to the Highlanders, however, as Flora recounts, the rebels had 'cut down [removed]' the planks on the bridge, 'excepting the two side beams', which they had greased. Moreover, far from being in retreat, 1,000 rebel militiamen were entrenched across the creek, and 'the Enemy', as she relates, had 'three piece[s] of cannon planted in front close to the bridge'.[37]

Struggling to find a purchase on the few and slippery planks remaining, the Highlanders fell victim to artillery or to musket fire either on the bridge or upon gaining the further bank. Macleod himself, though hit several times by enemy fire, rose again and again from the bridge, brandishing his broadsword and shouting encouragement to those behind him before succumbing to his wounds.[38] Before long the bridge, the water below and both banks of Moore's Creek were choked with corpses.

Caswell, more usually to be found in the assembly chamber, and his fellow militia commanders were triumphant. Those who remained in the depleted Highland army, in the wake of this disaster, retreated and the force rapidly dissolved. 'The men were not to be kept together, and the officers had no authority over the men', a loyalist eyewitness account was later to state.[39] Following a despondent council of war, Allan and the other leaders, with about 'ninety followers', retreated north, pursued all the way by enemy militia.[40] Though they did not know it, the promised fleet, with regulars, arms and ammunition, had still not arrived on the coast. Martin's plan to wrest power from the patriots had failed utterly.

Over a decade later, Flora's memory of her own sufferings in the wake of the failure of the Highland attack was acute. She was, she wrote in 1789, 'all this time in misery and sickness at home'. No one in Cross Creek knew for some days who had been killed, who was wounded and captive in the lower country. 'Being informed that her husband and friends were all killed or taken [prisoner]', her Memorial continues, she 'contracted a severe fever'.[41]

In the event, none of Flora's male relatives had been killed at Moore's Creek. The fates of her husband and her son Sandy, however, were ignominious. They and others were surrounded by a militia force in the far north of the colony, seized and confined in the common jail in Halifax, a town on the border with Virginia. Subsequently, on account of 'his being in a low state of health', Allan was allowed the freedom of the town.[42] Meanwhile Flora's woes at Cheek's Creek were compounded. As she later recalled with feeling, she was 'daily oppressed with straggling parties of plunderers from their [the patriots'] army'. Nor was that all she endured. 'Night robbers', she added, 'more than once threatened her life wanting a confession [of] where her husband's money was.'[43] Flora, racked by fever and sick with worry, yet kept her composure. No burglar succeeded in bearing off the Kingsburgh gold, such as there was. Did she wonder, though her mind was dulled by sickness, how it had come to this? She and Allan had successfully executed their plan of emigration and had bought this land only a year before. Now her husband was a prisoner, and she was prey to every passing marauder. Despite having no idea what the future might hold, Flora was not given to brooding. If she recovered from her fever, chief among her new duties would be the administration of the plantation.

15

'Almost Starved with Cold to Death'
February 1776–December 1779

While Flora lay on her sickbed in late February 1776, 2,000 patriot militiamen milled about Cross Creek, triumphant in the immediate wake of their victory over the Highland army. Some of these men were among those who, as she later wrote, 'daily' pillaged the Cheek's Creek plantation.[1] Marauders from the western counties came calling, too. Allan was later to give conflicting accounts of the Kingsburghs' losses, in 1784 pricing 'a Variety of articles plundered out of the house' at £150 and, a year later, the 'books, plate and furniture plundered' at £500. Similarly, in 1784 he assessed the horses and cattle lost on either farm as being worth £250, while noting a year later that 'the value of horses robbed and taken off both plantations' was £96.[2] For all his confused accounting, the losses were real. Flora also later recorded that several of the indentured servants who laboured in the house, in the fields and at the grist mill now deserted her. 'Such as stayed', she added, 'grew so very insolent, that they were of no service or help …'[3] With little money, ransacked possessions, stolen farm animals and a recalcitrant workforce, Flora can have expected, at best, to scratch a living.

She had, she was to relate, 'no comforter, but a young boy, her son'.[4] James, this fourth son, was then eighteen. Taken prisoner while a volunteer with the Highland army, he 'made his escape' and, evading further arrest, succeeded in gaining Cheek's Creek later in the spring.[5] James did not want courage and within a few years was to serve in an intrepid loyalist regiment, but his mother never placed great confidence in him. She had tried to interest no patron earlier in his preferment, while she had exerted herself for his elder and younger brothers.

On the Kenneth Black plantation in Cumberland County Annie Macleod was no better off than her mother and brother. Her husband Lochbay was 'a marked object of the enemy's resentment', as one who had played a principal role in raising the Highland army. His manservant was several times 'strangled almost to death' at the Macleods' house, 'in order to discover his master's effects [cash]'. The Highlander himself was forced to hide for 'six weeks in woods and swamps', before at length joining Josiah Martin on board the *Scorpion*.[6] There was no further thought of restoring order to the colony. When the fleet from England – which had belatedly arrived at Cape Fear – sailed south for Charleston in South Carolina, Lochbay and Martin went with it.

Annie Macleod, meanwhile, was helpless to prevent their home being 'plundered, and destroyed to a considerable extent'. The couple lost 'Household furniture, looking glasses, china' and 'Bedsteads, bedding, table and bed linen', including 'twenty-seven pair[s of] fine, new blankets'. Raiders drove off 'Twenty milch cows' and 'forty young [live]stock', later valued by Lochbay at £200. 'Corn, provisions and liquors', too, were 'carried away or wantonly destroyed'.[7]

At one point the three young Macleod children, Flora's grandchildren, were 'secreted in the woods' with their nurses. These stalwart women, Lochbay later averred, 'had the humanity to persist in declaring them [their charges] their own' when robbers threatened to 'carry off' the children. Annie herself, her husband recorded, was 'driven for refuge to a near relation twenty-four miles distant'.[8] The Macleods' home lay at that remove from the homes of Armadale, of the Cuidreach Macdonalds and of the Kingsburghs. Flora's stepfather, however, was now aged, and Annabella Macdonald at Cameron's Hill suffered 'cruelties' which exceeded even those which her niece experienced on the Black plantation. Her husband, Cuidreach, later wrote that his wife and five children were 'frequently plundered of the common necessaries of life, and at last stripped of even their body clothes, and turned out of their houses' – in Cumberland and Anson Counties – 'into the woods'. A humane Continental – patriot – officer provided safe conduct for them within British lines.[9] In all likelihood, Annie gave birth to Mary, a daughter, at the Cheek's Creek plantation, and the elder children joined their mother and grandmother there.

Lochbay, resident in New York from the autumn of 1776, was to centre his hopes on bringing his wife, children and mother-in-law out of danger and into that city, which was under British military occupation from September of that year. He was to find the means, as he later wrote, of 'supplying my family' – in which he included Flora – 'in North Carolina during my absence' to the tune of £250 over two years.[10]

Assuming that government reimbursement would soon follow, Lochbay and Allan had both spent lavishly in their efforts to raise and provision the Highland army. The former, however, was a rich man who could afford those and future disbursements. Kingsburgh had spent way beyond his limited income. Many years would pass before the Crown considered these Highlanders' claims on the public purse.[11] Allan had no funds with which to supply Flora, which only added to her misery at Cheek's Creek. While her husband and Sandy had been appointed, by the officers from Boston the previous summer, captain and lieutenant, in the Royal Highland Emigrants, loyalist regiments then forming in Quebec and Nova Scotia, neither of them had any opportunity to draw back-pay owed while they remained prisoners in patriot hands.[12]

Captive at first in Halifax, North Carolina, father and son were exiled from the colony to Philadelphia on 22 April 1776 with twenty-six other Highlanders judged, by a patriot committee, 'capable of doing us the Most Mischief'. The chairman of this body told the President of the Continental Congress, 'We are sorry to be compelled to an Act of such severity as this ...'[13] The North Carolina Provincial Congress, now de facto government of the colony, proclaimed, 'We war not with the helpless females which they left behind them.' Loyalist wives, daughters, mothers were 'rightful pensioners upon the charity and bounty of those who have aught [anything] to spare from their own necessities [essential needs]'.[14]

Whether or not Flora and Annie received any such aid, the former was determined to offer succour to the wives of those who had been dispatched prisoner out of the state with Allan. 'When she got the better of her fever,' her future Memorial details, 'she went to visit and comfort the other poor gentlewomen.' This task proved thankless, however. Though these ladies and their families had, only weeks before, cheered on the Highland army making for the coast, now 'they blamed him [Allan] as being the author of their misery, in rising the Highlanders'. If Flora felt there was some justice to these reproaches, she did not pause in what she saw as her Christian duty. To add to her troubles, on one of these 'charitable visits' she 'fell from her horse and broke her right arm'. She was subsequently 'confined [at home] ... for months', she wrote, because Murdoch Macleod, 'the only physician in the colony [Scots country]', was a prisoner in Philadelphia. Flora, now in her mid-fifties, was growing old, and the limb, for lack of medical attention, did not mend well. Her recollections of this time later were bleak: 'She remained in this deplorable condition' at the Cheek's Creek plantation for two years 'among Robbers and faithless servants'.[15]

Allan and Sandy were at first housed in the jail in Walnut Street, Philadelphia and were still in that city on 4 July, when Congress adopted the declaration that 'these United Colonies are, and of right ought to be, Free and Independent States'.[16] The British troops had evacuated Boston a few months earlier and sailed north to Halifax to regroup in Nova Scotia, a maritime province like Quebec still in British hands, and so named during the reign of James VI and I from the Latin for New Scotland. Many loyalist citizens followed them or sailed for New York, after it came under British military occupation in the autumn, or for new homes elsewhere. In the new state of Pennsylvania, Flora's husband and son obtained their parole later that summer and took up residence with two servants in Reading, a township fifteen miles distant from Philadelphia.[17] Ever the courtier, Kingsburgh made himself agreeable to the Continental Army general Thomas Mifflin, who had a fine country house nearby, and charmed funds out of him too. The following April Allan prevailed upon his new friend to deliver a petition to John Hancock, President of Congress, requesting his exchange and that of his son for patriot 'officers of the like denomination [rank]'.[18]

'His Excellency [Mifflin] and the [local] County Committee', Allan declared, would testify that he and Sandy had 'kept close to their parole, without giving the smallest offence to any person whatever'. Nonetheless, their allowance from Congress for the last three months had not been paid and they were living on an advance from Mifflin. Allan opined that it was but charity to allow him and Sandy to go to New York and negotiate their exchange with patriot officers of equivalent rank in conference with those recently appointed British and American commissaries of prisoners.[19] For all his claims of penury, in May Allan requested of a tailor in Philadelphia the makings of 'two summer waistcoats', 'an [sic] yard of scarlet cloth with furniture [accessories]' for another. He also required enough 'wheat corded [pale yellow corduroy] or plain stuff' to provide two pairs of breeches.[20]

After the failure of a further bid to get themselves exchanged, in July 1777 Allan petitioned Hancock for a third time.[21] A North Carolina delegate to Congress had written in March of some of those who had come north, prisoners with Allan and Sandy: 'They are incessant importuners.'[22] None was so persistent as Flora's husband. He asked the Congress President to consider 'the dispersed and distraught state of my family'. He wrote that Flora was then 'seven hundred miles from me, in a very sickly tender state of health'.

Allan was eager to make clear to Congress that he had no intention of returning to that territory where he had previously taken up arms against the nascent United States of America: 'Them [Flora, Annie and her children, and James] in Carolina, I can be of no service to in my present state,' he declared. Lochbay, indeed, was their sole support. Were he exchanged, however, Allan continued: 'I could be of service to the rest [his sons in America and Scotland]'.[23]

This last plea won a favourable hearing. Kingsburgh and Sandy
were allowed to travel to New York and secure an exchange with
Continental officers held by the British authorities there. Once
that was effected, they were expected in Nova Scotia. British
officers abounded in Halifax, the harbour town established in 1749
as the colony's capital. The 2nd Battalion of the Royal Highland
Emigrants, however, in which Allan and Sandy held commissions
as, respectively, a captain and a lieutenant, were doing garrison duty
at Fort Edward, Windsor, some sixty-five miles north-west, on the
Bay of Fundy. Captain Alexander Macdonald of Ardnamurchan,
battalion commander, told Allan, then in New York, that he
anticipated the 'pleasure of seeing you both soon here'.[24] While
the province was itself peaceful, the Emigrants guarded against the
possibility of an attack by sea from Maine, north-west across the
Bay and now a maritime district of the new state of Massachusetts.

Soon after his arrival on Manhattan Island in September, Flora's
husband had called on Josiah Martin, now an idle spectator of the
military scene with four other 'outcast' royal governors.[25] Where the
North Carolina official had once been entranced by Kingsburgh
and his fellow Highlanders, now he was sour: 'the Scotch officers
who have escaped from confinement', he wrote later, had 'forfeited
my good opinion by their avidity for money, and the high price
they put upon their short and ineffectual service in North Carolina
that they really seem to compute above all reward'.[26] Nevertheless,
Martin did, over the following months, reimburse Allan for some
part or all of his outlay on the 1776 Highland army.[27]

Meanwhile, it was becoming clear that an exit from North
Carolina for Flora and Annie was, if not the only option available
to them, certainly the best. In 1777 Richard Caswell became
Governor of the new state of North Carolina and presided over a
General Assembly, as he had over previous Provincial Congresses.
An act of confiscation was passed that November, passing to 'the
use of the state ... all the Lands, Tenements ... and moveable
Property within this State' of any who had 'during the present War
attached himself to, or aided or abetted, the Enemies of the United
States'.[28] This was a death knell for any hopes the two women

might have had to survive the war and prosper thereafter in this southern state. As wives of two Highlanders of rank and influence, who had raised and led companies 'against America', they could hope for no clemency. Flora herself was singled out some time before 30 November 1777 for questioning before either the General Assembly or an Anson County committee. If this body had hopes that she would swear allegiance to the revolutionary state, however, they were disappointed. In her youth, Flora had successfully parried questions from authorities including the Privy Council of the United Kingdom. Ardnamurchan in Nova Scotia was 'Happy to hear' from Allan in late December of 'Mrs Macdonald's … spirited behaviour, when brought before that committee of rascals'. Although admiring of Flora's courage, the officer, who was kin to Allan and his family, was concerned for her safety: 'Pray, for God's sake, it is possible to get Mrs Macdonald and the other poor women from North Carolina.'[29]

This question had for some time been agitating Flora's son-in-law, with whom Allan and Sandy were now reunited in New York. Although difficulties lay in his way, early in 1778 Lochbay paid £130 for 'freight and provisions of a [merchant] vessel' named the *Sucky and Peggy* 'with a flag [of truce]' and obtained permission from naval command at New York to proceed to North Carolina.[30] In March Flora and Annie received dispatches at Cheek's Creek from the latter's husband, then in Wilmington harbour on the merchant ship, with the intelligence 'of their having leave to depart the state'.[31] Patriot officials had greeted with mistrust the earlier arrival of this known 'traitor' to North Carolina. However, Richard Caswell, now Governor of the state, decreed that 'the paper signed by [British] Commodore [William] Hotham', which Lochbay proffered, must be 'considered as a proper flag [of truce]'. Caswell added this rider: 'The more expeditious he [Lochbay] is getting away [departing], the greater satisfaction he will give the State.'[32]

Upon receipt of her son-in-law's letter, Flora made haste to leave the plantations once so painstakingly cleared and cultivated, now looted of livestock and barren for lack of labourers and money. In the dwelling houses on either property at Cheek's Creek and nearby there remained furniture, books, clothing, bed and table linen, much of it brought from home in Skye. All was left behind to be seized by the state. When Flora and her party now struck out down the Cape Fear River for the coast, she took with her only personal property to a value of £40.[33] Although the venture to settle in North Carolina had proved disastrous, she was not one to repine. As head of her small family in the Scots country these two years, she had negotiated the vagaries of revolution as best she could. Now she looked to asylum within the British lines in New York.

Before leaving the state, apparently, she extracted from her small hoard of possessions two rhinestone and glass shoe buckles. These she gave to three Wilmington sisters, the Dunbidin ladies, in token of gratitude for some gesture of kindness. Then she embarked with the Lochbay family.[34] When Flora later recalled the voyage from Wilmington on the *Sucky and Peggy* in 'the dead of winter [March]', her Memorial slips into and stays in the first person. They were, she wrote, 'in danger of our lives for the most of the voyage by a constant storm'.[35] After weeks at sea, however, Manhattan came into sight and Flora was free to disembark and seek out her husband.

Two years had passed since Flora had last seen him. Both, rising fifty-six and fifty-eight, had suffered during their separation. Flora's broken arm had not mended well, and Allan had been mentioned by General Mifflin six months earlier as 'being in a Decay [poor health]'.[36] However, the Highlander had lost none of his enthusiasm to cut a figure in the great world. Although he had 'contracted a great deal of debt' while a prisoner, two years' back-pay was due him from the Royal Highland Emigrants, that regiment in which he was yet to serve.[37] Allan employed advances on that sum from Scottish merchants in New York to raise and outfit at his own expense 'a company of gentlemen volunteers' which he captained. They were, Flora commented, 'all dressed in scarlet and blue'.[38]

Ardnamurchan, in Nova Scotia, meanwhile wrote: 'I dare say you and your Volunteers make a formidable figure.'[39] The officer, however, would far rather see Kingsburgh at 'the head of your own company in our regiment than commanding a company of provincials'.[40] Like other volunteer forces which drilled in the city, Allan's company was probably tasked with little more than guarding stores. 'I wd earnestly recommend it to you to join the regt as soon as possible …'[41]

Ardnamurchan also counselled, 'I dare say you must have lived expensive [as a prisoner], but it is high time now, my dear Allan, to study economy …'[42] Economy was never a watchword with Allan, although there was now the more need for such a measure given the escalating price of food and other essentials in the occupied city. Though Kingsburgh received one advance of £1,690 among others, Ardnamurchan suspected he was 'straitened for cash' in June 1778.[43] Flora was fortunate that Lochbay could as ever be relied upon. He expended £150 'on his family' from April to October of that year.[44]

Even after Flora had joined him, however, Allan lingered in the city. It would be the late summer of 1778 before he consented to head further north; Ardnamurchan had to be satisfied with the presence, in the Emigrant barracks, of three of Kingsburgh's sons. Sandy sailed north to join his brother Charles, who had exchanged the Bengal army for service in America two years earlier. Ranald was there on detachment from the Marines.

Flora, meanwhile, was negotiating life in New York while looking to head north herself eventually. In her youth she had known London, a metropolis in the 1740s with well over half a million inhabitants. She was familiar, too, with Edinburgh, which was a tenth the size of the southern capital. New York, whose population then was 25,000, was a city of modest size by comparison. But conditions there were unstable. British soldiers and volunteer corps drilled and did guard duty in every corner. Continental prisoners occupied jails, prison ships and makeshift prisons, including churches. Loyalist fugitives crowded every lodging house and hostelry. General James Robertson, military commandant, was hard pressed to maintain order in this confused situation.

Flora, Allan and the Lochbay Macleods, while fugitives themselves, were embraced warmly by all the 'Scotch folks' in New York. Among these were many men of influence who were, as officeholders and members of a St Andrew's Society, accustomed to gather on the feast day of that tutelary saint of Scotland. Trader

William McAdam, source of numerous advance payments for Allan; Norman Macleod of Tolmie, a 'Skye man' made good and captain of other Highland volunteers; and Ardnamurchan himself were all enthusiastic members.[45]

The latter grew ever more insistent that Allan, with another laggard officer, should head north. 'Pray let them know', he wrote to McAdam, 'that I am very much surprised that I don't see or hear from them ... considering the number of men of war [naval ships] and armed vessels backwards and forwards ... All officers should be with their corps with recruits.'[46] In August 1778 he wrote still more forcefully: 'As I have said before, it's very surprising what keeps them there ... I will certainly stop their credit from receiving any more money [advances against back and current pay] if they don't join the regiment or assign sufficient reasons to the contrary.'[47]

Under this threat, Allan capitulated. Consigning his volunteer company to another, he set sail for Nova Scotia. Flora later recorded, 'I was obliged, though tender [in poor health], to follow.' Possibly she had the companionship of her daughter and Lochbay on the voyage, as that couple embarked from New York for London in October 1778, a passage which involved a stop at Halifax, the Nova Scotia port where Flora was bound.[48] She was to vividly recall the 'Rough Sea and long passage' northward a decade later. Falling victim to a 'violent disorder' while still at sea, she came 'very near death's door ... At last landing in Halifax', her Memorial continues, she was 'allowed to stay for eight days, on account of my tender state'.[49] The British garrison town on the Atlantic coast offered superior medical services. However, the battalion in which Allan served was doing duty at Fort Edward, a barracks forty miles north-west. 'The ninth day' after her arrival, Flora recorded, she 'set off for Windsor', the hamlet where the barracks were located, 'on the Bay of Minos [Minas]'.[50] The 2nd Battalion of the Royal Highland Emigrant Regiment there was tasked with repelling any Continental land attack on Nova Scotia. However remote that possibility might appear, the companies still drilled and marched in this peaceable corner of the Empire as though it were a present danger.

The journey to Windsor 'through woods and snow' occupied five long days. Nor were Flora's travails over when she arrived at the garrison, which was to be her home. Fort Edward comprised only a number of log cabins and a blockhouse, or small fortification, within bastion walls. 'There we continued all winter and spring,' she wrote. The ground was 'covered with frost and snow'. She 'almost starved with cold to death' in the officers' quarters. It was, she later reported, 'one of the worst winters ever seen there'.[51] It was, in fact, the coldest winter on record since the founding of the colony. Ink froze in Halifax, it was said, while letters were being written near a large fire, and temperatures fell to minus 40 degrees Fahrenheit.[52]

Flora could take joy, nevertheless, in being reunited with her son Charles, though Ranald, his younger brother, whom Ardnamurchan thought 'a fine young fellow' sure to 'make an excellent officer', had rejoined his ship.[53] Now in his late twenties, her eldest son was, according to Ardnamurchan, 'very sensible and clever when sober', but 'rather unhappy when … disguised with liquor [inebriated]'. Like father, like son, Charles had 'a propensity to extravagance'.[54]

There was a modicum of gaiety in the barracks to enjoy, even while snow and ice bound the earth outside. Every fortnight there was a *ceilidh*, or evening of Gaelic celebration, and, far from the Scottish Highlands, officers picked out the 'Guillicallum [*gille callum*, or sword dance] over two broad swords lain across'. Moreover, rather than 'sitting long after dinner and getting ourselves drunk', as was the custom on St Andrew's Day in November, Ardnamurchan informed a correspondent, this year the gentlemen of Fort Edward chose 'to entertain the ladies with a dance'.[55] Flora's sons and other younger comrades, not content with such 'sober and decent' entertainment, were instead 'fond of dancing and seeing the ladies' in Halifax.[56] Charles, tiring altogether of duty in the bleak and isolated garrison, departed to join his younger brother James in a new regiment, the British Legion, then mustering near New York.

When winter yielded in 1779 to spring and summer at Windsor, Flora had fresh troubles to surmount. She already had rheumatism in the arm which she had broken when in North Carolina. Now, in a further accidental fall at the barracks, she 'dislocated the wrist of the other hand and broke some tendons'. She had upon this occasion 'the assistance of the regimental surgeon', but in pain nonetheless, and doubly handicapped, she was, she later wrote, 'confined [to her bed] for two months'.

'When I got the better of this misfortune,' she recorded, 'I fixed my thoughts on seeing my native land, though in a tender state …'[57] Although she did not say as much, a return to Scotland brought the prospect of seeing once more her youngest children – Johnny, in Edinburgh, who was to turn twenty on 30 October, and Fanny on Raasay, who had become thirteen on 6 May.

Flora's brother Milton still occupied the family farms on the Long Island in the Outer Hebrides, and had prospered. Allan's sister Anne lived in material comfort with her second husband at Corriechatachan on Skye. Although Flora had no home on either island, her brother and sister-in-law would readily extend hospitality to her. Moreover, Flora's own daughter Annie, who had left New York in October 1778, settled the following year with her children at Dunvegan Castle on Skye. The Macleod, Lochbay's nephew, was soon to depart with a battalion to India. Lochbay himself, promoted major, was due to return to New York and report for duty. Annie, however, in occupation at the ancient stronghold, could offer Flora a home.

Flora did not delay long once she had made the decision to return to her native land. Allan obtained a berth for her in the *Dunmore*, a loyalist privateer of sixteen guns bound for London. On this vessel she duly embarked in October 1779 'with three young ladies and two gentlemen' on what would prove an eventful crossing. The ship was a 'letter of marque' and, as such, though a private vessel, had licence to board enemy craft and take prizes. Her captain, 'spying a sail [on the horizon], made ready for action'. Flora recorded that in then 'hurrying the ladies below to a place of safety' she slipped on 'a step in the trap [ladder]'. She fell and 'broke her dislocated arm in two'.[58] When later recounting this episode, according to her daughter Annie, Flora was 'accustomed to say that she had fought both for the House of Stuart and for the House of Hanover, but had been worsted in the service of each'.[59]

The pursuit of the craft with possible booty aboard ended without result, and Flora spent the rest of the voyage with her arm roughly 'set with bandages over slips of wood'. Keeping to her bed until they reached the Thames, she was still buoyed up with the prospect of making for her native land and her family in the Highlands. To her 'great sorrow', however, upon landing, she received the 'melancholy news' of the loss of her son Sandy at sea. He had been convalescent at Fort Edward when she last saw him, following an operation for a wound in his side. The voyage on which he had been embarked had been bringing him home for his health. This intelligence brought on a 'violent fit of sickness', and Flora was thereafter 'confined to her bed in London for half a year'.[60]

16

'All Possible Speed to the Highlands'
1780–1785

Flora lay dangerously ill in London through the winter of 1779 and into the spring of 1780. Her 'sickness', she later wrote, 'would have brought me to my grave if, under God's hand [providentially], Doctor Donald Munro' – a Scot with Skye connections – 'had not given his friendly assistance'.[1] Flora was indeed fortunate in her medical attendant. Munro, then in private practice in Piccadilly, was a renowned physician formerly responsible for the health of British forces in Germany.

This 'violent fit of sickness' that laid Flora low was only the latest in a catalogue of ills that had assailed her since her emigration to America. She had endured the attacks of 'night robbers' in North Carolina in the wake of the Moore's Creek fiasco four years earlier. Suffering agonies of uncertainty about the whereabouts and safety of her husband and sons, she had withstood interrogation by a revolutionary committee. Rough seas and winter storms had been her lot on long passages to New York and northward to Halifax, Nova Scotia, even before she embarked on the long transatlantic voyage to England. All this time Flora's constitution, formerly robust, was weakening. The breaks in both arms had not been well set, and rheumatism – probably rheumatoid arthritis – now afflicted both limbs.[2]

Although still convalescent, Flora travelled north in the late spring of 1780. While in Edinburgh she stayed with Mrs Macdonald, a celebrated druggist or pharmacist who sold a wide variety of medicines at her laboratory or pharmacy in the Lawnmarket. Although some of these remedies may have allayed the worst of Flora's ills, she was urged by her physicians to 'make for the benefit of the goats' whey'. She intended, she informed a Glasgow merchant also named Macdonald, 'to take up … residence in the Long Island'.[3]

The watery milk that Flora was advised to imbibe was then widely believed to have curative properties for a variety of ailments. Highland goats, it was noted with approval, fed 'amongst rocks and glens which abound with wild, aromatic plants'. The hills of South Uist where Flora, when young, had pastured her brother's livestock were still, as a local minister there was later to remark, 'covered with heath[er] and verdure, fit enough for pasturing black cattle, horses, sheep, and goats, during the summer and autumn months'.[4] Over thirty years earlier at midnight in that shepherd's hut on the Long Island, Flora had offered the famished Prince a bowlful of cream.[5] Now, in her late fifties, she herself might hope to grow fat on whey, cream, cheese and other wholesome Highland sustenance.

Flora wished Macdonald in Glasgow to convey 'some things [belongings]' of hers to the Long Island which she would send him 'by the [new Monkland] Canal'. Ever the woman of business, Flora suggested various ways whereby she might remit 'the freight' to the merchant.[6] Meanwhile she herself continued her journey north, pausing in Perthshire to pay her respects to Mrs John Mackenzie of Delvine.[7] Now a widow, this lady had been as a mother these past years in Edinburgh to Flora's son Johnny while he was at the high school and afterwards apprenticed to the law. Preferring a career in the military, the young man had secured a cadetship in the East India Company army, and had sailed for Bombay earlier in the year.[8] His mother had arrived in the Scottish capital too late to see him.

Continuing her travels north, Flora rested at Inverness some days before taking to the road again with a 'female companion' bound for Skye whom she had had 'the good luck to meet'. On Raasay, she reacquainted herself with her younger daughter. Flora wrote cheerfully to Mrs Mackenzie from Skye in July that Fanny, now fourteen, promised to be a 'stout Highland Caileag [Gaelic: young woman]', being 'quite overgrown [very tall] of her age'.[9]

Flora's odyssey from North Carolina, via New York and Nova Scotia, was nearly complete. She was writing from Dunvegan, the Macleod stronghold set high above the Minch on the western coast of Skye, where she and Fanny were staying with her elder daughter. Boswell had earlier commented on the 'many circumstances of natural grandeur' which made Dunvegan a worthy seat for the Macleod and his family.[10] Annie and her 'small family [children]' were now the castle's occupants. Lochbay, as Flora informed Mrs Mackenzie, was in the south and about to sail for America.[11] There, in common with Flora's sons Charles and James, he would engage in British manoeuvres in the southern states of America.

In her letter to Mrs Mackenzie in July, Flora expressed her relief that her progress north had been 'without any accidents, which I always dread'. Given that fall from her horse in America and the recent break in her arm on board the *Dunmore*, she had good reason for this apprehension about travel. She foretold years of rheumatism to come when she referred to having reached Raasay 'with difficulty', her hands being 'so pained with the [rough] riding' on the four days' journey beforehand from Inverness to the west coast.[12]

With no home of her own now on Skye, Flora must accept her daughter's hospitality while she rested after her peregrinations from London. At Dunvegan the landward views, 'wild, moorish [moorland], hilly, and craggy' in appearance, were desolate.[13] Beneath the castle, the sea pounded on glistening rocks and boulders. Here was a reminder to Flora, if reminder was required, that her husband and elder sons were located far across the Atlantic and Johnny further still, on the eastern rim of the Arabian Sea. The mother's thoughts flitted often to that youngest son, whom she had last seen six years earlier. She wrote to Mrs Mackenzie, 'Should you get a letter from my son Johnny sooner than I would get one from him, you would very much oblige me by dropping me a few lines communicating to me the most material part.'[14]

Flodigarry and Kingsburgh, Flora's former homes on Skye, had been comfortable and well-appointed dwellings. Dunvegan was cold even in summer and no place for a woman, like Flora, in 'tender health'. Every chimney in the house smoked, bar that in the drawing room, and a 'noble cascade' outside the window of this latter room made conversation often inaudible. Moreover, in consequence of the great size of the castle, food prepared in the kitchens was invariably cold when served in the dining room. Flora told Mrs Mackenzie in July, 'I wait here till a favourable opportunity for the Long Island shall offer itself ... Please direct to me, to Mrs Macdonald, late of Kingsborrow [Kingsburgh], South Uist, by Dunvegan.'[15]

Once the mistress of a home with plate and china, prints on the walls and beds hung about with tartan, she was now destitute of an abode of her own. Her son Johnny was later to write of his mother's 'pecuniary embarrassments' upon her return from America.[16] She did not, however, lack for male protectors in the absence of her husband. Her brother Milton was strong in support, once Flora had reached South Uist. He had recently given up the Balivanich farm on Benbecula, where the two had grown up. Now he lived at Milton, the tack on the shore of South Uist, where previously only a summer sheiling had existed.[17] Here, between the white strand bordering the Atlantic to the westward and hills stretching to the island's rocky eastward shore, Flora was on familiar territory, known to her from youth.

There was no reminder here of the latter years on Skye, when humiliating poverty had been her lot. Her brother and his wife, with a son in the army in America, sympathised, moreover, with her anxiety about Allan and her own sons on that continent.[18] Above all, Flora and Milton shared memories of their younger days, not least of that summer of 1746, when both had conspired in the Prince's escape from his pursuers. At Nunton Flora and Lady Clan had sewn those outsize robes for Betty Burke. Milton had escorted the mistress of that seat to the royal picnic on the shore at Rossinish. He had also been entrusted with the Prince's pistols before Flora, their cousin Neil and Betty Burke embarked for Skye.

Neil was long settled far away in France where he would die, still impecunious, in 1788. This autumn Lady Clan followed Young Clan, her rebel son, and Old Clan, her bibulous husband, to the grave. Survivors Flora and her brother made sure to hand down stories of their royal adventure to the Milton children, who in turn were to impress this family lore on their own descendants.[19]

Over the course of the next years Flora flitted between the homes of her brother and other relatives on the Long Island and Skye. Allan wrote to a cousin from Nova Scotia that he approved of some economical 'plan of living' his wife had adopted: 'I do think Flory judged right to take the world with so little trouble as possibly she can.'[20] Her thoughts, however, remained fixed on the fates of those far beyond the waves that churned on the shores of South Uist or below Dunvegan. She had described herself with some accuracy in July 1780 as 'Fond [anxious] to hear news, and yet afraid to get it'. Hoping that 'peace' (meaning British rule) would be soon 're-established' across the Atlantic, she declared that it would be 'for the utility of the whole nation – especially to [for] poor me, that has my all [Flora's husband and four sons] engaged'.[21]

Penurious and looking to others for support, devoid of the comfort of a husband or sons at home, often in pain and entering her seventh decade, Flora had reason to be bitter. Her spirits rose and fell, depending on the contents of the letters she received which often reached her months and even years after they had been written. Shortly after she had left Nova Scotia, a great force, which included Lochbay and Flora's sons Charles and James as officers in the new British Legion, now under the command of Banastre Tarleton, had sailed south from New York, its aim being to restore the southern states to Royal governance. Flora did not learn until two years later, however, that her eldest son had 'got the command of a troop of horse' and that his younger brother had secured a lieutenancy in the regiment.[22] By that time, both Charles, who served with distinction in skirmishes with patriot troops in the Carolinas, and James were once more in New York.[23] Like others who had been engaged in the southern campaign, they were soon to be sent home. Lochbay joined Annie and the children at Dunvegan in the autumn of 1781.

Flora was on the Long Island that December when a letter from her son Ranald of 10 October reached her. The Marine officer, then in New York, had written, 'No doubt you will be surprised to hear that Sandy is still in the land of the living.' Although the ship on which Flora's third son was embarked for home had been shipwrecked, Ranald related, 'They [her crew and passengers] were taken up at sea by a vessel from Lisbon and carried to the coast of Brazil.' This colony, with its mother country, Portugal, had remained neutral in the American war. Flora, quoting her son's words, wrote to her son-in-law on Skye, 'I have scarce power to write you the joyful news I received ...'[24] Ranald also regaled his mother with information about an expeditionary force that was then embarking to aid the British commander Lord Cornwallis, blockaded at Yorktown. 'This is two letters I received from him within this ten days ...' Flora wrote to a cousin on 10 December. 'God bless him [Ranald], poor man, he never misses an opportunity in writing to his mother.'[25]

Reports of Allan's welfare were, on the whole, encouraging. In 1779 his regiment had been placed upon the establishment, thanks to the exertions of some of his superior officers, as the 84th Regiment of Foot, and Flora wrote to Mrs Mackenzie of Delvine on 3 July 1782: 'I received a letter from Captain Macdonald, my husband, dated from [the garrison outside] Halifax, the twelfth of November '81. He was then recovering his health, but had been very tender for some time before.' She had apparently now heard that her shipwrecked son had found a passage from Brazil to Europe, but she was not optimistic: 'As for my son Sandy, who was a-missing, I had accounts of his being carried to Lisbon, but nothing certain ... I look upon the whole as a hearsay.' She took comfort in God having been 'pleased to spare his father and the rest [of her sons]'.[26] No further positive news was forthcoming, and Flora came to accept that the young Scot had indeed been lost at sea.

Sandy had been scholar enough to write his mother's petition to the Duke of Atholl begging fruitlessly for his own advancement.

He had proved a loyal servant of the King at Moore's Creek, in captivity and as a lieutenant at Fort Edward. He had, however, made little mark in his profession. Such was not the case with his younger brother, who had been gazetted captain of Marines in 1779. 'Ranald', Flora wrote proudly on 3 July 1782 to Mrs Mackenzie, '... was with [Admiral Lord] Rodney at the taking of St. Eustatia [Eustatius, in the Caribbean].'[27] That very month the *Ville de Paris*, an enemy flagship formerly 'the pride of the French navy', set sail in a convoy from Jamaica for England.[28] Ranald was made one of a Marine corps to serve on the vessel. Five hundred crew and troops in all were aboard. Most of them, like Ranald, were now veterans of some years' standing of the conflict in America and relished the coming opportunity for shore leave in England. In the early hours of 17 September, however, the convoy was battered off Newfoundland by a 'violent tempest'. The *Ville de Paris* foundered. Ranald and all others on board lost their lives, bar one who was later taken up from wreckage in the ocean.[29]

Seven years after Ranald had perished in this hurricane, in an envoi to the Memorial which she sent to Sir John Macpherson, former acting Governor General of Bengal, at his request, Flora was to cite her two sons' deaths as 'melancholy strokes'.[30] Her memory was at fault or she had her own motives when she described accounts of Ranald's decease as having reached her during that winter she spent in London, following her return from North America. 'Had they lived', she concluded, these sons might 'with God's assistance now be my support in my declined [decline and] old age'.[31]

Flora continued, however, to take pride in her youngest son's career. Still unaware of the loss of Ranald, she thanked Mrs Mackenzie in July 1782 for intelligence that Johnny had arrived safe in Sumatra in the East Indies, where he had recently been posted. 'The agreeable news', Flora wrote, 'relieved me of a great deal of distress, as that was the first accounts [sic] I had of him since he sailed [from Bombay] ... I am told by others', she added, 'that it will be in his power now to show his talents, as being in the engineer department.'[32]

Meanwhile, her relationship with Annie remained strong. Flora told Mrs Mackenzie that she was at her brother's house at Milton and, she reported, 'on my way to Skye, to attend my daughter who is to lie-in [give birth] in August'.[33] There was no happy outcome, however. A stillbirth may have been the result. A local surgeon and a minister were to declare on 16 December that Annie had 'for several months past laboured under a very tedious and dangerous disposition' at Dunvegan.[34] Mary Macleod, born in North Carolina in 1776 and now aged six, was to prove the last of the Lochbays' brood of four.

While the war in America did not officially conclude until the autumn of 1783, the majority of British troops, and the last of the loyalist civilians on that continent, came home over the course of the preceding year. Congress was now pondering what form the future government of the United States should take, and two gentlemen from Maryland even took it upon themselves to visit Florence in the autumn of 1782 and offer to make Charles Edward Stuart, long now in residence there, king of the new country. The Prince, having separated two years earlier from Princess Louise of Stolberg after a childless marriage of eight years, replied, 'I am too old. I have failed most of my life, and have no wish to fail more.'[35]

In London, meanwhile, an American Loyalist Claims office opened, where those who had suffered loss of property across the Atlantic could present demands for compensation.[36] Coffee houses across the capital thronged with would-be claimants, many of them Scots. Lochbay and Cuidreach were among those from Skye who pressed for payment. The latter, once owner of that fine Cameron's Hill plantation, was to declare that he had arrived in Britain 'destitute of friends or money to supply the common necessaries of life'.[37] The two men begged such government officials and military officers as they had known in America, now in England, for 'evidence' about their past loyal endeavours and the extent of their losses.

By contrast, Allan Macdonald was among those of the 2nd Battalion of the 84th Regiment, previously the Royal Highland

Emigrants, who chose to remain in Nova Scotia and claim their share of a blanket government grant of 105,000 acres on the Kennetcook River, some twenty-five miles from Fort Edward.[38] Kingsburgh, as captain of a company, was allotted at least 700 acres.[39] While he lodged with his nephew Kenneth, in the Hants County township created to accommodate the veterans and named Douglas, 'at the Red House behind Mrs Francklin's', Allan built what he described as a 'little neat hut' on land that he had cleared.[40] It was a forerunner, he hoped, of a more substantial home to come. Meanwhile, he employed Cuidreach to act as his agent in London and present to the government a memorandum of his North Carolina losses on Cheek's Creek.[41]

Did Flora have it in mind to join her husband in the British province which she had fled years earlier? It seems unlikely that she would be prepared to make a further transatlantic journey. She recalled with dread the freezing winter she had passed at Fort Edward. Moreover, the township the officers of the 84th were building on the Kennetcook was still makeshift and primitive. More probably, it was intended that Allan sell the bounty lands at some future date and retire home to Skye.

In the autumn of 1784 Kingsburgh had to stop work on his Nova Scotia acres, having run dry of money to make further improvements.[42] That winter he embarked for London, where he hoped that his application in person to the government for reimbursement would succeed where Cuidreach's earlier submission had failed. Thereafter, suitably equipped with capital, he meant to return to the Kennetcook and resume farming. Arriving in London in February 1785, Allan joined the queue of loyalists beating at the door of the American Loyalists Commission, whose office was in Lincoln's Inn Fields. Busy obtaining 'evidence' to bolster his claim from Governor Martin and others who had known and admired the Cheek's Creek plantation, awaiting a summons to bear witness himself before the government, Allan also provided at least one testimonial for another who had lost their all in the Scots country in North Carolina and, like him, was lodging in the capital.[43] The life of a half-pay officer in London was not disagreeable.

He was still in the southern capital when Flora, though living so secluded, shot to fame once more in the late autumn of 1785. The previous year Dr Johnson, whom Flora had once characterised as a 'young buck' and who had been graceful but succinct in her praise in his *A Journey to the Western Isles of Scotland* (1775), had died. James Boswell now published his own account of the northern 'peregrinations' on which he and the elderly lexicographer had embarked in the summer of 1773. *A Journal of a Tour to the Hebrides with Samuel Johnson* was, like its author, exuberant and entertaining. Boswell declared that the account of the Prince's adventures on Skye which he gave there contained 'some curious anecdotes which will, I imagine, not be uninteresting to my readers and even, perhaps, be of some use to future historians'.[44] A future editor of a later edition was to remark, rather, that there was little in the narrative, when published, that was not already known to the public.[45] Moreover, the diarist had taken down testimony from Flora and others nearly thirty years after the events they described. Nevertheless, Boswell's story of the meeting between Flora and Johnson, both constellations in their own firmaments, has verve and immediacy. It endures as a vivid account of that royal summer in the heather, even after the viva voce testimony of Flora and others collected by the Reverend Robert Forbes in Edinburgh immediately after the 'Forty-five was published by degrees in the nineteenth century.[46] Numerous newspapers extracted from the *Journal* that section which chronicles Flora's aid to the fugitive Prince. The poet Courtenay was moved to write:

> We see the Rambler [Johnson] with fastidious smile
> Mark the lone tree, and note the heath-clad isle:
> But when the heroic tale of Flora charms,
> Deck'd in a kilt, he wields a chieftain's arms:
> The tuneful piper sounds a martial strain,
> And Samuel sings 'The King shall have his ain [own]'.[47]

Not all were as impressed by the *Journal*. A satirical print entitled *The Ghost of Johnson* proved popular, in which a besuited doctor, standing on substantial clouds, berates the diarist. Boswell, who is seated, raises in alarm a small cushion inscribed 'Hebrides'. On the table in front of him meanwhile are spread further cushions and remnants of material, inscribed with names and phrases including 'Flora Macdonald', 'Wanderer [the Prince]', 'Drunkenness' and 'Savage Lord'. Beneath the design are lines from Congreve, as though spoken by Johnson:

> Thou art a retailer of Phrases;
> And dost deal in Remnants of Remnants,
> Like a maker of Pincushions.[48]

Boswell had more dangerous opprobrium to deal with in the wake of publication of the *Journal*. The 'Savage Lord' to whom the satirical print alludes was Sir Alexander Macdonald of Sleat, Baron Macdonald since 1776. Macdonald wrote to the diarist on 26 November 1785: 'Your violation of the acknowledged laws of hospitality by the wanton indignity put upon me in it [the book] after such a lapse of time is without a parallel in the annals of civilized nations.' The peer resented the attacks in the book on his character as chief. Nor, as he now made clear, had he forgiven Boswell for his insulting declaration on Skye, twelve years earlier, that 'his only errand' on the island 'was to visit the Pretender's conductress'.[49] Further, Macdonald reminded his correspondent, Boswell had then 'deemed every moment as lost which was not spent in her company'.[50] Flora had once been castigated by Lord Macdonald's mother, Lady Margaret, as a 'foolish girl' for bringing the Prince and 'trouble' to Skye.[51] Now her son rehearsed to Boswell the reasons why the Kingsburghs' emigration was in no part owing to his avarice as a landlord.[52] The good name of Flora Macdonald, as well as Boswell's own, was at stake, and her champion felt duty bound to issue the following challenge: 'Mr Boswell desires the honour of a personal meeting [duel] with Lord M in the ring in

Hyde Park at three o'clock this day [10 December 1785].'[53] At the eleventh hour, and to the relief of all, a compromise was effected, and no such 'personal meeting' took place.

The Sleat family, living all year in London, no longer had power to do Flora harm since she was no longer mistress of a tack on their land. Leading a vagabond existence on the Long Island and on Skye, she may have been saddened by Boswell's references in the *Journal* to a time when she and Allan could afford generous hospitality to visitors at a house once graced by royalty. In time, however, Flora was to turn to advantage the interest in her present circumstances which this publication evoked.

17

Royal Pensioner
1785–March 1790

For all the renewal of interest in Flora's exploits with the Prince
and curiosity about her meeting with Dr Johnson generated by
Boswell's *Journal*, she was still dependent on the charity of her
relations on Skye and on the Long Island. She and Allan, however,
hoped for a considerable amount from the 'memorial' that he
submitted to the government in February 1785. Claiming £1,341
for the loss of the Cheek's Creek farms and Macdonald possessions
there, and a little under £300 more for the outlay on raising and
arming his fellow Highlanders for the march to the coast in 1776,
the petitioner characterised himself as 'an old worn out officer ...
having ... an old wife, a daughter [Fanny] and himself to support
with only a very small income [regimental half-pay]'. Informing
the 'Honourable Commissioners [of American Claims]' that he
intended to return to his bounty lands in Nova Scotia, he declared
that the sum he sought would 'contribute to make his living easy
in his old days' there.[1] Presumably, he envisaged sending home to
Skye some portion of the profit he meant to reap there for the
maintenance of his wife and Fanny.

Flora's financial situation was not destined to improve
dramatically, nor did her husband obtain funds for further
agricultural improvements on the Kennetcook River. At a hearing
later that year Allan was awarded only £440 for his losses of land

and other property in North Carolina. Furthermore, the Audit Office determined that he had been reimbursed 'at different times' by Martin in New York for a part or the whole of what he claimed for mustering and equipping his fellow Scots for the march to the coast. The Commissioners declined to pay more.[2] It was a savage blow. Allan abandoned his plan to return to Nova Scotia, reckoning that he could not live 'easy' there on the income from this £440 and on half-pay, while taming his allotted bounty lands. He appears to have raised some further capital, however, disposing of his Douglas acreage to the Commission, as it was later reserved for the use of one of their number.[3] Leaving other Scots to petition further in Lincoln's Inn Fields, he undertook the journey north to Skye.

Upon his arrival there, Flora at least had the happiness of having a husband home to whom she remained devoted, and from whom she had been apart for six years. It was not in the character of this staunch Christian wife to be disappointed in her husband, and the couple had an understanding born of thirty-five years of marriage. Henceforward Flora spent less time on the Long Island where her brother had been her protector. Allan wished to be among his own kin on Skye. Referring to two advantageous matches that a McAllister niece and nephew had made there, he had written earlier that the island would be 'a good place to live on with so many young lairds'.[4] The fond uncle may have entertained hopes of subsidies from his young relations. Rather, Flora had her youngest son to thank for the 'abode' which she and Allan secured in 1787.

John Macdonald was making a fine career in the Bengal Engineers, a cadre charged by the East India Company with fortification duties in the Presidency of Bengal. Stationed at Bencoolen on the west coast of Sumatra in 1783, he was soon also given command of artillery duties at Fort Marlboro there. Marriage to a widow – 'the best of women', he told his mother in 1786 – and the birth of two daughters, however, provided short-lived happiness.[5] All three died within months of each other in a climate hostile to Europeans. Widowed, childless, Johnny relied henceforward for company and friendship on his fellow officers and worked tirelessly to advance his career. Appointed to head the garrison artillery, he proved also to be an able surveyor of the island's coast and those of other imperial possessions.[6]

Though living so far distant from his family on Skye, the young widower was painfully aware of his mother's financial woes there. He was to acknowledge, 'The latter part of the life of Flora Macdonald was marked by pecuniary embarrassments, which her son felt it his inclination, as well as his duty, to relieve, at least in proportion to his then very slender means.'[7] While on a voyage to Calcutta in May 1787, he wrote to his mother, 'I have ordered £100 to be given to you immediately for your and Fanny's use and £40 to Anny [Annie]. I have also ordered two-thirds of the interest of £1400 to be given to you annually and the other one third to Anny. If Fanny marries with her parents' consent, she is to have £100.'[8]

It is notable that John pursued these arrangements with his mother rather than with his father, although he may have been unsure whether the latter was as yet in Skye. In any event, following this bounty from his generous son, Allan leased Peinduin, a small tack on the Macdonald estate on the Trotternish peninsula.[9] Flora had a home once more on Skye, even if one where she must count every penny. A visitor who had known her when mistress of Kingsburgh was to observe with sorrow that she now lived in 'contracted circumstances'.[10] The gabled farmhouse overlooking Loch Snizort was not without its charms. Annie and Lochbay at Dunvegan were within easy reach across the water. Moreover, two of Flora's three sons now living were among those many Skye men who had returned to the island from America. Another, Donald Macdonald of Cuidreach, who had once been his grandfather Armadale's heir in North Carolina, now married his cousin Fanny.[11]

Flora, who had been vigilant in furthering her seven children's prospects since the early 1770s, could at last relax her guard. Remembering those two sons in their watery graves, she wore a locket inscribed 'In memory of my two beloved sons, Lieut. Alex. and Capt. Ranald Macdonald'.[12] Only Johnny was in harm's way in Sumatra, where '[malarial] fevers and consumption [tuberculosis]' accounted for the lives of scores of officers and men at Fort Marlboro in the years he was stationed there.[13]

Flora's life with Allan, however, was plagued by poor health as well as by financial hardship. She wrote, in 1789, when she was about sixty-seven, of having a 'cast [displaced fracture]' in both her arms, and she continued to suffer from painful 'rheumatism'. Allan, she recounted, had 'totally lost the use of his legs'.[14] Long gone were the days when visitors had trekked to Kingsburgh to pay homage to Flora, and when her now crippled husband had enthusiastically introduced into the island those 'three different sorts of potatoes' and a 'large brood of sheep'.[15]

Gone too were those years when Allan, in desperate financial straits, wrote, 'Was there anything in the world [in the way of employment] thrown in my way ... I would cheerfully submit to any slavery ...'[16] Now the ministrations of the couple's children and of younger members of their wider family were gratefully received at Peinduin, whose inhabitants were fading fast. Flora's younger Lochbay granddaughter, Mary Macleod, would long preserve souvenirs associated with her grandmother's Hebridean adventure with the Prince.[17] Other descendants treasured a pearl brooch said to contain her hair and that of the Prince, her wedding ring and silver utensils and receptacles engraved with her monogram.[18] Visitors have long pored over a pair of Flora's stays, 'worn and tattered', exhibited in a glass case at Dunvegan Castle. Miss Mary, their custodian, presented them to the Macleod of her day. Most poignant of all souvenirs of Flora's later life is a simple copper brooch which she gave to a young servant girl on the Long Island, and who handled it with pride till her death.[19]

Flora's once full life had dwindled, and she existed in a world of pain. Friends and family, however, later declared that she 'retained to the last that vivacity of character and that amiableness of disposition by which she was always distinguished.'[20]

In striking contrast, Charles Edward Stuart continued to alienate well-wishers with exhibitions of debauched and drunken behaviour in Florence and Rome. It was left to Charlotte, Duchess of Albany, his illegitimate daughter, to care for her father till his death at the latter place in January 1788. Following the 'Forty-five, he had never afterwards given thought, much less monetary reward, to one who had guided him, as Flora's son John was to declare, 'through multiplied perilous and hair-breadth escapes' and saved his life 'at the risk of her own.'[21] A year after that Prince's death, however, a member of the House of Brunswick was to prove Flora's unlikely champion. According to her son John, George, Prince of Wales came to hear 'accidentally' in London of the Bengal Engineer's recent provision for his mother. 'Rising superior to every narrow prejudice', the proud officer continued, this Hanoverian Prince 'nobly remarked that this remarkable woman [Flora] rescued from destruction a member of his family'. The royal scion, John wrote, forthwith 'settled a pension on her for life, from the privy purse'.[22]

While this tale of a youthful prince, more famous at this time for his romantic entanglements than for royal largesse, may appear fanciful, it is little more than the truth. George, Prince of Wales, afterwards Regent and King, had a keen sense of history and was alive, as were other members of his family, to slurs on the Hanoverian House as upstart rulers of the United Kingdom. At his death, Charles Edward Stuart had left no legitimate children. His brother Henry was barred, as a cardinal, from siring legitimate children and was now the last of the ancient Stuart dynasty. But even before this prelate's death the Hanoverian Crown began to claim Stuart history as its own. The pension that the Prince of Wales now afforded Flora, a year after Charles Edward's death, was a first graceful gesture. The traitorous nature of her 'escapes' with the Prince in 1746 was glossed over.

How did the Prince of Wales in London come to hear 'accidentally' of Flora's penury in the Hebrides and of her son John's efforts to ameliorate her finances? The skeins of Scottish kinship, ever a tangle, connect Prince and impoverished gentlewoman. Sir John Macpherson, a Skye man and administrator in Bengal in the 1780s, was the superior of Flora's son out east. Returning to the United Kingdom, and while on a spring visit in 1789 to his Highland birthplace, the baronet renewed an earlier acquaintance with Flora in the Trotternish peninsula. She appears to have been frank with him about the low ebb of her fortunes at Peinduin and to have made known to him her ill health.[23]

Macpherson was intimate with the Prince of Wales at this time and informed the Hanoverian heir in London of 'various interesting particulars relative to the celebrated Flora Macdonald'. The Prince was 'strongly affected' by this recital. When the baronet added that this interesting person was 'still living and in contracted circumstances, he [the Prince] instantly after' expressed 'his surprise and concern'. The Prince ordered Macpherson to 'wait on her in his name and to inform her that he should allow her a pension of fifty pounds for her life. "I make you the paymaster of my allowances", he continued, "and I rely on your carrying [taking] it to her." '24

Flora told Sir John in October 1789 that she sent up 'constant prayers to the Almighty to bliss [bless], protect and be your guide and director'. Her purpose in writing to him on the 21st of that month was to dispatch two long documents which he was later to endorse as 'Memorial of Mrs Macdonald Kingsburgh'. Her covering letter hints at the Prince's interest: 'Honoured dear Sir, Receive enclosed the papers you were so very good as to desire me to send you. I hope they are to the purpose, being exact truth. They are longer than I would wish, but shorter I could not make them.' Her hands stiff with rheumatism, Flora ended, 'Dear Sir, I ever am yours affectionately, while [still] able to sign ...'25

In the first document Flora provided, at the baronet's request, an account of her part in the 'Forty-five. Her adventures with the Prince appear as fresh in this narrative as if they had occurred weeks rather than over forty years earlier. The narrative opens: 'Miss Flora Macdonald was on a visit to her brother in South Uist, June 1746, when Prince Charles came to that country ... The Colonel [the Prince's Irish companion, Felix O'Neill] ... came to her to a sheiling of her brother's where she stayed and being about midnight sent in a cousin of her own [Neil MacEachen] to awake her ...'26

Over the course of ten pages, Flora reminisced about that passage to Skye, fraught with danger from the elements and from government militia: 'The night was dark and rainy. About daybreak it cleared up and they found themselves on the point [off the headland] of Waternish in Skye, where there was a party of militia stationed to intercept any boats that would come from the Long Island. They were so near the shore that they saw the men armed …'[27]

In the second document which Flora enclosed to Sir John in London, she wrote at equal length of her emigration and tribulations during the American Revolution and concluded in spirited fashion: 'The cast [twisted fractures] in both my arms are living monuments of my sufferings and distresses. And the long jail confinement which my husband underwent has brought on such disorders that he has totally lost the use of his legs. So that I may fairly say, we both have suffered in our person, family and interest, as much if not more than any two going under the name of refugees or loyalists – without the smallest [government] recompense.'[28]

Phenomenal as was the effort to recall events in searing detail from years before, welcome as was the prospect of a pension from the Prince of Wales, Flora yet seized the opportunity one last time to promote her children's interests. 'My husband had a letter from my John lately,' she told Macpherson. Her son was, she wrote, 'so ill in his passage from Calcutta to Bencoolen [on Sumatra] for two months, but is now, thank God, well and on the surveying business. I need not desire you to mention his name to any of the [East India] Directors you are acquainted with.' For her own part, she wrote, 'I am always oppressed with the rheumatism etc. since I saw you.'[29]

Flora had negotiated vicissitudes of fortune with the same courage with which she met physical danger. Lately she had achieved recognition in the literary world and now won a royal pension. Furthermore, the crusading Sir John, while on a subsequent visit to Italy, apparently mentioned 'the name of Flora' to Cardinal Henry of York. The Stuart prelate, according to Flora's son John, 'passed a high eulogium on the character of Flora, and unequivocally hinted, that could she be induced to change her religious tenets' – become a Catholic – 'he would grant her a splendid pension'.[30] She was not to learn, however, of this compliment or the conditional offer; she remained until death firm in the Presbyterian faith of her fathers.

Flora had not now long to live. The following year her life of intrepid adventure, celebrity and indigence came to an end on 4 March. She 'was taken suddenly ill with an inflammatory complaint', and the ailment 'refused to yield to all the medical skill available at that time'.[31] That medical skill was probably provided by Dr John Maclean, who was long the 'surgeon in Trotternish' and had once witnessed Flora's marriage contract. He wrote to his son on 24 March, 'Nothing has occurred since I wrote you, except the death of the famous Mrs Flora Macdonald, sometime of Kingsburgh. She suffered much distress for a long time …'[32] Annie Macleod was to tell a student of her mother's life, 'She possessed all her mental faculties to the very last, and calmly departed in the presence of her husband and two daughters.'[33] She 'died, as she lived, one of the best of Christians, of mothers, and of women, and a zealous member of the [Protestant] Church', her son John was to write.[34] The bedsheet on which the Prince had slept at Kingsburgh and which Flora had 'religiously and faithfully preserved' till now served as her shroud.[35]

The *Scots Magazine* informed its readers that Flora, 'spouse to Captain Allan Macdonald, late of Kingsburgh', was no more. The English press in April harked back instead to her earlier youth. 'Died … on the 4th ult. in the isle of Skye Mrs Flora Macdonald, famous in the annals of the late Pretender' read one of many similar paragraphs in different newspapers. The *European Magazine* added, '[See Mr Boswell's Tour.]'[36] It remained for those who had known and loved Flora to mourn her passing on a heroic scale. Her remains were conveyed after dark from Peinduin to Kingsburgh, a tack whose lease the Cuidreachs acquired that same year,[37] by a party of stalwart pallbearers. One among them was later to remember the 'dreadful' storm which broke above them as the coffin swayed over the rough ground. 'The night was pitch-dark except when the frequent flashes of lightning spread a momentary gleam over the scene. The thunder rolled with terrific peals. The rain fell in gushing torrents.'[38]

When the journey was at last effected and Flora had lain 'in state' some days at Kingsburgh, the procession of mourners, following the coffin to its burial further north, was 'more than a mile in length'. In the cemetery of Kilmuir, 'within a square piece of coarse wall', which enclosed earlier Kingsburgh tombs, the coffin was interred, while a dozen pipers played the 'Coronach', that 'melancholy lament for departed greatness'.[39]

At the wake that followed, island lore relates, 'Upwards of three hundred gallons' of whisky were consumed.[40] Under the verdant turf in the Kilmuir graveyard, which affords peerless views out over the Minch to the Long Island, Flora's remains lie to this day. The Gaelic blessing for travellers, so often spoken at Highland funerals, is an appropriate envoi:

> May the road rise up to meet you,
> May the wind be always at your back.
> May the sun shine warm upon your face;
> The rains fall soft upon your fields; and until we meet again,
> May God hold you in the palm of his hand.[41]

18

'Speed, Bonnie Boat, Like a Bird on the Wing' The Story

The 'Skye Boat Song', that haunting serenade, is sung the world over:

> Speed, bonnie boat, like a bird on the wing,
> Onward! the sailors cry;
> Carry the lad that's born to be king
> Over the sea to Skye.

Thousands, if not millions, in consequence know vaguely that Flora accompanied the Stuart Prince on a perilous sea voyage to Skye:

> Loud the winds howl, loud the waves roar,
> Thunderclaps rend the air ...

Many who sing those lines have no notion that four local men, and not Miss Macdonald herself, were at the oars of the vessel and a fifth at the helm. Has anyone ever remained so famous so long thanks to a single boat ride undertaken? Or was there something singular in the character that Flora displayed when acting as 'the Prince's preserver' and at other times that stays in the mind?

In the years following her interment at Kilmuir, interest in Flora Macdonald's story did not recede nor did the memories of those who had known her fade. While Allan survived his wife by only two years, their daughter Annie Macleod was eighty when she died a widow on Skye in 1834.[1] When a public appetite for all things Scottish developed in the 1820s, that island became a focus of Highland tours. 'Mrs Major' Macleod and her unmarried daughter, 'Miss Major' (Mary) Macleod, were on hand to reminisce in spirited fashion about their mother and grandmother. Alexander Macgregor, a scholarly minister, based much of his popular *Life of Flora Macdonald* (1882) on intelligence given him earlier by these ladies.[2]

Annie's younger brother John, who survived until 1831, was as imbued with filial piety as his sister. Publishing observations on military, scientific and other subjects while in Sumatra and after his return to England in 1796, he found recognition as a Fellow of the Royal Society and founding member of the Royal Asiatic Society.[3] Mrs Grant of Laggan, who in 1808 published a celebrated poem, *The Highlanders*, addressed these 'Lines' to a son whose potential his mother had so long before recognised when he was at the Portree Grammar School:

> Let those of wealth and empty titles proud
> Dazzle with idle pomp the vulgar crowd;
> 'Tis thine a nobler ancestry to boast,
> For courage famed, for virtue honoured most.
> …
> Such honours deck the gentle heroine's name,
> Who now to thee bequeaths her well-won fame.[4]

Acknowledging his debt, John paid for a marble gravestone to be engraved with the names of other forebears buried at Kilmuir and of his mother: 'who died March 1790, aged 68, a name that will be mentioned in history, and if courage and fidelity be virtues, be mentioned with honour'.[5] This slab, with its Johnsonian tribute, was duly installed in the Kingsburgh plot on Skye, although it had been fractured while being brought ashore after a long voyage north. 'In a few months every fragment had been carried off by relic-hunting tourists devoid of any sense of decency,' a later, scandalised visitor to the cemetery reported.[6] Over the years, a 'complete harvest of nettles' came to obscure Flora's last resting place, a state of affairs periodically lamented in newspapers and magazines as a national outrage.[7] While 'Miss Major' Macleod, born in the year of revolution in North Carolina, did not die on Skye until 1858, she lacked the funds to erect any lasting monument to her grandmother. 'Flora Macdonald's Lament', published in 1831 by James Hogg, the 'Ettrick Shepherd', seemed all too apt:

> The conflict is past and our name is no more
> There's nought left but sorrow for Scotland and me.[8]

Nevertheless, those on South Uist and Benbecula held their illustrious kinswoman's memory dear, as well as those of others concerned in the 'Forty-five. Echoes of that desperate time sounded in June 1825 when Étienne Macdonald, Marshal of France and Duc de Taranto, wrote in his diary: 'We are now under sail and heading for the Hebrides on a fair wind and choppy seas ... The purpose of my journey is to see the house where my father [Neil Macdonald, formerly MacEachen] was born, the cave where he hid with Prince Charles for three weeks, as well as what is left of our family.'[9]

The French Macdonald had imbibed in his youth in Sedan stories of his father's adventures with the Prince and Flora. Now at the MacEachen tack on South Uist he distributed sovereigns, pensions and a cask of whisky to newfound relations.[10] He was delighted to find that those events so dear to him were 'so present to the inhabitants' memory, that it seems they just happened yesterday'.[11] When climbing Glen Corradale with these 'countrymen', the Frenchman reflected: 'It is in these caves that Flora Macdonald, famed in history for her generous self-sacrifice, came to visit the Prince and took him over to Skye.'[12] In this error, he followed the narrative of Mrs Grant's *The Highlanders*:

Then to the cavern'd rock unseen she [Flora] steals,
And to the hapless PRINCE obsequious kneels …
With silent wonder, long the PRINCE survey'd
The beauteous guest, then thus: – 'Heroic maid,
'That com'st in pity to this secret cave,
'Unvisited, save by the rolling wave,
'To thy fair faith my wanderings I resign …'[13]

One of Flora's Milton great-nieces, married to a Uist minister, informed the Marshal that she had known her aunt 'quite well' before the latter's death thirty-five years earlier. 'She [Flora] was enthusiastic about her devotion to the Prince,' noted Macdonald, summarising her information. 'Had a lot of children. I am shown two of her portraits which bore a strong likeness.'[14] The Marshal slept that night at Nunton in what he was assured was 'the very room in which the celebrated and lovely Flora Macdonald slept'. The cutter in which he then embarked for Skye, he was told, 'took the very course which Prince Charles Stuart, attended by the celebrated Miss Flora Macdonald, took in sailing from Uist to Kingsburgh'.[15]

The past continued 'present to the inhabitants' memory' on South Uist in the decades that succeeded the Marshal's visit. Alexander Carmichael, Highland folklorist, confided to his field books in the 1860s and 1870s the lively reminiscences of those he questioned. In their minds Flora's grandfather, Angus Og, was still 'a celebrated soldier'.[16] They reported enthusiastically: 'Blood is [still] seen on the floor of the dining room at Cara,' where Flora's elder brother had died while she was still a girl.[17] The folklorist received as a present the fan that Lady Primrose had once given Flora in London,[18] and sketched the copper brooch which she herself had given her servant girl after the American war.[19] Pride in Flora's reputed birth on the island continues strong on South Uist to this day. In 1953 the Edinburgh and Glasgow Societies of Clan Donald inaugurated a 'cairn of remembrance' to their 'kinswoman' at Milton, which bears this inscription: 'She was born in 1722 near this place and spent her early years in the house that stood on this foundation.'[20]

While Flora lived for several years after her return from America at Milton, the tack at Balivanich on Benbecula was the family's principal residence during the long winter months when she was young. She would recognise there now only the ancient ruins of St Columba's Church. However, Nunton, the Clanranald seat, still stands and, in the bay below, Atlantic waves still wash the white strand. Although so much time has elapsed, those dangerous days in which Flora and Lady Clan sewed Betty Burke's vast garments at the latter's house come powerfully to the mind of the meditative visitor.

Flodigarry, that tack where Flora began married life, still stands on Skye,[21] although an avenue of trees alone marks the location of the Kingsburgh House of her time.[22] Her burial place on the island was at last accorded due honour when a tall 'Iona [Celtic] cross' was raised by public subscription in 1871.[23] Shortly afterwards, however, this monument was sundered in two by a gale. The damage was 'none too skilfully repaired' and within years 'a rank growth of nettles and weeds' once more festered in the plot.[24] A sturdier cross and a granite gravestone, again recording Dr Johnson's words, were installed a few years later. Rededicated in 1922, the bicentennial year of her birth, Flora's troubled grave site has now been a century at rest.[25]

A stained-glass window in the Episcopalian church in Portree, dedicated in 1896 and the gift of a descendant, commemorates Flora's 'risking her life for both the Houses of Stuart and Hanover'.[26] Further afield, Flora's portraits, taken from life, have long hung in British museums and galleries, including the Scottish National Portrait Gallery in Edinburgh, the Ashmolean Museum in Oxford and the National Portrait Gallery in London.[27] In each of these likenesses, her steady gaze, as much as the Jacobite emblems which adorn her dress, is compelling. And in Dr Johnson's house in the latter city, now a museum, there hangs a scene painted long after the encounter depicted took place. Flora, elegant in a rose-pink dress and jewellery, forever commands the attention of Dr Johnson and Boswell, seated at her tea table at Kingsburgh.[28] In her native Highlands, fittingly,

Flora is most powerfully represented. Her statue in bronze has guarded the front of Inverness Castle since the 1890s.[29] Portrayed as a young woman with a sheepdog at her side and a hand raised to shield her eyes, she gazes down Loch Ness towards the western seaboard of Scotland where she came to fame.

In North Carolina Flora's adventures in the American Revolution have always been afforded a respect granted to few other loyalists, and traces of her residence in that state are prized. A stone records the location of the Kingsburghs' home on Cheek's Creek, and her worship at Barbecue Church in Cumberland County is proudly remembered.[30] More recently, Diana Gabaldon set *A Breath of Snow and Ashes* (2005), the sixth of her time-travelling *Outlander* novels, in revolutionary North Carolina. Rich use is made in the chapter entitled 'Flora Macdonald's Barbecue' of material relating to the 'Forty-five and to the Kingsburghs' travails in America.[31] And historical markers in the state include the following in Fayetteville, formerly Cross Creek: 'Near this spot the Scottish heroine bade farewell to her husband, Allan Macdonald of Kingsburgh, during the march-out of his Highland troops to the battle of Moore's Creek Bridge, February 1776.'[32]

This loyalist Scot was afforded further recognition when the North Carolina Museum of Art acquired and displayed in the lobby at its 1956 inauguration in Raleigh her portrait by the eighteenth-century British artist Joseph Highmore.[33] Those glittering glass and rhinestone shoe buckles, bestowed by Flora on the Dunbidin sisters in Wilmington when she embarked for New York, and her monogrammed silver are to be found in the North Carolina Museum of History.[34]

Generations of young women, moreover, enjoyed higher education, learned Highland dancing and imbibed Presbyterian values at a college in Red Springs, North Carolina, given the name of Flora Macdonald College during the First World War.[35] Highland Games, inaugurated in 1978, following bicentennial celebrations of the Revolution, occupied the historic college campus for a number of years. The estate resounded to the music of bagpipes and drums, cabers were tossed, hammers thrown

and 'Flora Macdonald's Fancy' danced.[36] Highland Games now
continue elsewhere in the state under other names. In the twenty-
first century, however, a wider appreciation in America of the part
played by women and loyalists in the Revolution has seen a renewal
of focus on Flora Macdonald as a woman of purpose in North
Carolina, not least in the Museum of the American Revolution in
Philadelphia, founded in 2017.[37]

Flora's grave, now well tended, was lost to view at times beneath
a wilderness of nettles and weeds. So too her story has sometimes
been obscured in the public imagination, only to find the light once
more. This incomplete tally of monuments, windows, markers,
statues and portraits in the United Kingdom and in America does
not include china, locks of hair, rings and other items prized in
public and private collection for their association with her. It does,
however, make clear that the urgency to commemorate Flora's
character and her story and the desire to commit funds to such a
project have swelled and ebbed over two centuries. Often heightened
interest in her life has been in response to the publication of a work
of literature, the result of an author meditating on some aspect of
the 'Forty-five.

Walter Scott had known as a child in the Scottish Borders
'respected acquaintances' who had been 'out in the 'Forty-five'. He
was to recall 'their little idolatry of locks of hair, pictures, rings,
ribands [ribbons], and other memorials of the time in which they
still seemed to live'.[38] In 1808, by then a celebrated poet, he told a
friend, 'I became a valiant Jacobite at the age of ten years old; and,
even since reason and reading came to my assistance, I have never
quite got rid of the impression which the gallantry of Prince Charles
made on my imagination … I have always thought of a Highland
poem before hanging my harp on the willows.' He mused, 'Perhaps
it would be no bad setting for such a tale to suppose it related for
his [the Prince's] amusement, in the course of his wanderings after
the fatal field of Culloden. Flora Macdonald, Kingsburgh, Lochiel
… and many other characters … might be introduced.' The author
considered that the time was 'now passed away when the theme
would have had both danger and offence in it'.[39]

In the event, Scott abandoned poetry and published anonymously *Waverley*, a historical novel, which took the world by storm in 1814.[40] In that work, Edward Waverley, a young Englishman at the time of the 'Forty-five, falls under the spell of Flora MacIvor and signs up as a volunteer in the Prince's army under the command of her brother Fergus, a Highland chief. Scott's portrait of the young Highland woman upon her introduction to Waverley draws much on the appearance and character which the author ascribed to Flora Macdonald: 'at Glennaquoich', the MacIvor seat, 'every other sort of expenditure was retrenched as much as possible, for the purpose of maintaining, in its full dignity, the hospitality of the Chieftain …' Flora MacIvor's dress was arranged 'in a manner which partook partly of the Parisian fashion and partly of the more simple dress of the Highlands', and she 'bore a most striking resemblance to her brother Fergus … They had the same antique and regular correctness of profile; the same dark eyes, eye-lashes, and eye-brows; the same clearness of complexion …'[41] Early education had 'impressed upon her mind', as well as on that of her brother, 'the most devoted attachment to the exiled family of Stuart. She believed it the duty of her brother, of his clan, of every man in Britain, at whatever personal hazard, to contribute to that restoration which the partisans of the Chevalier St. George [James Edward Stuart] had not ceased to hope for. For this she was prepared to do all, to suffer all, to sacrifice all …'[42]

Most poignant, in consequence, is Flora's remorse when anticipating Fergus's execution the following day in the wake of the Rising: 'there is, Mr. Waverley, there is a busy devil at my heart that whispers – but it were madness to listen to it – that the strength of mind on which Flora prided herself has murdered her brother!' Her brother, she reflects, 'as volatile as ardent, would have divided his energies amid a hundred objects. It was I who taught him to concentrate them and to gage all on this dreadful and desperate cast … I spurred his fiery temper, and half of his ruin at least lies with his sister!'[43]

Flora MacIvor, as much a victim of her fanatical Jacobitism as her brother, is at once modelled on Flora Macdonald and a far cry from that rational woman, whose devotion to the Prince, though real, did not preclude a firm, if disastrous, attachment to the ruling House of Hanover when in North America. Regardless, following the immense success of *Waverley*, whose publication coincided with the close of the Napoleonic Wars, public interest in the Jacobite struggle revived.

In 1822 Scott masterminded a momentous 'King's Jaunt'.[44] George IV, recently crowned king, first of the Hanoverian sovereigns to visit Scotland, entered Holyroodhouse Palace in Edinburgh attired in an enormous kilt and flesh-coloured stockings.[45] Few did not contrast the corpulent and aged monarch with the slim Prince who had filled the ancestral Stuart seat with Jacobite supporters eighty years before. The mood, however, was festive. Highland chiefs and Lowland lairds alike donned plaid, bonnet and *skhian dubh* for the King's delectation. 'Stanzas for the King's Landing' – at Leith – and other paeans celebrated the union of Stuart and Hanoverian blood in the royal veins:

> Float fairly from Dun-Edin's brow,
>   Primeval pennon of his fathers;
> Nor tears nor blood shall stain thee now,
>   No gloom around thy blazon gathers.
> From Saxon firm and fiery Gael,
>   From moor and mart, from cot and hall,
> One voice, one heart, goes forth to hail
>   The King – the Sire of All.[46]

As part and parcel of this visit, the King and his government were eager to spread balm in the shape of pensions for the families of certain former Jacobites. Flora Macdonald had enjoyed that belated royal pension of £50 when the monarch was Prince of Wales. Sir John Macpherson, who paid it, later told a friend, 'She died at the end of two years but his Royal Highness entirely forgot to reimburse me, and the annuity came out of my own pocket.'[47] Now Flora's elder Lochbay granddaughter, a widow living quietly in Nairn, was amazed to receive an intimation from Sir Robert Peel, the Home Secretary, that she was granted a royal pension of the same sum.[48] Mrs Flora Mackay penned grateful thanks. Whether justified or not, her strong belief, as she informed a visiting poet in 1839, was that the £50 annuity was secured 'through the interest of Sir W. Scott'.[49]

The King returned to London, well satisfied with his reception north of the Border. Sir Walter Scott remained interested in Flora's character and story all his life. Acquiring her contract of marriage to Allan, he later dwelt, in *Tales of a Grandfather* – narratives from Scottish and French history written for the edification of the young – on Flora's 'spirit and presence of mind' during her adventures with the Prince. He remarked too 'The simplicity and dignity of her character' when Lady Primrose's honoured guest in London: 'She never thought she had done anything wonderful till she heard the world wondering at it.'[50]

Tourists now found majestic and wild the mountains and moors in the Highlands which had been abused as desolate bog by Hanoverian officers in the 'Forty-five. Scottish airs too gained in popularity. 'Wha'll be King but Charlie?', 'Charlie is my Darling' and 'Bonnie Charlie's Noo Awa', songs composed by Carolina Oliphant, Lady Nairne in the early 1820s, enjoyed an immediate vogue.[51] For the 'Skye Boat Song' the world had to wait until 1884, when Sir Harold Boulton and Anne Campbell Macleod, later Lady Wilson, published it in *Songs of the North*. Macleod had earlier heard the plaintive air when rowers broke into a Gaelic song as they were ferrying her across a loch on Skye. Boulton provided the famous lyrics.[52]

On coming to the throne in 1837, Queen Victoria followed her uncle, George IV, in taking a keen interest in her Stuart forebears. After she and Prince Albert had purchased the Balmoral estate in Aberdeenshire, her affection for this Royal House quickened, although she gave little credence to the dynastic claims of the Sobieski Stuarts. These two antiquarian brothers alleged they were legitimate grandsons of Charles Edward Stuart, offspring of an imagined son by his Stolberg bride who been spirited away and had grown up under an alias for fear of assassination. 'Sobieski' alluded to the Prince's maternal descent from John Sobieski, King of Poland. The publication of the brothers' *Costumes of the Clans* in 1844, however, encouraged many, including the Queen and Prince Consort, to adopt or design differentiated tartans.[53] A romantic portrait of Flora wearing a print dress and tartan plaid, the gift of Edward and Alexandra, Prince and Princess of Wales, joined the Royal Collection in 1869 at the Queen's Highland home.[54] Nearly twenty years later, the stamp of Hanoverian approval was firmly accorded to the 'Forty-five. The then heir presumptive and his sister, two of the Waleses' children, took the parts of 'Prince Charlie' and 'Flora Macdonald' in a *tableau vivant*, mounted and photographed at Balmoral. 'Flora', draped in a tartan shawl, tends a cooking pot. 'Charlie' lies on an animal skin at her feet, while two 'Highlanders', one armed with a fearsome axe, keep watch.[55] Queen Victoria judged the *tableau*, based on *Édouard en Écosse*, the painting of the same scene by French artist Paul Delaroche, 'extremely pretty & correct'.[56]

With the foundation of the Scottish History Society in 1886 and its commitment to publishing original sources, a golden epoch dawned for those interested in the life of Flora Macdonald. The three volumes of *The Lyon in Mourning*, that oral and written testimony of Flora and others collected by Forbes, appeared in 1895–6, edited by Henry Paton, and the following year the Society brought out Walter Biggar Blaikie's *Itinerary of Prince Charles Edward Stuart from his Landing in Scotland July 1745 to his Departure in September 1746*. In 1916, again with the Society, Blaikie also published *Origins of the 'Forty-Five*, Neil's narrative of the Prince's adventures on the Long Island, while *Prisoners of the '45*, the work of Sir Bruce Gordon Seton and his daughter Jean and a valuable source for the captivity of Flora and others in 1746 and 1747, followed in 1928. Relevant correspondence and documents abound in many archives, but historians owe a great debt to all those named above, as they do to Henrietta Tayler, who in 1948 published in *A Jacobite Miscellany* the two autobiographical narratives that Flora composed in her late sixties.

Local historians as well as scholars mined muniment rooms and folk memories in these years. *The Clan Donald* (1896–1904), a remarkable history of Macdonald families spanning 600 years and written by two Highland ministers, Angus and Archibald Macdonald, gives details unobtainable elsewhere of Flora's ancestry and connections to other branches of the clan. The Skye minister Alexander Macgregor too had the privilege of access to Flora's daughter and granddaughter for his *The Life of Flora Macdonald* (1882). But as valuable as any other source for historians is Allan R. Macdonald's pithy *The Truth about Flora Macdonald* (1938). The author, a Skye resident for most of his life and learned in 'Forty-five lore, is as meticulous in his critique of previous biographies as he is careful in the documentary presentation of his own brief but rich narrative.

By the time that Macdonald wrote *The Truth*, the story of Flora Macdonald was long interwoven with the folklore and literature of the Highlands. Flora Macdonald Wylde, one of John Macdonald's daughters, turned author when she was left a widow in the 1850s. Her fictional *Autobiography of Flora MacDonald*, which she published in 1870, is an engaging amalgam of authentic Kingsburgh family documents, later published in *Memorials of the '45* (1930), family lore, imagination and snippets from other narratives about her illustrious namesake and grandmother.[57] As one who would later detail the doings of a tortoise in *The Life and Wonderful Adventures of 'Totty Testudo': An Autobiography* (1873), Mrs Wylde was prone to flights of fancy. On reaching London in 1746, poor 'Flora', passing with her maid Kate through 'the wicket gate of the portcullis', was led by warders to rooms in the 'dismal dark' Tower of London and feared she would only leave it for the scaffold. A visit from Frederick, Prince of Wales, who expressed royal admiration for her exploits, cheered her spirits during a later stay at William Dick's.[58] 'Flora' was also pressed to sing a song, of her own composition, at her wedding to Allan:

> Oh! hie to the Highlands, my laddie,
> Be welcomed by hearts warm and true,
> For that's where you'll see, my ain laddie,
> The tartans and bonnets of blue.

> Ye'll hear of the chieftains of old,
> Those sons of valour and worth;
> But Charlie's own favourite clan was
> Macdonald, the pride of the North![59]

In the fastness of a Swiss sanatorium in 1881, meanwhile, Robert Louis Stevenson contemplated writing a *History of the Highlands*, in which Rob Roy and Flora Macdonald were to be among the *dramatis personae*. The opportunity to study the works of Boswell and Johnson, of Scott and Mrs Grant of Laggan, in preparation for this task, appealed to him.[60] Although he abandoned this project, he was to pen, in 1892, alternative verses to the 'Skye Boat Song' lyrics:

> Sing me a song of a lad that is gone,
> Say, could that lad be I?
> Merry of soul he sailed on a day
> Over the sea to Skye …
>
> …
>
> Billow and breeze, islands and seas,
> Mountains of rain and sun,
> All that was good, all that was fair,
> All that was me is gone.[61]

In 2014 those lyrics were in their turn – after the substitution of 'lass' for 'lad' and 'she' for 'he' – after adaptation, to become the theme song for the TV dramatisation of Gabaldon's *Outlander* series.[62]

Flora Macdonald's life has been greatly examined, embroidered and repurposed during and since her lifetime. Even her hours of secretly sewing Betty Burke's costume at Nunton with Lady Clan attracted their own homage. Abel Morrall, an enterprising needle manufacturer in the late nineteenth century, launched 'The Flora Macdonald Needle Packet Containing Sharps, Crewel, Darners, Bodkin'. Thousands of these items, all embellished on the cover with a portrait of the Heroine, were sold throughout the British Empire for more than forty years.[63] In its own way, 'The Flora

Macdonald Needle Packet' was an appropriate tribute. Practical and serviceable, this haberdashery item held an undisputed place of importance in parlours and kitchens while imperial grandeur waxed and waned. Walker's Shortbread Ltd, established in 1898 in Speyside, still pays tribute to Flora. Ever since its centenary year, when it acquired George William Joy's painting *Flora Macdonald's Farewell*, that image has been incorporated into the heart of the company logo, surrounded by swathes of ribbon. Against a background of distinctive Walker tartan, Bonnie Prince Charlie bows over Flora's hand countless times on shortbread-biscuit tins the length of the Royal Mile in Edinburgh and in many other parts of the world.[64]

In an era before Scottish devolution, a British law lord opined in 1971:

Scotland is not a nation in the eye of international law, but Scotsmen [and women] constitute a nation by reason of those most powerful elements in the creation of national spirit: tradition, folk memory and a sentiment of community. The Scots are a nation because of Bannockburn and Flodden, Culloden and the [bag]pipes at Lucknow, because of Jenny Geddes [an exuberant Edinburgh parishioner who sparked a riot, harbinger of the English Civil War] and Flora Macdonald, because of frugal living and respect for learning, because of Robert Burns and Walter Scott.[65]

Contemporary Scotland has forged new traditions and folk memories, but the memories of its people are also long. Robert Burns never used his pen in praise of Flora Macdonald. However, her story and character bring to mind one of his most famous compositions, 'For A' That', which was sung lustily at the opening of the Scottish Parliament in 1998:

A prince can mak a belted knight,
A marquis, duke, an' a' that …
The pith o' sense, an' pride o' worth,
Are higher rank than a' that.[66]

Flora Macdonald had sense and worth above many of her peers, male and female. Living in extraordinary times in Scotland and in America, she responded to the exigencies of civil war on both sides of the Atlantic with intelligence and wit, in which she was sustained by a strong Presbyterian faith. To some degree she reflected, in her grave demeanour and steely character, the customs and manner of the remote Western Isles where she grew up. Her moral courage was all her own.

Abbreviations

Am Baile	Am Baile: Highland History and Culture, ambaile.org.uk
Ashmolean	Ashmolean Museum, Oxford
BL	British Library, London, UK
BL Add MSS	British Library Additional Manuscripts
BM	British Museum, London
BNJ	*British Numismatic Journal*
Carmichael-Watson	Carmichael-Watson Collection, Edinburgh University Library, Special Collections
CSRNC	Colonial and State Records of North Carolina, https://docsouth.unc.edu/csr/
HMC	Royal Commission on Historical Manuscripts
HoC	House of Commons, London
HSP	Historical Society of Pennsylvania
JCC	Journals of the Continental Congress, https://memory.loc.gov/ammem/amlaw/lwjclink.html
JSAHR	*Journal of the Society for Army Historical Research*
LDC	Letters of Delegates to Continental Congress
LOC	Library of Congress, Manuscript Division, http://www.loc.gov/rr/mss
NA	National Archives, London

NA ADM	Admiralty Papers, National Archives, London
NA AO 12	American Loyalists Claims, Series I, Audit Office, National Archives, London
NA AO 13	American Loyalists Claims, Series II, Audit Office, National Archives, London
NA CO	Colonial Office Papers, National Archives, London
NA SP	State Papers, National Archives, London
NA T 79	American Loyalist Claims Commission, Records, National Archives, London
NA TS	Treasury Solicitor and HM Procurator General, Papers, National Archives, London
NCHR	*North Carolina Historical Review*
NCMA	North Carolina Museum of Art, Raleigh, NC
NCMH	North Carolina Museum of History, Raleigh, NC
NLS	National Library of Scotland, Edinburgh
NLS MSS.3733–6	Papers of John Campbell of Mamore, later 4th Duke of Argyll, National Library of Scotland, Edinburgh
NLS MSS.1306–10	Delvine Papers: Mackenzies of Delvine correspondence with Macdonalds of Sleat and Kingsburgh, National Library of Scotland, Edinburgh
NPG	National Portrait Gallery, London
NRAS	National Register of Archives for Scotland
NRAS NRAS3273	Macdonald estate papers, Museum of the Isles, Armadale, Skye
N-Y Hist. Soc.	New-York Historical Society
PCC	Papers of the Continental Congress, 1774–1789, National Archives, USA: https://catalog.archives.gov/id/1938489
PMHB	*Pennsylvania Magazine of History and Biography*

QMMR	*Quarterly Musical Magazine and Review*
RA	Royal Archives, Windsor
RA CP	Cumberland Papers, Royal Archives, Windsor
RA SP	Stuart Papers, Royal Archives, Windsor
RA VIC/MAIN/QVJ(W)	Queen Victoria's Journal, Royal Archives, Windsor
RCT	Royal Collection Trust
SNPG	Scottish National Portrait Gallery, Edinburgh
TGSI	*Transactions of the Gaelic Society of Inverness*
Yale Univ., Gen MSS 89	Boswell Papers, Yale University, New Haven, CT
YATJ	*Yorkshire Archaeological and Topographical Journal*

Notes

I A FUGITIVE PRINCE: 1745–1746

1 Blaikie, ed., *Origins of the 'Forty-Five*, 235
2 Paton, ed., *Lyon in Mourning*, II: 95
3 Blaikie, ed., *Origins of the 'Forty-Five*, 249–50
4 Fergusson, *Argyll in the Forty-Five*, 13
5 Fraser, ed., *Earls of Cromartie*, I: ccxii
6 *London Gazette*, 3 August 1745, https://www.thegazette.co.uk/London/issue/8455/page/1
7 Tayler, ed., *Jacobite Miscellany*, 40–1
8 NA SP 54/26/32, Charles Edward Stuart to James Edward Stuart, 20 September 1745
9 Duff, ed., *Culloden Papers*, 415
10 Pittock, *Culloden*, 104
11 Walpole, *Correspondence*, XIX: 287–8
12 McLaren, *Lovat of the '45*, 198
13 McLynn, *Bonnie Prince Charlie*, 262 and n. 106
14 Juries Act 1745, 19 Geo. 2, c. 9
15 Act of Proscription 1746, 19 Geo. 2, c. 39
16 Blaikie, ed., *Origins of the 'Forty-Five*, 218
17 Ibid., 230
18 Nicholas, ed., 'Account of Proceedings', 206
19 Blaikie, ed., *Origins of the 'Forty-Five*, 238–9
20 Ibid., 241
21 Ibid.
22 Ibid.

23 Paton, ed., *Lyon in Mourning*, II: 97

24 Blaikie, ed., *Origins of the 'Forty-Five*, 243

25 Tayler, ed., *Jacobite Miscellany*, 185

26 Blaikie, ed., *Origins of the 'Forty-Five*, 244

27 Ibid., 246

28 Ibid., 248–9

29 Ibid., 249–50

30 Paton, ed., *Lyon in Mourning*, I: 80

31 Blaikie, ed., *Origins of the 'Forty-Five*, 250

2 ILL MET BY MOONLIGHT: JUNE 1746

1 Macdonald, *The Truth*, 98: Flora's age of sixty-eight was given in the public press at the time of her death – March 1790 – and when the month and year of her death were later engraved at the behest of her youngest son on a marble slab erected over her grave. This accords with a birth year of 1722 or 1723. Her father is said in *The Truth* to have died in the latter year and in Macdonald and Macdonald, eds, *Clan Donald*, III: 281 in 1725. For a sketch of the qualifications of the author of the former work to pronounce with authority on Flora Macdonald's family, see *The Truth*, i–xi. *Clan Donald*, III: 278–82 has valuable genealogical information in addition

2 [Anon.], 'A Treatise on the Harmonic System, by John Macdonald …', 463n.

3 Macdonald, *The Truth*, 2; Macdonald and Macdonald, eds, *Clan Donald*, III: 280–1; Paton, ed., *Lyon in Mourning*, I: 300

4 Macdonald, *The Truth*, 2–3 and n. 9

5 Macdonald, *The French Macdonald*, 12 and nn. 21–2, 112–13

6 Macgregor, *Life of Flora Macdonald*, 26–7; Macgregor, a Skye native born in 1806 and later minister there in the 1840s, had the advantage of knowing personally Flora's daughter and granddaughter, Anne and Mary Macleod

7 Macdonald, *The Truth*, 2. See Macgregor, *Life of Flora Macdonald*, 27, for a different account of the boy's death

8 Paton, ed., *Lyon in Mourning*, I: 116

9 Ibid.

10 Richard Wilson, *Flora Macdonald* (1747), NPG 5848; Richard Wilson, *Flora Macdonald* (1747), SNPG PG 1162; Allan Ramsay, *Flora Macdonald* (1749), Ashmolean WA1960.76

11 Paton, ed., *Lyon in Mourning*, I: 117
12 Macmillan, *Flora Macdonald of Benbecula*, 29–30 and nn. 18–19; Macdonald, *The Truth*, 3 and n. 9
13 Paton, ed., *Lyon in Mourning*, I: 304, 296
14 NLS MS.3736/469, Angus Macdonald: Declaration, 16 August 1746
15 Paton, ed., *Lyon in Mourning*, I: 296
16 NA SP 54/32/f. 16, Flora Macdonald: Declaration, 12 July 1746
17 Blaikie, ed., *Origins of the 'Forty-Five*, 251
18 Tayler, ed., *Jacobite Miscellany*, 185; Blaikie, ed., *Origins of the 'Forty-Five*, 251; Tayler, ed., *Jacobite Miscellany*, 189
19 Paton, ed., *Lyon in Mourning*, I: 110
20 Tayler, ed., *Jacobite Miscellany*, 185
21 Macdonald, ed., *Memorials*, xxviii: Appendix B (2)
22 Paton, ed., *Lyon in Mourning*, I: 117
23 Tayler, ed., *Jacobite Miscellany*, 185; Blaikie, ed., *Origins of the 'Forty-Five*, 251
24 Paton, ed., *Lyon in Mourning*, I: 117
25 Tayler, ed., *Jacobite Miscellany*, 39–41
26 Paton, ed., *Lyon in Mourning*, II: 99
27 Ibid., 95
28 Ibid., I: 106
29 Tayler, ed., *Jacobite Miscellany*, 185
30 Paton, ed., *Lyon in Mourning*, I: 296
31 Ibid., 21, 26, 297; Chambers, *History of the Rebellion*, II: 161–2
32 Blaikie, ed., *Origins of the 'Forty-Five*, 251
33 NA TS 11/1082/5623, John Maclean: Declaration, 30 June 1746
34 Blaikie, ed., *Origins of the 'Forty-Five*, 251
35 Paul Delaroche, *Édouard en Écosse* (1827), sold at auction, Christie's, 12 June 1996
36 Marshall, *Our Island Story*, 431
37 Blaikie, ed., *Origins of the 'Forty-Five*, 251
38 Paton, ed., *Lyon in Mourning*, I: 176
39 Blaikie, ed., *Origins of the 'Forty-Five*, 252
40 Paton, ed., *Lyon in Mourning*, I: 296
41 Ibid.
42 Ibid., 176
43 RA SP/MAIN/276/37, John O'Sullivan to Daniel O'Brien, 4 August 1746
44 Paton, ed., *Lyon in Mourning*, I: 297

45 Ibid., II: 32, 46
46 Ibid., I: 297
47 NLS MS.3736/432, Flora Macdonald: Declaration, 12 July 1746
48 Blaikie, ed., *Origins of the 'Forty-Five*, 252–3

3 'GREAT FEARS': JUNE 1746

 1 Paton, ed., *Lyon in Mourning*, I: 279–80; NA SP 54/34/38, Ranald Macdonald of Clanranald to unknown [Andrew Stone?], 8 December 1746
 2 Paton, ed., *Lyon in Mourning*, I: 297
 3 Ibid., II: 95
 4 Blaikie, ed., *Origins of the 'Forty-Five*, 253–6
 5 Ibid., 256
 6 Ibid.
 7 Paton, ed., *Lyon in Mourning*, I: 107; Blaikie, ed., *Origins of the 'Forty-Five*, 258
 8 Blaikie, ed., *Origins of the 'Forty-Five*, 257
 9 Ibid.
10 Paton, ed., *Lyon in Mourning*, II: 99
11 Ibid., I: 107
12 Ibid., 327
13 Ibid., II: 98
14 NA SP 54/32/f. 16, Flora Macdonald: Declaration, 12 July 1746
15 Blaikie, ed., *Origins of the 'Forty-Five*, 259
16 Paton, ed., *Lyon in Mourning*, I: 330
17 Blaikie, ed., *Origins of the 'Forty-Five*, 259
18 Paton, ed., *Lyon in Mourning*, II: 18 n. 1
19 Ibid., I: 297
20 NA SP 54/32/f. 16, Flora Macdonald: Declaration, 12 July 1746; Blaikie, *Origins of the 'Forty-Five*, 259
21 Paton, ed., *Lyon in Mourning*, I: 297
22 Blaikie, ed., *Origins of the 'Forty-Five*, 259
23 Ibid., 259–60
24 Ibid., 260
25 Ibid.
26 Paton, ed., *Lyon in Mourning*, I: 297
27 Ibid., II: 79
28 Ibid., 99, 253

29 Ibid., I: 297–8

30 Blaikie, ed., *Origins of the 'Forty-Five*, 260

31 Paton, ed., *Lyon in Mourning*, I: III

32 Blaikie, ed., *Origins of the 'Forty-Five*, 260

33 RA CP/MAIN/68/xi:37/30, Rory Macdonald: Declaration, 9 July 1746

34 Paton, ed., *Lyon in Mourning*, I: III

35 Blaikie, ed., *Origins of the 'Forty-Five*, 260

36 Burton, *A Genuine and True Journal*, 24

37 Ibid.

38 NA SP 54/32/f. 16, Flora Macdonald: Declaration, 12 July 1746

39 Burton, *A Genuine and True Journal*, 24

40 NA SP 54/32/f. 16, Flora Macdonald: Declaration, 12 July 1746

41 Blaikie, ed., *Origins of the 'Forty-Five*, 260–1

42 RA CP/MAIN/68/xi:37/30, Rory Macdonald: Declaration, 9 July 1746

43 Boulton and Macleod, eds, *Songs of the North*, I: 20

4 'A MAN IN A WOMAN'S DRESS': JUNE 1746

1 Wordsworth, *Last Poems*, 305–7

2 Mackay, ed., *Jacobite Songs and Ballads of Scotland*, 272–3

3 Blaikie, ed., *Origins of the 'Forty-Five*, 261

4 Paton, ed., *Lyon in Mourning*, I: III

5 Blaikie, ed., *Origins of the 'Forty-Five*, 261

6 Paton, ed., *Lyon in Mourning*, I: III

7 Ibid., 305

8 Ibid., III

9 Ibid., 305

10 Anon., *Alexis*, 10–12

11 Blaikie, ed., *Origins of the 'Forty-Five*, 261

12 Ibid.

13 Tayler, ed., *Jacobite Miscellany*, 186

14 RA CP/MAIN/68/xi:37/30, Rory Macdonald: Declaration, 9 July 1746

15 Blaikie, *Origins of the 'Forty-Five*, 262

16 Tayler, ed., *Jacobite Miscellany*, 186

17 Blaikie, ed., *Origins of the 'Forty-Five*, 262–3

18 Paton, ed., *Lyon in Mourning*, I: 300

19 Ibid., II: 17 n. 1

20 See NLS MS.1306/1-48, John Mackenzie of Delvine: correspondence with Alexander Macdonald of Kingsburgh, 1733–46

21 Macleod, ed., *Book of Dunvegan*, II: 41

22 Paton, ed., *Lyon in Mourning*, II: 13

23 Ibid.

24 RA CP/MAIN/68/xi:37/30, Rory Macdonald: Declaration, 9 July 1746

25 Paton, ed., *Lyon in Mourning*, II: 17 n. 1

26 Ibid., I: 300

27 Macdonald, ed., *Memorials*, xxi: Appendix B (2)

28 Paton, ed., *Lyon in Mourning*, II: 17 n. 1

29 Ibid., 13

30 RA CP/MAIN/68/xi:37/30, Rory Macdonald: Declaration, 9 July 1746; Chambers, *History of the Rebellion*, II, 163

31 RA CP/MAIN/17/144, John Macleod of Talisker to Lord Loudoun, 8 July 1746

32 Paton, ed., *Lyon in Mourning*, I: 300

33 Ibid., 300–1

34 Chambers, *History of the Rebellion*, II: 164–5

35 Paton, ed., *Lyon in Mourning*, I: 300–1

36 Mahon, *History of England*, II: 361

37 Blaikie, ed., *Origins of the 'Forty-Five*, 265

38 Chambers, *History of the Rebellion*, II: 165–6

39 Paton, ed., *Lyon in Mourning*, II: 117

40 Ibid., I: 117–19

41 Ibid., 121

42 Tayler, ed., *Jacobite Miscellany*, 187

43 Paton, ed., *Lyon in Mourning*, I: 301–2

44 Ibid., 119

45 Macdonald, *The Truth*, 44 and nn. 26–9

46 Macdonald, ed., *Memorials*, xxv: Appendix B (2)

47 Paton, ed., *Lyon in Mourning*, II: 75

48 Ibid., I: 112

49 Ibid., 76

50 Ibid., 81

51 Ibid., 302

5 'FAREWELL TO THE LAD': JULY 1746

1   Tayler, ed., *Jacobite Miscellany*, 187

2   Paton, ed., *Lyon in Mourning*, II: 18–19

3   Ibid., 19–21

4   Ibid., 22–3

5   Ibid., 21

6   Ibid., 17 n. 1

7   Ibid., 22

8   Ibid., 20

9   Ibid., 22

10 Ibid., 27

11 Ibid., 23

12 NLS MS.3736/420, Charles MacNab: Declaration, 9 July 1746; Paton, ed., *Lyon in Mourning*, II: 24

13 Paton, ed., *Lyon in Mourning*, II: 23

14 George William Joy, *Flora Macdonald's Farewell* (1891), held since 1997 at Walker's Shortbread Head Office, Aberlour on Spey, Scotland. See also Nicholson, *Bonnie Prince Charlie and the Making of Myth*, 142

15 Paton, ed., *Lyon in Mourning*, II: 25

16 Ibid., 25–6

17 Ibid., 26–7

18 NLS MS.3736/420, Charles MacNab: Declaration, 9 July 1746

19 [Hogg], *Songs by the Ettrick Shepherd*, 11–12

20 *Flora Macdonald's Lament*, Valentine card, Am Baile, ID: QZP40_CARD_2631, https://www.ambaile.org.uk/asset/34534/

21 NLS MS.3736/420, Charles MacNab: Declaration, 9 July 1746

22 Paton, ed., *Lyon in Mourning*, I: 302

23 Ibid., II: 32

24 Blaikie, ed., *Itinerary*, 55ff.

25 RA CP/MAIN/16/380, 'Mr Tolme' [Norman Macleod of Tolmie] to Norman Macleod of Macleod, 30 June 1746

26 NLS MS.3735/406, George Anderson to unknown, 3 July 1746

27 NLS MS.3736/411, General Campbell to Capt. Colin Campbell of Skipness, 5 July 1746

28 RA CP/MAIN/16/339, Duke of Cumberland to Duke of Newcastle, 26 June 1746

29 Paton, ed., *Lyon in Mourning*, II: 253

30 NLS MS.3735/409, 'A Detail of what has been done by the Party with Capt Fergusson, since ... July 4th 1746'

31 NA TS 11/1082/5623, John McLean: Declaration, 30 June 1746

32 NLS MS.3735/409, 'A Detail of what has been done by the Party with Capt Fergusson, since ... July 4th 1746'

33 RA CP/MAIN/17/144, John Macleod of Talisker to Lord Loudoun, 8 July 1746

34 Ibid.

35 Paton, ed., *Lyon in Mourning*, I: 303

36 Ibid., II: 31

37 Ibid., I: 303

38 RA CP/MAIN/17/248, Donald Macdonald of Castleton to Sir Alexander Macdonald, 11 July 1746

39 Paton, ed., *Lyon in Mourning*, I: 303

40 Ibid., II: 32

6 PRISONER ON THE *FURNACE*: JULY–AUGUST 1746

1 NLS MS.3736/421, Campbell of Mamore: Proclamation, 9 July 1746

2 NLS MS.3736/425, Campbell of Mamore to Duke of Cumberland, 10[–11] July 1746

3 NLS MS.3735/407, George Anderson to unknown, 3–27 July 1746

4 NLS MS.3736/420, Charles MacNab: Declaration, 9 July 1746

5 NLS MS.3736/425, Campbell of Mamore to Duke of Cumberland, 10[–11] July 1746

6 RA CP/MAIN/17/175, Norman Macleod of Macleod to Sir Alexander Macdonald, 10 July 1746

7 Ibid.

8 NLS MS.3736/436, Campbell of Mamore to Duke of Cumberland, 13 July 1746

9 NLS MS.3736/427, David Campbell to Campbell of Mamore, 11 July 1746

10 NLS MS.3736/428, Alexander Macdonald of Kingsburgh: Declaration, 11 July 1746

11 HMC, 11th Report (1887), Appendix, Part IV, 360–1

12 NLS MS.3736/425, Campbell of Mamore to Duke of Cumberland, 10[–11] July 1746

13 RA CP/MAIN/17/248, Donald Macdonald of Castleton to Sir Alexander Macdonald of Sleat, 11 July 1746

14 Duff, ed., *Culloden Papers*, 290

15 NLS MS.3736/432, Flora Macdonald: Declaration, 12 July 1746;
    Macdonald, ed., *Memorials*, xliv: Appendix B (3)
16 NLS MS.3736/432, Flora Macdonald: Declaration, 12 July 1746
17 Macdonald, ed., *Memorials*, xxvii–xxviii: Appendix B (2)
18 NLS MS.3736/430, John Mackinnon of Elgol: Declaration, 12 July 1746
19 NLS MS.3736/426, Duke of Cumberland to John Campbell of
    Mamore, 10 July 1746
20 NLS MS.3736/436, Campbell of Mamore to Duke of Cumberland,
    13 July 1746
21 NLS MS.3736/434, Duke of Cumberland to Campbell of Mamore,
    13 July 1746
22 Paton, ed., *Lyon in Mourning*, III: 377
23 NLS MS.3736/434, Duke of Cumberland to Campbell of Mamore,
    13 July 1746
24 NLS MS.3736/431, [Sir Everard Fawkener, secretary to the] Duke of
    Cumberland: Proclamation: 12 July 1746
25 NLS MS.3736/434, Duke of Cumberland to Campbell of Mamore,
    13 July 1746
26 NLS MS.3736/440, Duke of Cumberland to Campbell of Mamore,
    18 July 1746
27 RA CP/MAIN/17/299, Duke of Cumberland to Duke of Newcastle,
    16–17 July 1746
28 RA CP/MAIN/17/380, Lord Albemarle to Duke of Cumberland, 22
    July 1746
29 Walpole, *Correspondence*, XXXVII: 250
30 Terry, *Albemarle Papers*, II: 405
31 Paton, ed., *Lyon in Mourning*, I: 113
32 NLS MS.3736/438, Colin Campbell of Skipness to Campbell of
    Mamore, 14 July 1746
33 Paton, ed., *Lyon in Mourning*, I: 303
34 NLS MS.3736/447, Campbell of Mamore to Lord Albemarle, 24
    July 1746
35 Paton, ed., *Lyon in Mourning*, I: 112
36 Browne, *History of the Highlands*, III: 309n.

7 'THE FAMOUS MISS FLORA MACDONALD': AUGUST–
DECEMBER 1746

1 *Scots Magazine*, VIII (1746), 341

2 Walpole, *Correspondence*, XXX: 102: from Henry Fox to Horace Walpole, 22 July 1746

3 Ibid., XXXVII: 252: from Henry Conway to Horace Walpole, 12 August 1746

4 Tayler, ed., *Jacobite Miscellany*, 187

5 *Scots Magazine*, VIII (1746), 574

6 Paton, ed., *Lyon in Mourning*, I: 116

7 Smith, ed., *Grenville Papers*, I: 57

8 NLS MS.3736/467, Ranald MacDonald of Clanranald to Campbell of Mamore, 14 August 1746

9 Jurors (Scotland) Act 1745, 19 Geo. 2, c. 9

10 Paton, ed., *Lyon in Mourning*, I: 116

11 HMC, 11th Report (1887), Appendix, Part IV, 362

12 Wylde, *Autobiography of Flora Macdonald*, II: 16–17

13 *Caledonian Mercury*, 8 September 1746

14 Paton, ed., *Lyon in Mourning*, I: 116

15 *Derby Mercury*, 26 December 1746

16 Paton, ed., *Lyon in Mourning*, I: 116–17

17 Ibid., 111–12

18 Ibid., 117

19 Ibid., 116–17

20 Ibid., 114

21 Terry, *Albemarle Papers*, I: 209

22 Paton, ed., *Lyon in Mourning*, II: 106

23 Ibid., I: 112

24 Ibid., 116

25 Ibid., 115–16

26 Ibid., 112

27 Ibid., 115

28 Ibid., 112

29 'The Following is said to be a Genuine account of the Young Pretender's Escape after the Battle of Culloden', *Caledonian Mercury*, 21 October 1746, 2–3

30 Terry, *Albemarle Papers*, I: 297

31 NA ADM 52/551, Masters' logs (1744–9), including *Bridgewater* (17 August 1746–10 January 1747)

32 NLS MS.3736/511, Charles Knowler to Campbell of Mamore, 30 November 1746

33 NA SP 42/31, f. 37, 'Letter announcing the arrival at the Nore ... of Miss Flora Macdonald'

34 NA ADM 52/710, Masters' logs (1741–7), including *Royal Sovereign* (17 August 1746–16 October 1747)

35 NA SP 44/84, Transportation warrants, 4 December 1746: Duke of Newcastle to William Dick; same to commander of *Royal Sovereign*

36 NA SP 36/92/1/28, 'List of prisoners in the custody of [William] Dick ...' [1746]

37 NA SP 36/89/3/54, Aeneas Macdonald to unknown [Andrew Stone?], 26 November 1746

38 NA SP 36/90/2/18, Aeneas Macdonald et al. to Andrew Stone, 22 December 1746

39 NA SP 54/34/58, Roderick Macleod to Ranald Macdonald of Clanranald, December 1746

40 NA SP 54/34/163, Ranald [Macdonald of] Clanranald to Andrew Stone, 8 December 1746

41 Burton, *A Genuine and True Journal*, preface

42 Ferriar, *Illustrations of Sterne*, II: 129–45

43 Burton, *A Genuine and True Journal*, 39

44 Ibid., 20

45 Anon., *Female Rebels*, 53–5

46 Anon., *Alexis*, 6–10

47 'London. Dec 30. The famous Miss Flora Macdonald ... From St James's Evening Post, 30 December 1746', *Caledonian Mercury*, 5 January 1747

48 NA SP 36/83/2/84, Dr John Burton to Andrew Stone, 8 May 1746; Davies, 'A Memoir of Dr John Burton, M.D., F.S.A.', 414

49 Macleod, ed., *Book of Dunvegan*, I: 132

50 'London. Dec 30. The famous Miss Flora Macdonald ... From St James's Evening Post, 30 December 1746', *Caledonian Mercury*, 5 January 1747

8 HIGH TREASON: JANUARY–JULY 1747

1 NA SP 54/34/58, Roderick Macleod to Ranald Macdonald of Clanranald, December 1746

2 NA SP 36/94/2/121–2, '[Jacobite prisoner] Lady A [Anne] MacKinon [Mackinnon] to Andrew Stone' [1746]

3 NA SP 36/94/2/121, 'The Case of Lady Mackinnon'

4   NA SP 36/104/1/80, 'Petition for release sent to the Duke of Newcastle from Ann, Lady Stewart …' [1746]

5   Seton and Arnot, eds, *Prisoners of the '45*, I: 169

6   NA SP 36/93/2/63, 'Minutes of Cabinet …', 21 January 1747

7   Ibid.

8   Duff, ed., *Culloden Papers*, 290

9   NLS MS.1308/206-7, Ranald McAllister to John Mackenzie of Delvine, 23 November 1746

10 Warrand and Barron, eds, *More Culloden Papers*, V: 140

11 [Griffiths], *Ascanius*, 45–7

12 *The Pretender's Flight*, etching and engraving with vignettes, BM 1862,1213.29

13 *Miss Macdonald* [*c*.1746], RCT, RCIN 658352

14 *Miss Cameron. Miss Macdonald. How happy could I be with Either Were t'other dear Charmer away*, 1746, RCT, RCIN 658353

15 Act of Proscription 1746, 19 Geo. 2, c. 39

16 NA SP 54/38/65, 'Remarks … concerning the state of the Highlands …' [1746]

17 Paton, ed., *Lyon in Mourning*, II: 110–11

18 Act of Proscription 1746, 19 Geo. 2, c. 39; https://www.britishmuseum.org/collection/search?keyword=Flora&keyword=Macdonald

19 NA SP 36/94/1/101, Minutes of meeting between Duke of Newcastle and government law officers, 13 February 1747

20 NA SP 36/104/1/98–103, List of state of cases against named prisoners sent latterly from Scotland … [1747]

21 Ibid.

22 Ibid.

23 NA SP 36/95/1/87–8, 'Report of the Attorney General [Dudley Ryder] and Solicitor General', 23 March 1747

24 NA SP 36/95/1/124, 'Minutes of Cabinet …', 31 March 1747

25 'London. 7 April. Several ladies … Macdonald', *Derby Mercury*, 3 April 1747

26 NA SP/36/98/1/21, 'List of 26 prisoners held at Mr Dick's', 9 June 1747

27 Macdonald, ed., *Memorials*, xx: Appendix B (2)

28 Pinkerton, *General Collection*, III: 323

29 Croker, *Letters of Lady Hervey*, 257

30 https://www.christies.com/lot/lot-follower-of-allan-ramsay-portrait-of-anne-5714565/

31 Scott, *Tales of a Grandfather*, III: 231

32 Chambers, *History of the Rebellion*, II: 329

33 Wylde, *Autobiography of Flora Macdonald*, II: 24–5

34 http://carmichaelwatson.blogspot.com/2012/09/objects-in-focus-flora-macdonalds-fan.html

35 Paul Mellon Centre, http://www.richardwilsononline.ac.uk/index.php ?a=QuickSearch&qsv=Flora+Macdonald&WINID=1631461492829

36 Ibid.

37 Ibid.

38 Thomas Hudson, *Flora Macdonald* (1747), sold at auction, Bonham's, Edinburgh, 5 December 2013; *Mrs. Flora Macdonald* ('Tho. Hudson ad vivum Pinx. 1747'), mezzotint by John Faber the Younger, BM 1838,0420.169

39 Scott, *Tales of a Grandfather*, III: 231

40 Indemnity Act 1747, 21 Geo. 2, c. 9

41 Paton, ed., *Lyon in Mourning*, I: 283

42 Seton and Arnot, eds, *Prisoners of the '45*, I: 169

43 Boswell, *Life of Johnson*, ed. Hill and Powell, V: 201

9 A JACOBITE DOWRY: AUGUST 1747–APRIL 1751

1   *The Scotsman*, 6 January 1927: W. Forbes Gray, citing letter, David Beatt to James Burnet of Barns, Peeblesshire, September 1747

2   Paton, ed., *Lyon in Mourning*, I: 152

3   Chambers, *Jacobite Memoirs*, xii–xiii

4   Paton, ed., *Lyon in Mourning*, I: 297

5   Ibid., II: 43

6   Ibid., 70

7   Ibid., I: xviii, 112

8   Ibid., II: 82–3

9   Chambers, *Jacobite Memoirs*, xii

10 Paton, ed., *Lyon in Mourning*, I: xviii, 81

11 Ibid., II: 105

12 Ibid., 178

13 Ibid., 46

14 Macgregor, *Life of Flora Macdonald*, 124n.

15 Paton, ed., *Lyon in Mourning*, II: 43

16 Ibid., 80

17 Ibid., 178

18 Ibid., 124n.

19 HMC, 9th Report (1884), Part 2, 478

20 *The Athenaeum Journal for the Year 1844*, 525

21 Macgregor, *Life of Flora Macdonald*, 124n.

22 Zimmermann, *The Jacobite Movement in Scotland and in Exile*, 89 and n. 99

23 Thomas Hudson, *Flora Macdonald* (1747), sold at auction, Bonham's, Edinburgh, 5 December 2013; *Mrs. Flora Macdonald* ('Tho. Hudson ad vivum Pinx. 1747'), mezzotint by John Faber the Younger, BM 1838,0420.169; Miles, *Thomas Hudson*, 13

24 Langford, *Catalogue of Paintings of Richard Mead*, 7; *Mrs Flora Macdonald*, after Allan Ramsay, mezzotint by James McArdell, 1749, NPG D1348; *Flora Macdonald*, engraving by George Greatbach, BM 1847, 1113.3

25 Allan Ramsay, *Flora Macdonald* (1749), Ashmolean WA1960.76

26 Stephens, 'Among the Portraits at South Kensington', 392–3

27 Macgregor, *Life of Flora Macdonald*, 124n.

28 *BNJ*, III (1906), 404–6, https://www.britnumsoc.org/publications/Digital%20BNJ/pdfs/1906_BNJ_3_32.pdf: British Numismatic Society, Proceedings, 30 November 1906

29 Paton, ed., *Lyon in Mourning*, I: xviii–xx

30 Paton, ed., *Scottish National Memorials*, 152–4

31 Stephens, ed., *Exhibition of the Royal House of Stuart*, 113–15

32 http://carmichaelwatson.blogspot.com/2012/09/objects-in-focus-flora-macdonalds-fan.html

33 Paton, ed., *Lyon in Mourning*, II: 321, 324 and n.

34 *Scots Magazine*, XII (1750), 550

35 Macdonald, *The Truth*, 77 and n. 6

36 Macgregor, *Life of Flora Macdonald*, 125. And see *Oban Times*, 8 July 2021: 'a 30cm square of "hard [stiff] tartan" in storage at the West Highland Museum in Fort William, dating from the eighteenth century and once part of a much larger piece now divided between the Glencoe Museum and a private collection, was recently rediscovered. The whole length was originally owned by Flora's granddaughter, Flora Macdonald Wylde, and the 30cm square bears a 1964 label, identifying it as Flora's "wedding dress". Research to investigate this claim is ongoing at the time of publication'

37 https://www.tartanregister.gov.uk/tartanDetails?ref=2377:   unnamed
    19th century – a plaid belonging to Flora Macdonald
38 Macdonald, *The Truth*, 70n.; NRAS NRAS3273/5608, John Macleod,
    4 January 1740: Receipts for payments, school wages for Allan
    Macdonald
39 Macdonald, *The Truth*, 76; NA AO 13/87/59, Allan Macdonald,
    Memorial, 8 February 1785
40 Macdonald, *Memorials*, lvii: Appendix E
41 Paton, ed., *Lyon in Mourning*, III: 81
42 Ibid., 82
43 Macdonald, *The Truth*, 112–15, Appendix V: Marriage contract, 3
    December 1750
44 *The Athenaeum Journal for the Year 1844*, 525: Flora Macdonald
45 Ibid.
46 Ibid.
47 Macdonald, *The Truth*, 69–79 and nn. 22–3
48 *The Athenaeum Journal for the Year 1844*, 525: Flora Macdonald
49 Ibid.

10 MARRIED LIFE: APRIL 1751–1770

1   Kyd, ed., *Scottish Population Statistics*, 60
2   McLynn, *Bonnie Prince Charlie*, 552–3
3   Voltaire, *Age of Louis XIV and Louis XV*, II: 46
4   Ibid., 48
5   Ibid., 33–4 and ff.
6   RA SP/MAIN/421/210, Neil Macdonald [formerly MacEachen] to
    unknown, 7 June 1764; RA SP/MAIN/421/169, Neil Macdonald
    [formerly MacEachen] to Andrew Lumisden, 4 October 1765;
    Maclean, *A Macdonald for the Prince*, 72–3
7   RA SP/MAIN/M/Box 1/347, Henry Goring to Charles Edward
    Stuart, 6 June 1752; McLynn, *Bonnie Prince Charlie*, 406
8   NA SP 54/44/15A, Humphrey Bland to Lord Holdernesse, 13 June
    1754
9   Ibid.
10 NA SP 54/44/24B, Humphrey Bland to Lord Holdernesse, 'Sequel',
    encl., 15 July 1754
11 NA SP 54/44/24B, Humphrey Bland to Lord Holdernesse, 13 August
    1754

12 Boswell, *Life of Johnson*, ed. Hill and Powell, V: 257–8

13 NRAS NRAS3273/5438, Macdonald of Sleat, Bills and receipts [1754–5]

14 Macdonald, *The Truth*, 113–17

15 Ibid., 110–11

16 NLS MS.1306/78, Edmund McQueen to John Mackenzie of Delvine, 6 June 1767

17 NLS MS.1306/59–60, Allan Macdonald to John Mackenzie of Delvine, 18 November 1763

18 NLS MS.1306/61-62, Allan Macdonald to John Mackenzie of Delvine, 6 June 1767

19 Ibid.

20 Ibid.

21 Macdonald, *The Truth*, 76 and n. 15

22 Macdonald, *Memorials*, 70. See Macgregor, *Life of Flora Macdonald*, 102–3 for the information from Anne Macleod that her mother was also buried in a royal shroud. And see Boswell, *Life of Johnson*, ed. Hill and Powell, V: 190, where biographer and subject appear unaware that one bedsheet was still extant in 1773

23 Macdonald, *The Truth*, 108

24 Ibid.

25 Ibid.

26 NLS MS.1309/141-2, Lady Margaret Macdonald to John Mackenzie, 3 November 1763

27 Ibid.

28 Ibid., Sir James Macdonald to John Mackenzie of Delvine, 16 October 1763

29 NLS MS.1309/249-50, Sir James Macdonald to John Mackenzie of Delvine, 15 October 1763

30 NLS MS.1309/249-50, Sir James Macdonald to John Mackenzie of Delvine, 16 October 1763

31 NLS MS.1306/59-60, Allan Macdonald to John Mackenzie of Delvine, 18 November 1763

32 Ibid.

33 Macdonald, *The Truth*, 108

34 Ibid.

35 NRAS NRAS3273/416, John Maclean to John Mackenzie of Delvine, 27 March 1766

36 Macdonald, *The Truth*, 113–17
37 Ibid., 108
38 Ibid.
39 NLS MS.1306/61-2, Allan Macdonald to John Mackenzie of Delvine, 6 June 1767
40 NRAS NRAS3273/4284, Journal of Sir Allan Macdonald of Kingsborrow [Kingsburgh], 25 September 1769

11 'WE HAVE HARDLY WHAT WILL PAY OUR CREDITORS': 1771–1774

1 NLS MS.1306/78, Edmund McQueen to John Mackenzie of Delvine, 2 October 1771
2 NLS MS.1306/54-5, Alexander Macdonald to John Mackenzie of Delvine, 30 April 1771
3 Macdonald, *The Truth*, 109–10
4 NLS MS.1306/65-6, Allan Mackenzie to John Mackenzie of Delvine, 30 November 1772
5 Macdonald, *The Truth*, 111
6 Ibid.
7 NLS MS.1306/67-8, Allan Macdonald to John Mackenzie of Delvine, 2 March 1773
8 NA AO 13/121/734, Alexander Macleod, Memorial [1779]
9 NA AO 13/121/736, Alexander Macleod, Memorial, 10 June 1783
10 Macdonald, *The Truth*, 111
11 Ibid., 110–11
12 [Scotus Americanus], *Informations concerning … North Carolina*, 16
13 *Caledonian Mercury*, 2 September 1771
14 CSRNC 9:248-52, Board of Trade Memorandum for George III, 26 February 1772
15 *Caledonian Mercury*, 2 September 1771
16 CSRNC 8:620, Petition from James Macdonald et al., [before 14 June] 1771
17 CSRNC 9:303-04, Privy Council Order re Petition from James Macdonald et al., 19 June 1772
18 NLS MS.1306/67-8, Allan Macdonald to John Mackenzie of Delvine, 2 March 1773
19 NA AO 13/121/214, Allan Macdonald, Affidavit, 24 June 1786, in Donald Macdonald, Memorial [1784–6]; NA AO 13/121/185,

Alexander Macleod, Minutes of Evidence, 15 October 1784 in Alexander Macdonald, Memorial [1786]

20 NA AO 12/36/4, Alexander Macdonald, Minutes of Evidence, 7 October 1786; NLS MS.1306/67-8, Allan Macdonald to John Mackenzie of Delvine, 2 March 1773

21 Johnson, *Journey to the Western Islands*, ed. Fleeman, 79

22 NLS MS.1306/67-8, Allan Macdonald to John Mackenzie of Delvine, 2 March 1773

23 Yale Univ., Gen MSS 89, Series II, Box 26, Folder 637, Sir Alexander Macdonald to James Boswell, 12 July 1773

24 Macdonald, *The Truth*, 109–10

25 *Caledonian Mercury*, 2 September 1771

26 CSRNC 9:248-52, Board of Trade Memorandum for George III, 26 February 1772

27 Macdonald, *The Truth*, 110

28 Yale Univ., Gen MSS 89, Series II, Box 26, Folder 638, Sir Alexander Macdonald to James Boswell, 26 November 1785

29 CSRNC 9:248-52, Board of Trade Memorandum for George III, 26 February 1772

30 CSRNC 9:52-59, Josiah Martin to Marquess of Downshire, 1 March 1772

31 Murdoch, ed., 'Scottish Document', 449–50

32 Boswell, *Life of Johnson*, ed. Hill and Powell, V: 277–8

33 Johnson, *Journey to the Western Islands,* ed. Fleeman, 1 and n. 1

34 Boswell, *Life of Johnson*, ed. Hill and Powell, V: 221–2

35 Johnson, *Journey to the Western Islands,* ed. Fleeman, 46

36 Boswell, *Life of Johnson*, ed. Hill and Powell, V: 161

37 Ibid., 277

38 Redford, ed., *Letters of Samuel Johnson*, II: 77

39 Boswell, *Journal of a Tour to the Hebrides*, ed. Pottle and Bennett, 113–14

40 Boswell, *Life of Johnson*, ed. Hill and Powell, V: 151

41 Yale Univ., Gen MSS 89, Series II, Box 26, Folder 638, Sir Alexander Macdonald to James Boswell, 26 November 1785

42 Ibid., Folder 637, Sir Alexander Macdonald to James Boswell, 12 September 1769

43 Pennant, *Tour in Scotland, 1772,* 343–6

44 Boswell, *Journal of a Tour to the Hebrides*, ed. Pottle and Bennett, 160

45 Chambers, *History of the Rebellion*, II: 330

46 Wylde, *Autobiography of Flora Macdonald,* II: 109

47 Pennant, *Tour in Scotland, 1772,* 346

48 Macdonald, *Memorials,* xxv: Appendix B (2)

49 See Boswell, *Life of Johnson,* ed. Hill and Powell, V:532

50 Pennant, *Tour in Scotland, 1772,* 346

51 Boswell, *Journal of a Tour to the Hebrides,* ed. Pottle and Bennett, 159–60

52 Ibid., 159

53 Johnson, *Journey to the Western Islands,* ed. Fleeman, 54

54 Boswell, *Journal of a Tour to the Hebrides,* ed. Pottle and Bennett, 159

55 Ibid.

56 Boswell, *Life of Johnson,* ed. Hill and Powell, V: 185

57 Redford, ed., *Letters of Samuel Johnson,* II: 90–1

58 Boswell, *Life of Johnson,* ed. Hill and Powell, V: 186–7

59 Prior, *Poems on Several Occasions,* I: 126

60 Boswell, *Life of Johnson,* ed. Hill and Powell, V: 187 n. 2; *London Gazette,* 3 August 1745

61 Boswell, *Life of Johnson,* ed. Hill and Powell, V: 187

62 Redford, ed., *Letters of Samuel Johnson,* II: 90

63 Boswell, *Life of Johnson,* ed. Hill and Powell, V: 187

64 Ibid., 188 and n. 2

65 Ibid., 188

66 Boswell, *Journal of a Tour to the Hebrides,* ed. Pottle and Bennett, 162

67 Redford, ed., *Letters of Samuel Johnson,* II: 90

68 Johnson, *Journey to the Western Islands,* ed. Fleeman, 54

69 Redford, ed., *Letters of Samuel Johnson,* II: 71

70 Ibid., 91

71 Johnson, *Journey to the Western Islands,* ed. Fleeman, 58

72 Boswell, *Life of Johnson,* ed. Hill and Powell, V: 208, 212

73 Yale Univ., Gen MSS 89, Series II, Box 26, Folder 640, Allan Macdonald to James Boswell, 1774

74 Macdonald, *The Truth,* 110

75 Yale Univ., Gen MSS 89, Series II, Box 27, Folders 647-8, John Macleod of Raasay to James Boswell, 1775; ibid., Box 28, Folder 638, Sir Alexander Macdonald to James Boswell, 26 November 1785

76 NA AO 13/121/743, Lt Gen. Simon Fraser evidence in Alexander Macleod, Memorial [rec'd 16 March 1784]

77 DeWolfe, *Discoveries of America,* 172–3

12 CHEEK'S CREEK, NORTH CAROLINA: 1774–APRIL 1775

1 NA CO 5/115/24, Memorial of Charles Macdonald to Viscount Barrington, Secretary of War, requesting an appointment that will enable him to better assist peace efforts, 24 October 1775

2 MacInnes, *Brave Sons of Skye*, 16

3 Murdoch, ed., 'Scottish Document', 449

4 NA AO 13/121/748–9, Alexander Macleod, Memorial, Inventories of Losses [1779]

5 NA AO 13/87/59, Allan Macdonald, Memorial, February 8, 1785

6 Murdoch, ed., 'Scottish Document', 448

7 Treason Act 1766, 6 Geo. 3, c. 53

8 Wood, *This Remote Part of the World*, 110–11 and n. 1

9 Robertson, 'Mentioned with Honour', 165

10 NA CO 5/115/24, Memorial of Charles Macdonald to Viscount Barrington, Secretary of War, requesting an appointment that will enable him to better assist peace efforts, 24 October 1775

11 Murdoch, ed., 'Scottish Document', 449

12 Maclean, *Flora Macdonald in America*, 32

13 *Virginia Gazette*, 12 May 1774

14 Macdonald, *The French Macdonald*, 160

15 Foote, *Sketches of North Carolina*, 155; Bartram, *Travels through North and South Carolina*, 475–6

16 NA AO 13/122/139–41, Neill McArthur evidence, 11 August 1784, and Norman Macleod evidence, 11 August 1784, in Murdoch Macleod, Memorial

17 NA AO 12/34/83, Neill McArthur, Account of Losses, 28 May 1785

18 See NA AO 13, former North Carolina residents, Memorials, passim, c.1783–6

19 Redford, ed., *Letters of Samuel Johnson*, II: 90

20 Jesse, *Memoirs of the Pretenders and their Adherents*, 431–2

21 Lossing, *Hours with Living Men and Women of Revolution*, 106–7

22 Banks, *Life and Character of Flora Macdonald*, 6

23 Jesse, *Memoirs of the Pretenders and their Adherents*, 431–2

24 Mackenzie, ed., *History of Barbecue Church*, 14–16

25 Foote, *Sketches of North Carolina*, 155

26 Lossing, *Hours with Living Men and Women of Revolution*, 108

27 Presbyterian Historical Society, Philadelphia: Museum Collection 1367

28 NA AO 13/121/198, Alexander Macdonald, Memorial [rec'd 19 March 1784]

29 NA AO 13/121/187, Alexander Morrison evidence, 4 November 1785, in Alexander Macdonald, Memorial [1786]

30 NA AO 13/121/189, Alexander Macleod of Lochbay evidence, 18 April 1786, in Alexander Macdonald, Memorial [1786]

31 NA AO 13/121/198, Alexander Macdonald, Memorial [rec'd 19 March 1784]

32 NA AO 13/121/189, Alexander Macleod of Lochbay evidence, 8 April 1786, in Alexander Macdonald, Memorial [1786]

33 Fowler, *They Passed This Way: Harnett County*, 74

34 NA AO 13/121/745, Alexander Macdonald, Account of Losses [rec'd 19 March 1784]

35 CSRNC 8:620, Petition from James Macdonald et al., [before 14 June] 1771

36 NA AO 13/121/745–50, Alexander Macdonald, Account of Losses [rec'd 19 March 1784]

37 Egerton, ed., *Royal Commission on the Losses and Services of American Loyalists*, 214–15

38 NA AO 13/121/209, Donald Macdonald, Estimate of Losses, 19 March 1784

39 NA AO 13/121/212, James Macdonald evidence, 9 July 1784, in Donald Macdonald, Memorial [1784–6]

40 Tayler, ed., *Jacobite Miscellany*, 187

41 NA AO 13/122/28-9, Allan Macdonald, Account of Losses [rec'd 12 March 1784]

42 Ibid.

43 Tayler, ed., *Jacobite Miscellany*, 187

44 NA AO 13/122/28–9, Allan Macdonald, Account of Losses [rec'd 12 March 1784]

45 Macdonald, *The Truth*, 111

46 Ibid., 110

13 'KING AND COUNTRY': APRIL–JUNE 1775

1 Wicker, *Miscellaneous Ancient Records of Moore County*, 373

2 CSRNC 9:1016–17, Resolutions by inhabitants of Wilmington district, 21 July 1774

3 CSRNC 9:1029, Minutes of North Carolina Governor's Council, 12 August 1774

4 CSRNC 9:1090–1, Minutes of Wilmington Committee of Safety, 26 November 1774

5 CSRNC 9:1083, Josiah Martin to Lord Dartmouth, 4 November 1774

6 NA AO 13/121/741, Alexander Macleod, Memorial [rec'd 16 March 1784]

7 Egerton, ed., *Royal Commission on the Losses and Services of American Loyalists*, 214–15

8 CSRNC 9:1166–8, Josiah Martin to Thomas Gage, 16 March 1775

9 NA AO 13/121/741, Alexander Macleod, Memorial [rec'd 16 March 1784]

10 NA AO 13/87/59, Allan Macdonald, Memorial, 8 February 1785

11 CSRNC 9:1174–6, Josiah Martin to Lord Dartmouth, 23 March 1775

12 Tayler, ed., *Jacobite Miscellany*, 187

13 NA AO 13/121/741, Alexander Macleod, Memorial [rec'd 16 March 1784]

14 CSRNC 9:1255–7, Josiah Martin to Lord Dartmouth, 18 May 1775

15 NA AO 13/121/196, Alexander Macdonald, Memorial [rec'd 19 March 1784]

16 Tayler, ed., *Jacobite Miscellany*, 187

17 NA AO 13/87/59, Allan Macdonald, Memorial, 8 February 1785

18 CSRNC 10:41–4, Josiah Martin to Lord Dartmouth, 30 June 1775

19 Inman, 'Losses of the Military and Naval Forces Engaged in the War of the American Revolution', 189

20 NA AO 13/121/741, Alexander Macleod, Memorial [rec'd 16 March 1784]

21 Tayler, ed., *Jacobite Miscellany*, 187

22 Ibid.

23 NA AO 13/87/59, Allan Macdonald, Memorial, 8 February 1785

24 NA AO 13/121/764, Josiah Martin to Alexander Macleod, 4 July 1775, in Alexander Macleod, Memorial

25 Boswell, *Life of Johnson*, ed. Hill and Powell, V: 184

26 NA AO 13/87/60, Allan Macdonald, Memorial, 8 February 1785

27 NA AO 13/121/764–5, Josiah Martin to Alexander Macleod, 4 July 1775, in Alexander Macleod, Memorial

28 CSRNC 10:64–5, Minutes of Wilmington Committee of Safety, 3 July 1775

29 CSRNC 10:45–6, Josiah Martin to Lord Dartmouth, 30 June 1775

30 NA AO 13/117/360, Josiah Martin to John Burnside, 10 July 1775, in John Burnside, Memorial

31 Tayler, ed., *Jacobite Miscellany*, 187

14 'ALL KILLED OR TAKEN': JULY 1775–FEBRUARY 1776

1 CSRNC 10:124, Minutes of Wilmington Committee of Safety, 31 July 1775

2 CSRNC 10:230–7, Josiah Martin to Lord Dartmouth, 28 August 1775

3 Tayler, ed., *Jacobite Miscellany*, 187

4 Ibid., 188

5 See NA AO 13/121/741, Alexander Macleod, Memorial; NA AO 13/121/196, Alexander Macdonald, Memorial; NA AO 13/122/374, Alexander Morrison

6 Rankin, 'Moore's Creek Bridge Campaign, 1776', 32 and nn. 49–52

7 NA AO 13/121/766, Lt Col. Donald Macdonald, Evidence, in Alexander Macleod, Memorial [rec'd 4 August 1779]

8 NA CO 5/232, *A [Narrative] of the proceedings of a body of [loyalists] in North Carolina* [Alexander McLean et al.], [1776], encl. in NA CO 5/93 Part 1, General Howe to Lord George Germain, 25 April 1776

9 https://www.archives.gov/founding-docs/declaration-transcript, Declaration of Independence: A Transcript

10 CSRNC 10:325, Josiah Martin to Lord Dartmouth, 12 November 1775

11 NA AO 13/121/741, Alexander Macleod, Memorial [rec'd 16 March 1784], 4

12 CSRNC 10:321–8, Josiah Martin to Lord Dartmouth, 12 November 1775

13 CSRNC 10:299–300, Lord Dartmouth to Josiah Martin, 27 October 1775

14 CSRNC 10:299–300, Commission to appoint Allan Macdonald et al. as officers of loyalist militias, 10 January 1776

15 NA CO 5/232, *A [Narrative] of the proceedings of a body of [loyalists] in North Carolina* [Alexander McLean et al.], [1776], encl. in NA CO 5/93 Part 1, General Howe to Lord George Germain, 25 April 1776

16 Lossing, *Hours with Living Men and Women of Revolution*, 107

17 NA AO 13/87/60, Allan Macdonald, Memorial, 8 February 1785

18 Lossing, *Hours with Living Men and Women of Revolution*, 107

19 Macgregor, *Life of Flora Macdonald*, 124n.

20 Advocates Library, EP/ABB; http://lib1.advocates.org.uk/flora

21 Boswell, *Life of Johnson*, ed. Croker, IV: 204

22 CSRNC 10:443–4, Manifesto by Donald Macdonald, 5 February 1776

23 NA CO 5/232, *A [Narrative] of the proceedings of a body of [loyalists] in North Carolina* [Alexander McLean et al.], [1776], encl. in NA CO 5/93 Part 1, General Howe to Lord George Germain, 25 April 1776

24 NA AO 13/122/374–5, Alexander Morrison, Memorial [rec'd 20 December 1783]

25 NA AO 13/121/741, Alexander Macleod, Memorial [rec'd 16 March 1784]

26 NA AO 13/121/767, Alexander Macleod, Losses on Public Account, 5 June 1777

27 NA AO 13/87/60, Allan Macdonald, Memorial, 8 February 1785

28 NA AO 13/06/394–5, Neill McArthur, Memorial and account, 4 February 1785

29 NA AO 13/122/130, Murdoch Macleod, Account of Losses, 25 September 1783

30 NA CO 5/232, *A [Narrative] of the proceedings of a body of [loyalists] in North Carolina* [Alexander McLean et al.], [1776], encl. in NA CO 5/93 Part 1, General Howe to Lord George Germain, 25 April 1776

31 Ibid.

32 Tayler, ed., *Jacobite Miscellany*, 187

33 Lossing, *Hours with Living Men and Women of Revolution*, 108

34 Foote, *Sketches of North Carolina*, 157

35 Tayler, ed., *Jacobite Miscellany*, 187

36 NA CO 5/232, *A [Narrative] of the proceedings of a body of [loyalists] in North Carolina* [Alexander McLean et al.], [1776], encl. in NA CO 5/93 Part 1, General Howe to Lord George Germain, 25 April 1776

37 Tayler, ed., *Jacobite Miscellany*, 187

38 NA CO 5/232, *A [Narrative] of the proceedings of a body of [loyalists] in North Carolina* [Alexander McLean et al.], [1776], encl. in NA CO 5/93 Part 1, General Howe to Lord George Germain, 25 April 1776

39 Ibid.

40 Tayler, ed., *Jacobite Miscellany*, 187–8

41 Ibid., 188

42 CSRNC 10:509, Minutes of the Provincial Congress of North Carolina, 11 April 1776

43 Tayler, ed., *Jacobite Miscellany*, 188

15 'ALMOST STARVED WITH COLD TO DEATH': FEBRUARY
1776–DECEMBER 1779

1 Tayler, ed., *Jacobite Miscellany*, 188

2 NA AO 13/122/30-31, Allan Macdonald, letter of 3 January 1784, in Memorial [recd. 12 March 1784]; NA AO 13/87/59, Allan Macdonald,

Memorial, 8 February 1785. Preserved in North Carolina and Virginia are NCMH, H. 19XX.244.1, 'Flora Macdonald's Silver' – a silver tray, sauce boat, jug and ladle, engraved with the monogram 'FMcD' – and Patrick Henry Memorial Foundation, 76.2.1a, 'Flora Macdonald China' – a willow-pattern tea service, including a teapot with an oriental handle and spout edged with gold, and a coffee pot with a dark-blue band, similarly gilded. If these are plunder and not given, sold or abandoned later, they have been well looked after.

3 Tayler, ed., *Jacobite Miscellany*, 188
4 Ibid., 8
5 NA AO 13/87/59, Allan Macdonald, Memorial, 8 February 1785
6 NA AO 13/121/763, Alexander Macleod, Memorial [rec'd 4 August 1779]
7 NA AO 13/121/769, Alexander Macleod, Account of Losses [rec'd 4 August 1779]
8 NA AO 13/121/763, Alexander Macleod, Memorial [rec'd 4 August 1779]
9 NA AO 13/121/267, Alexander Macdonald, Memorial [rec'd 19 March 1784]
10 NA AO 13/121/742, Alexander Macleod, Account of Losses … for his loyal exertions [rec'd 16 March 1784]
11 NA T 79, American Loyalist Claims Commission: Records
12 *London Gazette*, 16 January 1779; Macdonald, *Letter Book*, 388
13 CSRNC 11:293, Thomas Burke to John Hancock, 22 April 1776
14 CSRNC 11:547–8, Minutes of North Carolina Provincial Congress, 29 April 1776
15 Tayler, ed., *Jacobite Miscellany*, 188
16 https://loc.gov/resource/bdsdcc.02101. *In Congress, July 4, 1776. The unanimous declaration of the thirteen United States of America.*
17 LOC/JCC/5:743, 7 September 1776
18 LOC/JCC/7:250, 10 April 1777, citing Thomas Mifflin letter to Congress, 8 April 1777; PCC 5:41, Allan Macdonald to John Hancock, 5 April 1777
19 PCC 5:41, Allan Macdonald to John Hancock, 5 April 1777
20 HSP Misc. Coll. Allan Macdonald to Alexander Bartram, Reading, 10 May 1777
21 LOC/JCC/8:570, 22 July 1777; PCC 15/232, Allan Macdonald to John Hancock, 18 July 1777

22 LOC/LDC/6:386, Thomas Burke to Richard Caswell, 2 March 1777

23 PCC 15/232, Allan Macdonald to John Hancock, 18 July 1777

24 Macdonald, *Letter Book,* 377

25 CSRNC 11:765–8, Josiah Martin to Lord George Germain, 15 September 1777

26 Ibid.

27 Egerton, ed., *Royal Commission on the Losses and Services of American Loyalists,* 345–6

28 CSRNC 24:124, Acts of North Carolina General Assembly, 15 November 1777

29 Macdonald, *Letter Book,* 387–9

30 NA AO 13/121/742, Alexander Macleod, Account of Losses ... for his loyal exertions [rec'd 16 March 1784]; CSRNC 13:55–6, John Ashe to Richard Caswell, 23 February 1778

31 CSRNC 13:64–5, Richard Caswell to John Ashe, 7 March 1778

32 Ibid.

33 NA AO 13/87/59, Allan Macdonald, Memorial [8 February 1785]

34 NCMH, Shoe buckles, with Flora Macdonald history, 19XX.332.104

35 Tayler, ed., *Jacobite Miscellany,* 188

36 LOC/LDC/8:96–7, Elbridge Gerry to Elias Boudinot, 10 October 1777

37 Macdonald, *Letter Book,* 389

38 Tayler, ed., *Jacobite Miscellany,* 188

39 Macdonald, *Letter Book,* 389

40 Ibid., 387

41 Ibid., 401

42 Ibid., 389

43 Ibid., 420

44 NA AO 13/121/742, Alexander Macleod, Account of Losses ... for his loyal exertions [rec'd 16 March 1784]

45 Morrison, *History of St Andrew's Society, New York,* 184–5

46 Macdonald, *Letter Book,* 429–30

47 Ibid., 441

48 NA AO 13/121/742, Alexander Macleod, Account of Losses ... for his loyal exertions [rec'd 16 March 1784]

49 Tayler, ed., *Jacobite Miscellany,* 188

50 Ibid.

51 Ibid.

52 Town, ed., Detail of *Some Particular Services Performed in America*, 70
53 Macdonald, *Letter Book*, 388–9
54 Ibid., 394
55 Ibid., 475
56 Ibid., 484–5
57 Tayler, ed., *Jacobite Miscellany*, 188
58 Ibid., 188–9
59 Macgregor, *Life of Flora Macdonald*, 134
60 Tayler, ed., *Jacobite Miscellany*, 189

16 'ALL POSSIBLE SPEED TO THE HIGHLANDS': 1780–1785

1 Tayler, ed., *Jacobite Miscellany*, 189
2 Ibid.
3 Macdonald, *The Truth*, 111–12
4 Cruttwell, *A Tour through Great Britain, Divided into Journeys*, V: 325
5 Blaikie, ed., *Origins of the 'Forty-Five*, 251
6 Macdonald, *The Truth*, 111–12
7 Macgregor, *Life of Flora Macdonald*, 135
8 Macdonald, *Treatise on Telegraphic Communication*, 133–4n.
9 Macgregor, *Life of Flora Macdonald*, 135–6
10 Boswell, *Life of Johnson*, ed. Hill and Powell, V: 223
11 Macgregor, *Life of Flora Macdonald*, 135
12 Ibid.
13 Boswell, *Life of Johnson*, ed. Hill and Powell, V: 207
14 Macgregor, *Life of Flora Macdonald*, 135–6
15 Ibid., 136
16 Macdonald, *Treatise on Telegraphic Communication*, 133–4n.
17 Carmichael-Watson, Coll-97/CW150/77, Notes and stories relating to Flora Macdonald, 12 April 1870
18 Fraser-Mackintosh, 'The Kingsburgh and Milton Families', 165
19 Carmichael-Watson, Coll-97/CW150/77, Notes and stories relating to Flora Macdonald, 12 April 1870
20 Macdonald, ed., *Memorials*, lii: Appendix D (3)
21 Macgregor, *Life of Flora Macdonald*, 135
22 Ibid., 136
23 Tarleton, *History of the Campaigns of 1780 and 1781*, 97–8, 161–2
24 BL Add MSS 45524, Flora Macdonald to Alexander Macleod, December 1781

25 Macdonald, ed., *Memorials*, l: Appendix D (2)
26 Macgregor, *Life of Flora Macdonald*, 136
27 Ibid.
28 Mahon, *History of England*, VII: 175
29 *Nautical Magazine for 1848*, 459–60
30 Tayler, ed., *Jacobite Miscellany*, 189
31 Ibid.
32 Macgregor, *Life of Flora Macdonald*, 136
33 Ibid.
34 NA AO 13/121/760, William Bethune and John McCaskill, 16 December 1782, in Alexander Macleod, Memorial
35 Stewart, *Forgotten Monarchy of Scotland*, 365
36 NA T 79, American Loyalist Claims Commission: Records
37 NA AO 12/36/2, Alexander Macdonald, Minutes of Evidence, 7 October 1786
38 Allen, ed., *Loyal Americans*, 69
39 Duncanson, *Rawdon and Douglas*, 309–10
40 Maclean, *Writings of Loyalist-Era Settler*, 100; NA AO 13/87/59, Allan Macdonald, Memorial, 8 February 1785
41 NA AO 13/122/30–1, Allan Macdonald, 3 January 1784, endorsed by Alexander Macdonald in Allan Macdonald, Memorial [rec'd 12 March 1784]
42 NA AO 13/87/59, Allan Macdonald, Memorial, 8 February 1785
43 NA AO 12/34/214, Allan Macdonald, Affidavit, 24 June 1786, in Donald Macdonald, Memorial [1784–6]
44 Boswell, *Life of Johnson*, ed. Hill and Powell, V: 187
45 Boswell, *Life of Johnson*, ed. Croker, III: 111
46 Chambers, *Jacobite Memoirs*; Paton, ed., *Lyon in Mourning*
47 Boswell, *Life of Johnson*, ed. Croker, III: 111
48 See BM 1864,0611.141 (1803)
49 Yale Univ., Gen MSS 89, Series II, Box 26, Folder 638, Sir Alexander Macdonald to James Boswell, 26 November 1785
50 Ibid.
51 Duff, ed., *Culloden Papers*, 290
52 Yale Univ, Gen MSS 89, Series II, Box 26, Folder 638, Sir Alexander Macdonald to James Boswell, 26 November 1785
53 Ibid., Series I, Box 5, Folder 168, James Boswell to Sir Alexander Macdonald, 10 December 1785

17 ROYAL PENSIONER: 1785–MARCH 1790

1 NA AO 13/87/59, Allan Macdonald, Memorial, 8 February 1785

2 Egerton, ed., *Royal Commission on the Losses and Services of American Loyalists*, 345–6

3 Duncanson, *Rawdon and Douglas*, 309

4 Macdonald, ed., *Memorials*, liv: Appendix D (3)

5 Macdonald, *The Truth*, 112

6 [Anon.], *Memoir of John Macdonald*, 7–10

7 Macdonald, *Treatise on Telegraphic Communication*, 133–4n.

8 Macdonald, *The Truth*, 112

9 Ibid., 97 and n. 21

10 Wraxall, *Historical and Posthumous Memoirs*, ed. Wheatley, V: 357

11 Macdonald, *The Truth*, 117

12 Paton, ed., *Scottish National Memorials*, 153

13 Harfield, 'Lieutenant Colonel John Macdonald', 207

14 Tayler, *Jacobite Miscellany*, 189

15 NLS MS.1306/61-2, Allan Macdonald to John Mackenzie of Delvine, 6 June 1767

16 Macdonald, *The Truth*, 109

17 Macgregor, *Life of Flora Macdonald*, 77n.

18 Stephens, ed., *Exhibition of the Royal House of Stuart*, 152–4

19 Carmichael-Watson, Coll-97/CW119/24, Notes on a copper brooch and sketch, 1871; Carmichael-Watson, Coll-97/CW126f/16, Notes on Isabel Ross née Macdonald, 1892

20 Macgregor, *Life of Flora Macdonald*, 138

21 [Anon.], 'A Treatise on the Harmonic System, by John Macdonald ...', 462n.

22 Ibid.

23 See Tayler, ed., *Jacobite Miscellany*, 189

24 Wraxall, *Historical and Posthumous Memoirs*, ed. Wheatley, V: 357

25 Tayler, ed., *Jacobite Miscellany*, 189

26 Ibid., 185

27 Ibid., 186–7

28 Ibid., 189

29 Ibid.

30 Macdonald, *Treatise on Telegraphic Communication*, 133–4n.

31 Macgregor, *Life of Flora Macdonald*, 139

32 Macdonald, *The Truth*, 98 and n. 23; *The Times*, 4 June 1991, Letter from General Sir Patrick Palmer

33 Macgregor, *Life of Flora Macdonald*, 139

34 Macdonald, *Treatise on Telegraphic Communication*, 133–4n.

35 Macgregor, *Life of Flora Macdonald*, 139

36 *Scots Magazine*, LII (1790), 205; *Newcastle Courant*, 1 May 1790; *Northampton Gazette*, 1 May 1790; *European Magazine*, XVII (January–July 1790), 398

37 Macdonald, *The Truth*, 97

38 Macgregor, *Life of Flora Macdonald*, 139–40

39 Ibid., 140–1

40 Ibid., 141

41 Mayhew-Smith, 'An Irish Blessing for Travellers', in *Landscape Liturgies* [unpaginated]

18 'SPEED, BONNIE BOAT, LIKE A BIRD ON THE WING': THE STORY

1 *Scots Magazine*, LIV (1792), 518; *Inverness Courier*, 24 December 1834

2 Macgregor, *Life of Flora Macdonald*, 77, 130

3 Harfield, 'Lieutenant Colonel John Macdonald', 209

4 Wylde, *Autobiography of Flora Macdonald*, II: 170

5 Macgregor, *Life of Flora Macdonald*, 142; Macdonald, *Treatise on Telegraphic Communication*, 133n.; Boswell, *Journal of a Tour to the Hebrides*, ed. Carruthers, 144

6 Donaldson, *Wanderings in the Western Highlands*, 173

7 E.E.G., 'The Grave of Flora Macdonald', 600

8 [Hogg], *Songs by the Ettrick Shepherd*, 11–12

9 Macdonald, *The French Macdonald*, 156–8

10 Ibid., 159–61

11 Ibid., 160

12 Ibid., 164

13 Grant, *Highlanders*, 81

14 Macdonald, *The French Macdonald*, 161

15 Ibid., 194–5 (quoting NLS press account of 1825 Tour)

16 Carmichael-Watson, Coll-97/CW108/64, Notes on the family of Flora Macdonald, 8 May 1877

17 Carmichael-Watson, Coll-97/CW150/77, Notes and stories relating to Flora Macdonald's family, 12 April 1870

18 http://carmichaelwatson.blogspot.com/search?q=Flora+Macdonald

19 Carmichael-Watson, Coll-97/CW119/24, Notes on copper brooch and sketch, 1871

20 *Clan Donald Magazine* no. 12 (1991) online, https://www.clandon ald.org.uk/cdm12/cdm12a08.htm; https://canmore.org.uk/site/9848/ south-uist-milton-flora-macdonald-memorial

21 https://canmore.org.uk/site/11391/skye-flodigarry-flora-macdonalds-cottage

22 https://canmore.org.uk/site/253811/skye-kingsburgh-house, showing later Kingsburgh House

23 Macdonald, *The Truth*, 79

24 Donaldson, *Wanderings*, 173–4

25 https://canmore.org.uk/site/173033/skye-kilmuir-church-graveyard-flora-macdonald-monument

26 Macdonald, *The Truth*, 99–100

27 Richard Wilson, *Flora Macdonald* (1747), SNPG PG 1162; Allan Ramsay, *Flora Macdonald* (1749), Ashmolean WA1960.76; Richard Wilson, *Flora Macdonald* (1747), NPG 5848

28 Unknown artist (19th century), *Johnson and Boswell with Flora Macdonald*, Dr Johnson's House, 142

29 https://victorianweb.org/sculpture/davidson/1.html

30 http://www.ncmarkers.com/Markers.aspx?MarkerId=K-38;   http:// www.ncmarkers.com/Markers.aspx?MarkerId=H-57, text and essay

31 Gabaldon, 'Flora MacDonald's Barbecue', in *A Breath of Snow and Ashes*, 643ff.

32 https://www.waymarking.com/waymarks/WMHC8_Flora_MacDonald

33 Joseph Highmore, *Flora Macdonald* (1747–50), NCMA G.48.4.1

34 Flora Macdonald's silver, NCMH, H. 19XX.244.1; Shoe buckles, with Flora Macdonald history, NCMH, 19XX.332.104

35 Page, *Flora Macdonald College*, 1–16

36 https://www.laurinburgexchange.com/features/12286/hist ory-of-the-highland-games

37 'The Legendary Flora Macdonald', https://www.ncmuseumofhist ory.org/legendary-flora-macdonald

38 Scott, *Waverley Novels*, 35: xx–xxi

39 Scott, *Familiar Letters*, I: 67

40 Walter Scott, esquire, first published *Waverley; Or, 'T is Sixty Years Since* anonymously in three volumes in Edinburgh in July 1814. Over the next several years, eight thousand copies were to be sold in various editions.

41 Scott, *Waverley: Or, 'Tis Sixty Years Since*, ed. Garside, 106–7

42 Ibid., 107

43 Ibid., 344

44 Prebble, *The King's Jaunt*, 49

45 Sir David Wilkie, *George IV* (1829), RCT RCIN 401206; Sir David Wilkie, *The Entrance of George IV at Holyroodhouse* (1822–39), RCT RCIN 401187

46 *Blackwood's Magazine*, XII (1822), 350–1

47 Wraxall, *Historical and Posthumous Memoirs*, ed. Wheatley, V: 357

48 BL Add MS 40351, ff. 19, 20, Flora Mackay of Nairn: Correspondence with Sir Robert Peel, 1822

49 MacColl, 'Extracts from Notes of a Tour in the North of Scotland, 1838–39', 143

50 Scott, *Tales of a Grandfather*, II: 302

51 See Smith, ed., *Scotish* [sic] *Minstrel*, 6 vols, for works by Carolina Nairne, using the pseudonym Mrs Bogan of Bogan

52 Boulton and Macleod, eds, *Songs of the North*, I: 18–20

53 Trevor-Roper, 'The Invention of Tradition: The Highland Tradition of Scotland', 35–42

54 Alexander Johnston, *Flora Macdonald* (1869), RCT RCIN 406295

55 Charles Albert Wilson, *Balmoral Tableaux Vivants*: 'Charles Edward', 6 October 1888, RCT, RCIN 298001

56 RA VIC/MAIN/QVJ (W): QVJ(W) 6 October 1888 (Princess Beatrice's copies)

57 Macdonald, *Memorials*; Wylde, *Autobiography of Flora Macdonald*

58 Wylde, *Autobiography of Flora Macdonald*, II: 8–14

59 Ibid., 109–14

60 Colvin, *Letters of Robert Louis Stevenson*, II: 23–4

61 Stevenson, *Songs of Travel*, ed. Colvin, 82–3

62 Frankel, *Symbolism and Sources of Outlander*, 75–6

63 Grey Roots Museum and Archives, ON, Canada: https://greyroots.pastperfectonline.com/bycreator?keyword=Abel+Morrall+Limited

64 Walker's Shortbread Ltd, Aberlour, Speyside, Scotland: https://www.walkersshortbread.com/the-story-of-bonnie-prince-charlie-flora-macdonald/

65 *Ealing London Borough Council* v *Race Relations Board* [1971]: House of Lords 3 (16 December 1971), 10, Lord Simon of Glaisdale, observations

66 Harvie, *Scotland and Nationalism*, 1–2

Select Bibliography

NEWSPAPERS AND PERIODICALS

Blackwood's Magazine
Caledonian Mercury
Celtic Magazine
Derby Mercury
Dalhousie Review
London Gazette
Macmillan's Magazine
Mirror of Literature
Nautical Magazine
Oban Times
Scots Magazine
The Scotsman
Virginia Gazette

BOOKS, ARTICLES, ETC.

Allen, Robert S., ed., *The Loyal Americans: The Military Role of the Loyalist Provincial Corps and their Settlement in British North America, 1775–1784* (Ottawa, 1983)

[Anon.], *Alexis, or The Young Adventurer* (London, 1746)

[Anon.], *The Female Rebels* (Dublin, 1747)

[Anon.], *Memoir of Lt.-Col. John Macdonald* (London, 1831)

[Anon.], 'A Treatise on the Harmonic System, by John Macdonald …', *QMMR*, 4 (1822), 462–7

The Athenaeum Journal for the Year 1844 (London, 1844)

Atkinson, Rick, *The British Are Coming: The War for America: Lexington to Princeton, 1775–1777* (London, 2019)

Banks, James, *Life and Character of Flora Macdonald* (Fayetteville, NC, 1857)

Bartram, William, *Travels through North and South Carolina, Georgia, East and West Florida*, ed. Gordon DeWolf (Charlottesville, VA, 1980)

Becker, Laura Leff, 'The American Revolution as a Community Experience: A Case Study of Reading, Pennsylvania', PhD dissertation (University of Pennsylvania, 1978)

Blaikie, Walter Biggar, ed., *Itinerary of Prince Charles Edward Stuart from his Landing in Scotland July 1745 to his Departure in September 1746*, Scottish History Society Publications, First Series, vol. XXIII (Edinburgh, 1897)

——, ed., *Origins of the 'Forty-Five, and Other Papers Relating to That Rising*, Scottish History Society Publications, Second Series, vol. II (Edinburgh, 1916)

Boswell, James, *Journal of a Tour to the Hebrides with Samuel Johnson, now first published from the original manuscript*, ed. F. A. Pottle and C. H. Bennett (London, 1936)

——, *Journal of a Tour to the Hebrides with Samuel Johnson, LL.D.*, ed. Robert Carruthers (London, 1852)

——, *The Life of Dr Samuel Johnson, LL.D., and Journal of a Tour to the Hebrides*, ed. John Wilson Croker, 5 vols (London, 1831)

——, *The Life of Samuel Johnson, LL.D., Together with Boswell's Journal of a Tour to the Hebrides and Johnson's Diary of a Journey into North Wales*, ed. G. B. Hill and L. F. Powell, 2nd edn, 6 vols (Oxford, 1934–64), vol. V (1964): *The Tour to the Hebrides* and *The Journey into North Wales*

Boulton, Sir Harold, and Anne Campbell Macleod, eds, *Songs of the North, Gathered from the Highlands and Lowlands of Scotland*, 3 vols (London, 1884, 1894)

Brooke, John, *King George III* (London, 1972)

Browne, James, *A History of the Highlands and of the Highland Clans*, 3 vols (Edinburgh, 1849–50)

Burns, Robert, *The Complete Poems and Songs* (Glasgow, 2017)

Burton, John, *A Genuine and True Journal of the Most Miraculous Escape of the Young Chevalier, from the Battle of Culloden to his Landing in France* (London, 1749)

Chambers, Robert, *History of the Rebellion in 1745, 1746*, 2 vols (Edinburgh, 1827)

Chambers, Robert, ed., *Jacobite Memoirs of the Late Rebellion of 1745, Edited from the Manuscripts of ... Robert Forbes* (Edinburgh, 1834)

Clyde, Robert, *From Rebel to Hero: The Image of the Highlander, 1745–1830* (East Linton, 1995)

Cole, Robert, 'Curious particulars respecting Flora Macdonald', *The Mirror of Literature*, 43 (1844), 378–9

Colonial and State Records of North Carolina, in *Documenting the American South*, https://docsouth.unc.edu/csr/

Colvin, Sidney, ed., *The Letters of Robert Louis Stevenson*, 4 vols (London, 1911)

Craig, Maggie, *Damn' Rebel Bitches: The Women of the '45* (Edinburgh, 1997)

Croker, John Wilson, ed., *Letters of Mary Lepel, Lady Hervey* (London, 1821)

Cruickshanks, Eveline, and Edward Corp, eds, *The Stuart Court in Exile and the Jacobites* (London, 1995)

Cruttwell, Clement, *A Tour through the Whole Island of Great Britain, Divided into Journeys*, 5 vols (London, 1801)

Davies, Robert, 'A Memoir of Dr John Burton, M.D., F.S.A.', *YATJ*, 2 (1873), 403–40

Devine, T. M., *To the Ends of the Earth: Scotland's Global Diaspora, 1750–2010* (London, 2011)

DeWolfe, Barbara, *Discoveries of America: Personal Accounts of British Emigrants to North America during the Revolutionary Era* (Cambridge, 1997)

Donaldson, M. E. M., *Wanderings in the Western Highlands and Islands*, 2nd edn (Paisley, 1923)

Douglas, Hugh, *Flora MacDonald: The Most Loyal Rebel*, rev. edn (Stroud, 1999)

Duff, H. R., ed., *Culloden Papers, Comprising an Extensive and Interesting Correspondence from the Year 1625 to 1748. Published from the Originals in the Possession of Duncan Forbes of Culloden* (London, 1815)

Duncanson, John Victor, *Rawdon and Douglas: Two Loyalist Townships in Nova Scotia* (Belleville, Ontario, 1989)

Dziennik, Matthew P., *The Fatal Land: War, Empire, and the Highland Soldier in British America* (New Haven, CT, 2015)

E.E.G., 'The Grave of Flora Macdonald', *Gentleman's Magazine*, New Series, V (January–May 1868), 600–11

Egerton, H. E., ed., *The Royal Commission on the Losses and Services of American Loyalists, 1783 to 1785. Being the Notes of Mr. D. P. Coke, M.P., one of the Commissioners during that Period* (Oxford, 1915)

Fergusson, Sir James, *Argyll in the Forty-Five* (London, 1951)

Ferriar, Johns, *Illustrations of Sterne; with Other Essays and Verses*, 2 vols (New York, 1971)

Foote, William Henry, *Sketches of North Carolina, Historical and Biographical* (New York, 1846)

Forsyth, David, ed., *Bonnie Prince Charlie and the Jacobites* (Edinburgh, 2017)

Fowler, Malcolm, *They Passed This Way: A Personal Narrative of Harnett County History* (Lillington, NC, 1946)

Frankel, Valerie Estelle, *Symbolism and Sources of Outlander: The Scottish Fairies, Folklore, Ballads, Magic and Meanings that Inspired the Series* (Jefferson, NC, 2015)

Fraser, Sarah, *The Last Highlander: Scotland's Most Notorious Clan Chief* (London, 2012)

Fraser, Sir William, ed., *The Earls of Cromartie*, 2 vols (Edinburgh, 1876)

Fraser-Mackintosh, Charles, 'The Kingsburgh and Milton Families', *TGSI*, 14 (1887–8), 158–71

Gabaldon, Diana, *A Breath of Snow and Ashes*, Outlander Series, Book 6 (London, 2005)

Grant, Mrs Anne, of Laggan, *The Highlanders, and Other Poems* (London, 1808)

[Griffiths, Ralph], *Ascanius, or The Young Adventurer: A True History* (London, 1747)

Guthrie, Neil, *The Material Culture of the Jacobites* (Cambridge, 2013)

Harfield, Alan, 'Lieutenant Colonel John Macdonald', *JSAHR*, 66 (1988), 204–11

Harvie, Christopher, *Scotland and Nationalism: Scottish Society and Politics 1707 to the Present*, 4th edn (London, 2004)

Heard, Kate, and Kathryn Jones, eds, *George IV: Art & Spectacle* (London, 2019)

Henderson, Andrew, *The Life of William Augustus, Duke of Cumberland*, ed. Roderick Macpherson (London, 2010)

Hibbert, Christopher, *George IV: Prince of Wales, 1762–1811* (London, 1972)

——, *George IV: Regent and King, 1811–1830* (London, 1973)

HMC, 9th Report (1884), Part II: Appendix and Index

——, 11th Report (1887), Appendix, Part IV

[Hogg, James], *Songs by the Ettrick Shepherd* (Edinburgh, 1831)

Inman, George, 'Losses of the Military and Naval Forces Engaged in the War of the American Revolution', *PMHB*, 27 (1903), 176–205

Jesse, John Heneage, *Memoirs of the Pretenders and their Adherents* (London, 1858)

Johnson, Samuel, *A Journey to the Western Islands of Scotland*, ed. J. D. Fleeman (Oxford, 1985)

Kyd, James Gray, ed., *Scottish Population Statistics, Including Webster's Analysis of Population, 1755* (Edinburgh, 1952)

Langford, Abraham, *Catalogue of Paintings of Richard Mead, deceased* (London, 1754)

Logan, G. Murray, *Scottish Highlanders and the American Revolution* (Halifax, Nova Scotia, 1976)

Lossing, Benson, *Hours with the Living Men and Women of the Revolution* (New York, 1889)

MacColl, Evan, 'Extracts from Notes of a Tour in the North of Scotland, 1838–39', *Celtic Magazine*, VI (1881), 139–49

Macdonald, Alexander, *Letter Book, 1775–1779* (New York, 1883)

Macdonald, Allan R., *The Truth about Flora Macdonald* (Inverness, 1938)

Macdonald, Angus, and Archibald Macdonald, *The Clan Donald*, 3 vols (Inverness, 1896–1904)

Macdonald, Rev. A. [Archibald], ed., *Memorials of the '45* (Inverness, 1930)

Macdonald, Étienne, *The French Macdonald: The 1825 Travel Diary of Jacques Étienne Joseph Alexandre Macdonald*, trans. and ed. Jean-Didier Hache and Domhnall Uilleam Stiùbhart (Port of Ness, Lewis, 2007)

Macdonald, John, *A Treatise on Telegraphic Communication* (London, 1808)

Macgregor, Alexander, *The Life of Flora Macdonald*, 2nd edn (Inverness, 1882)

MacInnes, John, *The Brave Sons of Skye* (London, 1899)

Mackay, Charles, ed., *The Jacobite Songs and Ballads of Scotland: From 1688 to 1746* (London, 1861)

Mackenzie, James D., *History of Barbecue Church* (Raleigh, NC, 1965)

McLaren, Morag, *Lord Lovat of the '45* (London, 1957)

Maclean, Alasdair, *A Macdonald for the Prince: The Story of Neil MacEachen* (Stornoway, Lewis, 1982)

Maclean, Hector, *Writings of a Loyalist-Era Military Settler in Nova Scotia*, ed. Jo Currie, Keith Mercer and John G. Reid (Kentville, Nova Scotia, 2015)

Maclean, J. P., *Flora Macdonald in America* (Lumberton, NC, 1909)

MacLeod, R. C., ed., *The Book of Dunvegan: Being Documents from the Muniment Room of the MacLeods of MacLeod at Dunvegan Castle, Isle of Skye*, 2 vols (Aberdeen, 1938, 1939)

MacLeod, Ruairidh, *Flora MacDonald: The Jacobite Heroine in Scotland and North America* (London, 1995)

McLynn, Frank, *Bonnie Prince Charlie: Charles Edward Stuart* (London, 1988, 2003)

Macmillan, Angus, *Flora Macdonald of Benbecula* (Benbecula, 2010)

Mahon, Philip, Lord, *History of England from the Peace of Utrecht to the Peace of Versailles, 1713–1783*, 7 vols (Paris, 1841)

Marsden, *The History of Sumatra*, ed. John Bastin (Oxford, 1986)

Marshall, Henrietta, *Our Island Story* (Edinburgh, 1905)

Mayhew-Smith, Nick, *Landscape Liturgies* (Norwich, 2021)

Medley, Mary M., *History of Anson County, North Carolina, 1750–1976* (Charlotte, NC, 1976)

Meyer, Duane, *The Highland Scots of North Carolina, 1732–1776* (Chapel Hill, NC, 2014)

Miles, Ellen G., *Thomas Hudson: Portraitist to the British Establishment* (New Haven, CT, 1976)

Morrison, G. A., *History of the St Andrew's Society of the State of New York, 1756–1906* (New York, 1906)

Murdoch, Alexander, 'A Scottish Document Concerning Emigration to North Carolina in 1772', *NCHR*, 67 (1990), 438–49

Nicholas, Donald, ed., 'Account of Proceedings from Prince Charles's Landing to Prestonpans', in *Miscellany of the Scottish History*

Society: Ninth Volume, Scottish History Society Publications, Third Series, vol. L (Edinburgh, 1958), 199–216

Nicholson, Robin, *Bonnie Prince Charlie and the Making of Myth: A Study in Portraiture* (London, 2002)

O'Shaughnessy, Andrew, *The Men Who Lost America: British Command during the Revolutionary War and the Preservation of the Empire* (London, 2013)

Page, Ralph W., *Flora Macdonald College: An Aftermath of History* (Charlotte, NC, 1920)

Paton, Henry, ed., *The Lyon in Mourning; or a Collection of Speeches, Letters, Journals etc. … by the Rev. Robert Forbes, 1746–1775*, Scottish History Society Publications, First Series, 3 vols (Edinburgh, 1895–6)

Paton, James, Sir Arthur Mitchell et al., eds, *Scottish National Memorials: A Record of the Historical and Archæological Collection in the Bishop's Castle, Glasgow, 1888* (Glasgow, 1890)

Pennant, Thomas, *A Tour in Scotland, 1769* (London, 1771)

——, *A Tour in Scotland, and Voyage to the Hebrides, 1772*, rev. edn (London, 1790)

Pinkerton, John, ed., *A General Collection of … Voyages and Travels*, 17 vols (London, 1809–14)

Pittock, Murray, *Culloden* (Oxford, 2016)

Prebble, John, *The King's Jaunt: George IV in Scotland, August 1822: 'One and twenty daft days'* (London, 1988)

Prior, Matthew, *Poems on Several Occasions*, 3 vols, 5th edn (London, 1741)

Rankin, Hugh F., 'The Moore's Creek Bridge Campaign, 1776', *NCHR* 30 (1953), 23–60

——, *The North Carolina Continentals*, ed. Lawrence Babits (Chapel Hill, NC, 1971/2005)

Redford, Bruce, ed., *The Letters of Samuel Johnson*, 3 vols, vol. II: *1773–1776* (Oxford, 1992)

Riding, Jacqueline, *Jacobites: A New History of the '45 Rebellion* (London, 2016)

Roberts, Andrew, *George III* (London, 2021)

Robertson, Beth Whatley, 'Mentioned with Honour: The Story of Flora MacDonald', *Dalhousie Review*, 45 (1965), 165–81

Schaw, Janet, *Journal of a Lady of Quality*, ed. Evangeline Walker Andrews and Charles MacLean Andrews (New Haven, CT, 1934)

Scott, Hew, *Fasti Ecclesiæ Scoticanæ: The Succession of Ministers in the Parish Churches of Scotland, from the Reformation, A.D. 1560, to the Present Time*, 3 vols (Edinburgh, 1866–71)

Scott, Sir Walter, *Familiar Letters*, ed. David Douglas, 2 vols (Edinburgh, 1894)

——, *Tales of a Grandfather*, 3 vols (Philadelphia, 1827)

——, *The Waverley Novels*, 36 vols (Edinburgh, 1829–33): vol. 35 (1832)

[——], *Waverley; Or, 'Tis Sixty Years Since*, 3 vols (Edinburgh, 1814)

——, *Waverley; Or, 'Tis Sixty Years Since*, ed. P. D. Garside, rev. edn (Edinburgh, 2014)

[Scotus Americanus], *Informations concerning the province of North Carolina addressed to emigrants from the Highlands and Western Isles of Scotland by an impartial hand* (Glasgow, 1773)

Seton, Sir Bruce, ed., *Miscellany of the Scottish History Society: Fourth Volume*, Scottish History Society Publications, Third Series, vol. IX (Edinburgh, 1926)

Seton, Sir Bruce Gordon, and Jean Gordon Arnot, eds, *Prisoners of the '45*, Scottish History Society Publications, Third Series, vols. XIII–XV, 3 vols (Edinburgh, 1928–9)

Sinclair, Sir John, *Analysis of the Statistical Account of Scotland; with a general view of the history of that country* (Edinburgh, 1825)

Smith, R. A., ed., *The Scotish* [sic] *Minstrel*, 6 vols (Edinburgh, 1820–4) [Carolina Nairne authored works under name of Mrs Bogan of Bogan]

Smith, W. J., ed., *The Grenville Papers: Being the Correspondence of Richard Grenville, Earl Temple, and the Right Hon. George Grenville, their Friends and Contemporaries*, 4 vols (London, 1852–3)

The Statistical Accounts of Scotland, 1791–1845, https://stataccscot.edina.ac.uk/static/statacc/dist/home

Stephens, Frederick G., 'Among the Portraits at South Kensington', *Macmillan's Magazine*, XVI (May–October 1867), 383–93

Stephens, Frederick George, ed., *Exhibition of the Royal House of Stuart*, catalogue, (London, 1889)

Sterne, Laurence, *Works*, ed. George Saintsbury, 6 vols (London, 1894)

Stevenson, Robert Louis, *Songs of Travel, and Other Verses*, ed. Sidney Colvin (London, 1896)

Stewart, Michael, *The Forgotten Monarchy of Scotland* (Shaftesbury, 1998)

Stumpf, Vernon O., *Josiah Martin: The Last Royal Governor of North Carolina* (Durham, NC, 1986)

Tarleton, Lieutenant-Colonel Banastre, *A History of the Campaigns of 1780 and 1781, in the Southern Provinces of North America* (Dublin, 1787)

Tayler, Henrietta, ed., *A Jacobite Miscellany: Eight Original Papers on the Rising of 1745–1746* (Oxford, 1948)

Terry, Charles Sanford, ed., *The Albemarle Papers*, 2 vols (Aberdeen, 1902)

Thompson, Andrew C., *George II: King and Elector* (London, 2011)

Tindley, Anne, 'The Scottish History Society: 130 Years of Promoting the Best in Scottish History Scholarship', *Scottish Archives*, XXI (2015), 8–17, http://scottishhistorysociety.com/wp-content/uploads/2020/05/2282.Scottish-Archives-21.2-Tindley.web_.2017-02-02.pdf

Toffey, John J., *A Woman Nobly Planned: Fact and Myth in the Legacy of Flora Macdonald* (Durham, NC, 1997)

Town, Ithiel, ed., *A Detail of Some Particular Services Performed in America, during the Years 1776–79. Compiled from journals and official papers, supposed to be chiefly taken from the journal kept on board the Rainbow, commanded by Sir G. Collier* (New York, 1835)

Trevor-Roper, Hugh, 'The Invention of Tradition: The Highland Tradition of Scotland', in Eric Hobsbawm and Terence Ranger, eds, *The Invention of Tradition* (Cambridge, 1983), 15–42

Troxler, Carole Watterson, *The Loyalist Experience in North Carolina* (Raleigh, NC, 1976)

Voltaire, *The Age of Louis XIV and Louis XV*, trans. Ralph Griffiths, 3 vols (London, 1779–81)

Walpole, Horace, *Yale Edition of Horace Walpole's Correspondence*, ed. W. S. Lewis, 48 vols (New Haven, CT, 1937–83), https://walpole.library.yale.edu/collections/digital-resources/horace-walpole-correspondence

Warrand, Duncan, and Evan Macleod Barron, eds, *More Culloden Papers*, 5 vols (Inverness, 1923–30)

Watt, Patrick, and Rosie Waine, *Wild and Majestic: Romantic Visions of Scotland* (Edinburgh, 2019)

Wicker, Rassie E., *Miscellaneous Ancient Records of Moore County* (Southern Pines, NC, 1971)

Wood, Bradford J., *This Remote Part of the World: Regional Formation in Lower Cape Fear, North Carolina, 1725–1775* (Columbia, SC, 2004)

Wordsworth, William, *Last Poems, 1821–1850*, ed. Jared Curtis et al. (Ithaca, NY, 1999)

Wraxall, Sir Nathaniel, *Historical and Posthumous Memoirs, 1772–84*, ed. H. B. Wheatley, 5 vols (London, 1884)

Wylde, Flora Macdonald, *Autobiography of Flora Macdonald: Being the Home Life of a Heroine, Edited by her Granddaughter*, 2 vols (London, 1870)

——, *The Life and Wonderful Adventures of 'Totty Testudo': An Autobiography* (Edinburgh, 1873)

Zimmermann, Doron, *The Jacobite Movement in Scotland and in Exile, 1746–1759* (London, 2003)

Illustration Credits

Edouard en Ecosse (Edward in Scotland) by Hippolyte (Paul) Delaroche, 19th century. Oil on canvas. Private Collection. (© Christie's Images/ Bridgeman Images)

Prince Charles Edward Stuart as Betty Burke by J. Williams, c.1746. Mezzotint. National Library of Scotland, Edinburgh. (© National Library of Scotland)

Tableau vivant at Balmoral Castle, showing Princess Victoria of Wales as Flora Macdonald and Prince Albert Victor of Wales as Charles Edward Stuart by Charles Albert Wilson, 1888. Albumen print. The Royal Collection, London. (The Royal Collection Trust/© Her Majesty Queen Elizabeth II, 2022)

Flora Macdonald, embarked for Skye, with oarsman from W. E. Aytoun, *Lays of the Scottish Cavaliers and other Poems*, illustrated by J. N. and W. H. Paton (Edinburgh, 1863). (©Pictorial Press Ltd / Alamy Stock Photo)

During the Wandering of Charles Edward Stuart by Robert Alexander Hillingford, 19th century. Oil on canvas. Private collection. (© Christie's Images/Bridgeman Images)

The Baptism of Prince Charles Edward Stuart by Antonio David, 1725. Oil on canvas. Scottish National Portrait Gallery, Edinburgh. (© National Galleries of Scotland)

Bonnie Prince Charlie Entering the Ballroom at Holyroodhouse by John Pettie, 1891–92. Oil on canvas. The Royal Collection, London. (Royal Collection Trust/© Her Majesty Queen Elizabeth II, 2022/Bridgeman Images)

Charles Edward Stuart by Hugh Douglas Hamilton, c.1785. Oil on canvas. National Portrait Gallery, London. (© National Portrait Gallery, London)

Flora Macdonald by Richard Wilson, 1747. Oil on canvas. Scottish National Portrait Gallery, Edinburgh. (© National Galleries of Scotland/ Bridgeman Images)

William Augustus, Duke of Cumberland from the studio of David Morier, c.1760. Oil on canvas. Anglesey Abbey, Cambridgeshire. (© Anglesey Abbey, Cambridgeshire, UK/National Trust Photographic Library/ Bridgeman Images)

Anne Drelincourt, Lady Primrose by a follower of Allan Ramsay, 18th century. Oil on canvas. Private collection. (© Christie's Images/Bridgeman Images)

'Home of Flora Macdonald', Flodigarry, Skye. Postcard, c.1920s. Author's collection. (Photograph © Mike Trow)

Johnson and Boswell with Flora Macdonald by an unknown artist, 19th century. Oil on canvas. Dr Johnson's House Museum, London. (Reproduced by courtesy of the Trustees of Dr Johnson's House)

Boswell and the Ghost of Samuel Johnson by an unknown artist, 1803. Engraving. Private Collection. (Private Collection/Bridgeman Images)

Flora Macdonald on Way to Barbeque Church, North Carolina, by Elenore Plaisted Abbott, c.1900. Oil on canvas. Presbyterian Historical Society, Philadelphia. (Reproduced courtesy of the Presbyterian Historical Society, Philadelphia, Pennsylvania)

May Day at Flora MacDonald College, Red Springs, North Carolina, c.1916. From James Alexander Macdonald, *Flora Macdonald; a history and a message* (Washington D.C., 1916)

Historical marker on site where Flora waved off Highland army, 1776. Placed by the Cumberland County Historical Society, Fayetteville, North Carolina. (Waymarking.com)

Flora Macdonald's Monument, Kilmuir, Skye from *Illustrated London News*, 27 January 1872. Engraving. (Private Collection/Look and Learn/ Illustrated Papers Collection/Bridgeman Images)

A still from the film *Bonnie Prince Charlie*, 1948. David Niven as Prince Charles Edward Stuart and Margaret Leighton as Flora Macdonald. (© Pictorial Press Ltd / Alamy Stock Photo)

Index

The index is organised so that names of individuals who are associated with a clan – or a specific branch of one clan – are alphabetised by their clan, and, where possible, by branch. This is in order to avoid having multiples of the same name next to one another and to keep the members of each clan together.

A Note on the Type

The text of this book is set in Adobe Garamond. It is one of several versions of Garamond based on the designs of Claude Garamond. It is thought that Garamond based his font on Bembo, cut in 1495 by Francesco Griffo in collaboration with the Italian printer Aldus Manutius. Garamond types were first used in books printed in Paris around 1532. Many of the present-day versions of this type are based on the *Typi Academiae* of Jean Jannon cut in Sedan in 1615.

Claude Garamond was born in Paris in 1480. He learned how to cut type from his father and by the age of fifteen he was able to fashion steel punches the size of a pica with great precision. At the age of sixty he was commissioned by King Francis I to design a Greek alphabet, and for this he was given the honourable title of royal type founder. He died in 1561.